Urban Ministry in the 21st Century: Global Faiths

Volume 1

Engaging Muslims and Islam

Lessons for 21st-Century American Evangelicals

Dr. Amit A. Bhatia

Editor: Andrew Wood

Urban Loft Publishers | Skyforest, CA

Engaging Muslims and Islam
Lessons for 21st-Century American Evangelicals

Urban Loft Publishers
P.O. Box 6
Skyforest, CA 92385
www.urbanloftpublishers.com

Senior Editors: Stephen Burris & Kendi Howells Douglas
Series Editor: Andrew Wood
Copy Editor: Adrienn Vasquez
Graphics: Elisabeth Arnold

ISBN-13: 978-0-9989177-0-2

Made in the U.S

ENDORSEMENTS

The research discussed in this book is an important contribution to the ongoing conversation of Christian-Muslim relations in the US. It presents a Biblical foundation for ministering to our Muslim neighbors, providing helpful suggestions for Christians to connect with Muslims and begin spiritual conversations. I hope this book ignites a new compassion for reaching Muslims with the Gospel.

Fouad Masri

Founder and President

Crescent Project

Engaging Muslims and Islam: Lessons for 21st Century American Evangelicals is a timely book in these days of conflicting views regarding Islam and Muslims. It deserves careful reading. This practical work, grounded in careful primary research, will help all Evangelicals in the United States and beyond in their relationships with the Muslims they encounter. Highly recommended.

Tite Tiénou

Research Professor, Theology of Mission and Dean Emeritus

Trinity Evangelical Divinity School

Engaging Muslims and Islam is a timely, practical guide for followers of Jesus. Dr. Bhatia's research debunks the negative media about Muslims and provides a well-researched, balanced and biblical perspective. This is a great resource for those who want to follow Jesus and love their Muslim neighbors.

Rick Love, Ph.D. President

Peace Catalyst International

DEDICATION

For my parents, who never let me lose sight of the
importance of education,
and for Kathy, my constant encourager and
partner in ministry.

ACKNOWLEDGEMENTS

I want to thank Andrew Wood, the series editor,
for his painstaking editing work and helpful suggestions.

I want to thank my wife Kathy,
who encouraged me and prayed for me
throughout the dissertation and book writing process.

EDITOR'S PREFACE

Urban Mission in the 21st Century is a series of monographs that addresses key issues facing those involved in urban ministry whether it be in the slums, squatter communities, *favelas*, or in immigrant neighborhoods. It is our goal to bring fresh ideas, a theological basis, and best practices in urban mission as we reflect on our changing urban world. The contributors to this series bring a wide-range of ideas, experiences, education, international perspectives, and insight into the study of the growing field of urban ministry. These contributions fall into four very general areas: 1––the biblical and theological basis for urban ministry; 2––best practices currently in use and anticipated in the future by urban scholar/activists who are living working and studying in the context of cities; 3––personal experiences and observations based on urban ministry as it is currently being practiced; and 4––a forward view toward where we are headed in the decades ahead in the expanding and developing field of urban mission. This series is intended for educators, graduate students, theologians, pastors, and serious students of urban ministry.

More than anything, these contributions are creative attempts to help Christians strategically and creatively think about how we can better reach our world that is now more urban than rural. We do not see theology and practice as separate and distinct. Rather, we see sound practice growing out of a healthy vibrant theology that seeks to understand God's world as it truly is as we move further into the twenty-first century. Contributors interact with the best scholarly literature available at the time of writing while making application to specific contexts in which they live and work.

Each book in the series is intended to be a thought-provoking work that represents the author's experience and perspective on urban ministry in a particular context. The editors have chosen those who bring this rich diversity of perspectives to this series. It is our hope and prayer that each book in this series will challenge, enrich, provoke, and cause the reader to dig deeper into subjects that bring the reader to a deeper understanding of our urban world and the ministry the church is called to perform in that new world.

Dr. Kendi Howells Douglas and Stephen Burris,
Urban Mission in the 21st Century Series Co-Editors

SERIES PREFACE

In previous eras, knowledge of world religions and cultural proficiency in communicating with people of other faiths were within the purview of a select group of academics and missionaries with the motivation and means to travel internationally. In the 21st century, urbanization and globalization have brought large numbers of ordinary people of diverse cultures and religious beliefs into unavoidable daily contact in the workplace, educational institutions, local and national politics, and through social media.

For Christians, as for the rest of society, these social changes represent a challenge. Many church members are experiencing role conflict between their statuses as members of a particular nationality, class, and culture versus their status as citizens of the world-encompassing Kingdom of God. They waver between fear and faith as they try to reconcile the confusing and anxiety-provoking messages of the media with the imperatives of Scripture to love one's neighbor—even if one's neighbor seems like an enemy. Church leaders may find traditional means of evangelism and discipleship proving ineffective in demographically changing communities. Those who do succeed in bridging cultural divides in the community to communicate the gospel compellingly may find it difficult to integrate ethnically diverse new Christians into the existing cultural majority of the church. Already overwhelmed with the demands of ministry, leaders typically do not have the time to do an in-depth cultural study to arrive at culturally appropriate, biblically sound, and effective means of communicating Jesus to people of non-Christian religious communities, especially given the great diversity of religious others one encounters every day in a major metropolitan area.

However, we must not allow the difficulties of rapid cultural change to overshadow the enormous opportunity this change represents to the church. For the first time, large numbers of ordinary Christians and members of other faiths can share and model their beliefs simply and directly with one another, unmediated by religious leaders. The "priesthood of all believers" (see 1 Pet. 2:9) can thus become a reality with respect to cross-cultural outreach in an unprecedented way. Moreover, learning and spiritual growth may very well go in both directions. As they lead religious others to become followers of Jesus, Christians themselves are challenged by the questions, devotional practices, and theologies of other faiths in ways that cause them to reexamine the reasons for their own beliefs and redouble their efforts to live consistently with their own profession of faith in Christ. The need to adjust ministry practices to communicate clearly to people of a wide variety of other faiths may cause Christian leaders to focus more carefully upon the true essentials of the Christian faith, stripping away the cultural syncretism that so easily entangles the church in materialism, nationalism, and other subtle idolatries. The result can be a church more focused on its mission with an increased capacity to love others in clearer emulation of the self-sacrificial model of Christ himself.

Urban Ministry in the 21st Century: Global Faiths is a monograph series intended to help the church overcome the challenges and rise to the opportunities represented by the growing religious diversity of the burgeoning cities of the world. Each volume focuses upon a different non-Christian religious faith, providing the reader with tools to understand that faith better as well as practical suggestions and examples for biblically faithful and culturally appropriate contextualization. The authors are ministry professionals and academics who write not only from a basis of careful research, but also from thoughtful reflection upon their own real life experiences listening, dialoging, and sharing faith with people of religious backgrounds different from their own. We hope these volumes will be of practical assistance to ministers, educators, college students, Christian nonprofit workers, and inquisitive laypeople who will discern the Lord's hand at work in the cultural changes in their communities and respond eagerly to His call, "Here am I. Send me!" (Isa 6:8 New International Version).

Dr. Andrew Wood
Series Editor
Urban Ministry in the 21st Century: Global Faiths

TABLE OF CONTENTS

FOREWORD

The early 21st century brings both daunting challenges and unprecedented opportunities to American Christians. American society itself is rapidly changing, becoming increasingly diverse in terms of ethnicity, culture, and moral values. The religious demographics are also shifting, as the numbers of Christians decrease while those of adherents of other religious traditions grow. Although many Americans welcome the religious diversification of society, many others resist this, with some longing for recovery of an imagined past when America was a "Christian nation". The United States is undergoing a period of profound transformation, which is forcing a new conversation about what it means to be American.

For American evangelicals in particular the issues involve more than simply clarification of the social, cultural, and political contours of a nation in transition; evangelicals must also come to grips with what it means to be disciples of Jesus Christ in a nation with very different ideological and religious traditions. What is needed, in other words, is for evangelicals to formulate a biblically faithful and culturally relevant "theology of religions" that enables Christians to think responsibly about, and to interact appropriately with, adherents of other religious traditions. Nowhere is this need more urgent than with respect to evangelicals' thinking about Islam and Muslims.

I write this in December 2016, in the aftermath of an especially ugly and contentious presidential election that made the question of Muslims, among other issues, a highly contentious and polarizing subject of political discourse. Ever since the rise of radical Islamist

terrorism in the 1990s—and especially after the tragic events of 9/11,—
Americans have tended to view Muslims through the lenses of violence
and terrorism. In some respects, American evangelicals have been
among those most suspicious of Muslims, often regarding Islam as
inherently violent and incompatible with American norms. While
perhaps understandable, this perspective is simplistic and misleading,
and it prevents the church from formulating an appropriate and
effective missiological framework for engaging with Muslims in
American society. What is needed today is a fresh look at what "real
Muslims" are like and what Scripture says about how Christ's disciples
are to relate to those who are religiously different from—and yes, even
hostile to—Christians. An essential first step in this effort to craft an
appropriate theological and missiological framework for encountering
Muslims is a careful examination of how evangelicals today actually do
think about and relate to Muslims. And this is where Engaging Muslims
and Islam makes such an important contribution.

Three things distinguish this unusual book. First, the author,
Dr. Amit Bhatia, is uniquely prepared to guide us through the issues.
Although he has lived for many years in the United States and is
thoroughly familiar with American evangelical culture, he brings the
perceptive insight of an "outsider", someone with life experiences very
different from most American evangelicals. Dr. Bhatia was born into a
Hindu home in India, living in a diverse and eclectic environment. The
opportunities and challenges of religious diversity are not new to him.
Moreover, since becoming a disciple of Jesus Christ, Dr. Amit Bhatia
has been actively involved in evangelism and ministry among those of
other religious traditions, including Muslims. He is a gifted evangelist,
and his observations come from years of personal experience with
religious others. Moreover, Dr. Bhatia has extensive formal training in
theology, culminating in a PhD in intercultural studies, so he brings a

theoretically informed and critical reflection upon what he observes in real life encounters.

Second, the book is unusual in that it draws upon both the significant theoretical literature in the field and Dr. Bhatia's own original research into the views and practices of evangelicals in the Chicago area. Dr. Amit Bhatia is at home in the academic literature in American religious history, religious studies, and the theology of religions, and he provides an informative overview of significant factors that frame how American evangelicals approach Muslims and Islam today. But the heart of the book is the material he gleans from the extensive interviews with evangelicals about their perceptions of Muslims and Islam. What is uncovered by way of evangelical perceptions of Muslims is both encouraging in some respects and deeply disturbing in others.

Finally, the book includes some wise and helpful suggestions for Christians who are concerned about how we should respond to the increasing religious diversity of American society. Religious diversity is here to stay, and an integral part of the diversification of American society will be the growing prominence of Muslims and Islam throughout American life. Dr. Bhatia offers some important guidelines for evangelical Christians as they serve as both good citizens and faithful disciples of Jesus in the days ahead.

Dr. Harold A. Netland
Professor of Philosophy of Religion and Intercultural Studies
Trinity Evangelical Divinity School

CHAPTER 1

WHY A BOOK ON ENGAGING MUSLIMS AND ISLAM?

Some of my significant early childhood memories are of engagement with people of other religious backgrounds. I grew up in India as a Hindu, interacting with Muslims, Jains, and Christians, participating in religious festivals of other religions and seeing non-Hindus participate in Hindu festivals. As a "practicing" Hindu, I came to the United States and got the opportunity to engage born-again Christians as well as Muslims. Five years after my encounter with the person of Jesus Christ and hearing for the first time the exclusive claims of Jesus I was convinced of the truth of Christianity and became a disciple of Jesus.

Since coming to Christ I have engaged Hindus, Buddhists, Muslims, Jews, and others in the American culture of religious diversity lived out and experienced in an urban work setting as an IT professional. When God called me into full-time ministry as a pastor, I spent nine years engaging people from a variety of cultural and religious backgrounds, including Muslims. In one setting I served as a leader in a house church geared towards ministering to people of Hindu and Muslim backgrounds as well as working with a help-based ministry that was started to reach out to Hindus and Muslims from India and Pakistan. After serving in local congregations in a pastoral capacity, Christ called me into the role of adjunct professor at Trinity International University. Here I have taken evangelical Christian students enrolled in intercultural ministry courses on field trips that allowed us to engage Muslims from a variety of countries around the globe living in an urban setting in the US. During the course of this venture for the past nearly four decades I have learned to appreciate religious others as well as developed a longing to engage them with the good news of Jesus Christ better. If you, the reader, want to develop an understanding of Islam and get better at engaging Muslims living in urban settings in the US, then this book is for you.

It is also through this engagement that Jesus gave me a desire to understand the ways in which evangelical Christians are, and should be, engaging Islam and Muslims as far as their perspectives, attitudes, and practices are concerned. It was this desire to increase my understanding that gave rise to the research project that forms the basis of this book. As I began working on this project, the journey that Jesus took me on included both academic learning and learning from the experience of American evangelicals who have spent a significant portion of their lives engaging Muslims, both overseas and in the US. It is this knowledge that I have acquired, as well as lessons that I have learned over the course of this study, that I wish to share with those who will encounter Islam and Muslims living in the US. In this chapter I begin with a brief introduction of the current religious situation in the US as it pertains to the presence of Islam and Muslims in our context.

In the more than fifty years since the enactment of the United States' Immigration and Nationality Act of 1965 that opened immigration to non-European countries, an increasing number of non-European immigrants have been coming to the US. Many of these immigrants are non-Christians who bring their religions with them and contribute to the religious diversity of the US. Islam is one of these religions, and it has become increasingly visible. Evangelical Christians, who in the past might only have encountered Islam on the mission field, are now finding that they have Muslim coworkers and neighbors, and their children study in schools with Muslim children. In the context of this increasing presence of Muslims, Christ exhorts His disciples to be "salt" and "light" (Matt 5:13-16, NIV) in order that Jesus may be presented to them in a winsome manner, so that they may come to know Him.

In a world rife with violence and bigotry in the name of religion, this is not an easy task. Take for example the terrorist attacks that took place on 9/11 under the leadership of Osama bin Laden, the now-deceased leader of al-Qaeda, a militant Islamic organization regarded as a terrorist group by numerous countries. Osama bin Laden masterminded the bombing of the World Trade Center and the Pentagon, killing over 3000 people. Even though the Bush administration communicated that American retaliation to this event should not be viewed as an act of religious violence, Thomas Kidd (2009) asserts that the numerous events related to the 2001 terrorist attacks were perceived by American Christians partly as a clash between Christianity and Islam (p. 144). The events of 2001 have also given rise to a plethora of literature on terrorism and Islam by leading American evangelicals such as John MacArthur (2001), Dave Hunt (2005), and Randall Price (2001), to name just a few.

The events of 9/11 have also given rise to rash statements by a number of influential evangelicals. A few examples illustrate this tendency. Pat Robertson commented, "Somehow I wish the Jews in America would wake up, open their eyes and read what is being said about them. This is worse than the Nazis. Adolf Hitler was bad, but what the Muslims want to do to the Jews is worse" (Kidd, 2009, p. 145). During an October 6, 2002 interview on CBS 60 Minutes, Jerry Falwell commented that Muhammad was a terrorist.

> I read enough of the history of his life written by both
> Muslims and non-Muslims [to know] that he was a violent

man, a man of war. In my opinion... Jesus set the example for love, as did Moses. And I think that Muhammad set an opposite example. (McKay, 2002)

Franklin Graham said that the God of Islam is "a different God" and that Islam is "a very evil and wicked religion" (Cox, 2001, p. 30). Jerry Vines asserted that "Muhammad was a 'demon-possessed pedophile' and that Islam teaches the destruction of all non-Muslims" (Falwell, 2002, para. 1). Terry Jones, pastor of the Dove World Outreach Center in Gainesville, FL, expressed his distaste for Islam by publically burning a Qur'an. Many other evangelicals have labeled Islam a "demonic" and "violent" religion (Kidd, 2009). These actions are reflective of the long history of Christian-Muslim animosity ever since Islam was founded in the early seventh century.

On the other hand, some evangelicals diminish problems with Islam, highlighting only its positive elements. For instance, Miroslav Volf (2011) disavows that the God of the Qur'an is a "fierce and violent deity in opposition to the God of Jesus Christ, who is sheer love," and claims that Christians and Muslims worship the same God (p. 14). In his view, while their understanding of God's character is "partly" different, "the object of their worship is the same," and "the one and only God" worshipped by both Muslims and Christians commands people to love their neighbor (Volf, 2011, p. 14). Even though what it means to love one's neighbor is "partly" different in Islam and Christianity, in the end it does not matter whether you are a Muslim or a Christian, but that you love God with all your heart and "trust and obey Jesus Christ, the Word of God and Lamb of God" (Volf, 2011, p. 15).

As I began to read and reflect on the beliefs and actions of evangelicals, it became clear to me that these perspectives and attitudes, and the resulting practices, are not shaped in a vacuum. In light of Jesus' exhortation to "love your neighbor as yourself" (Matt 19:19), it is imperative that evangelicals understand these perspectives, attitudes, and practices – how they are shaped, formed, and justified; how theologically and missiologically sound they are; and how we should respond to them as well as to the Muslims in our midst. Evangelical views of Islam as a religion and Muslims as adherents of Islam highlight the need to develop a set of theological and missiological principles that answer questions such as: What theological themes and doctrines aid evangelicals in gaining a theological understanding of Islam and Muslims? and What biblical values should guide our understanding of how evangelicals should live among and relate to their Muslim neighbors in the US?

Forming this set of theological and missiological principles in order to address this host of questions necessitates the development of: first, a robust theological framework that will shape our understanding of Islam; second, a set of biblical guidelines to shape evangelicals' response to Muslims; and third, practical steps evangelicals can take to engage Muslims and Islam. In order to do this, the initial step must be to become cognizant of how evangelicals perceive Islam and how they relate to Muslims.

Gaining Awareness of Perceptions and Relationships

Beginning in April 2013 I conducted a 2-year qualitative study, including an analysis of the qualitative data, to gain an understanding of American evangelicals' perspectives, attitudes, and practices toward immigrant Muslims.[1] Through this study I attempted to answer two research questions. First: What perspectives, attitudes, and practices toward Muslims and Islam are found among evangelical laypeople and

---

[1] The research methodology of this study is discussed in detail in Appendix 1.

pastors? And second: How have these perspectives, attitudes, and practices been formed and justified?

In this study I interviewed forty middle-class lay American evangelicals (twenty-three men and seventeen women) and four pastors, all white males, from four different evangelical congregations in four suburbs in the Chicago area. The qualitative data to answer the two research questions were gathered via one-on-one interviews that lasted on average anywhere from thirty to sixty minutes. The American evangelical respondents were for the most part self- selecting, which means that the clear patterns that emerge from their responses may not be indicative of the perspectives, attitudes, and practices of all American evangelicals, who number some 92 million members (Mandryk, 2010, p. 862). Because these respondents had an interest in this topic, they may have had an agenda and hence were more likely to articulate in stronger terms the kinds of things they said than would a randomly selected subset of American evangelicals. Extrapolating these results would mean that the perspectives, attitudes, and practices of American evangelicals in general would be less extreme than what emerged from the interviews of the respondents. However, the responses that they gave were helpful, because their interest in this topic led them to read and dialogue about as well as reflect on the issues related to the research topic; hence, the information they provided allowed me to answer the two research questions. Furthermore, in spite of the fact that my research sample is small and limited theologically, geographically, and demographically, the insights and missiological principles that emerged from this study are pertinent even in settings that differ from those of my interviewees.

To deepen the understanding of this issue I also conducted a focus group study of Christian Outreach Ministry to Muslims

(COMM),[2] a friendship center and helps-based ministry serving Hindus and Muslims. This study included a group interview of nine leaders at COMM as well as a one-on-one interview of COMM's staff apologist to Muslims and provided additional information to help answer the two research questions. COMM also served as a concrete example of an effective way in which American evangelicals can engage Muslims in an urban setting.

To facilitate the understanding and analysis of the data it was helpful to think about the qualitative information from three vantage points: perspectives, attitudes, and practices. Perspectives includes general views that evangelicals have of Muslims and Islam, whether they consider Islam/Muslims to be evil or peaceful, whether they think there is any truth in Islam, or whether they see Muslims as good people. Attitudes includes general dispositions that evangelicals have towards Islam and Muslims, characterized by a propensity to view Muslims or Islam either positively or negatively. There may also be a mismatch between perspectives and attitudes of evangelicals – they may have a fairly positive perspective towards Islam but a negative attitude towards Muslims, or vice versa. Practices includes specific actions that evangelicals take to engage Islam and Muslims at different levels, including developing relationships with Muslims or avoiding interaction with them, trying to learn about Islam and Muslims by taking courses, reading literature on Islam and Muslims, blogging, engaging others in discussion, or passing on negative or positive perspectives and attitudes they hold about Islam, etc.

In this research study I not only probed these perspectives, attitudes, and practices in order to assess how American evangelicals gain their information about Islam but also analyzed the theological and missiological soundness of these perspectives, attitudes, and

---

[2] A pseudonym

practices. Furthermore, I interacted with and drew from the writings of scholars who have written about an evangelical theology of religions, including Islam, for the development of a set of theological and missiological principles that were then used to analyze the information obtained through the two research questions and the focus group. These principles helped me develop recommendations to help shape evangelicals' understanding of Islam as well as a set of biblical guidelines to shape evangelicals' response to Muslims.

Significance Of The Research Study

A number of Christians have written about American perspectives, attitudes, and practices toward American religious others in general and American Muslims in particular. From their research it becomes clear that the popular understanding of Islam is strongly shaped by media reports (Eck, 2002; Wuthnow, 2007; Kidd, 2009). However, a systematic study based on qualitative interviews of evangelical pastors and laypeople to gather comprehensive information on what these perspectives, attitudes, and practices are and how they are formed and justified has not been conducted. This research sought to contribute this information on evangelicals in the US to make them cognizant of this gap in their understanding of American Muslims and of how it is shaped.

Christian scholars, some evangelicals and others not, have also presented a number of ways in which evangelicals should respond to religious others in general (Muck, 1990; Marty, 2005; Wuthnow, 2007; Numrich, 2009), and developed models for evangelizing Muslims (Richardson, 1988) and responding to Islam and Muslims in particular (Chapman, 2007). But a theological and missiological response to American evangelicals' perspectives, attitudes, and practices toward Muslims, based on a robust qualitative study of American evangelicals, and a theology of religion regarding Islam has not yet been developed. This research study was an attempt to fill this gap.

Overview Of The Book

A bird's-eye view of the book, leading to a theological and missiological response, is as follows.

PART I: The Past Experience of Americans with Religious Others. In this section I summarize literature on a variety of topics, moving from the broader discussion of religious diversity in the US to the growth of Islam and the development of Christian-Muslim relationships in the US. Chapter 2, setting the broader context of this book, offers a brief discussion about the growth of religious diversity in the US and ways in which American Christians have responded to religious others in their midst. In Chapter 3 I discuss briefly the growth of Islam in the US and the experiences of Muslims in the religiously diverse climate of America. Chapter 4 presents a few works of literature by American non-evangelicals as well as American evangelical Christians that discuss Christian-Muslim relationships in the US.

PART II: The 21st–Century Experience of American Evangelicals with Muslims. Chapters 5, 6, and 7 discuss the qualitative data gathered through the research project. Set in the context of the literature review of the previous chapters, Chapter 5 discusses the qualitative information obtained from the forty-four interviews of American evangelicals directly pertaining to the perspectives, attitudes, and practices they espouse regarding Islam and Muslims. Chapter 6 discusses how these perspectives, attitudes, and practices were formed and justified. Chapter 7 considers data gathered through the focus group study of COMM. It looks at the perspectives, attitudes, and practices of American evangelical ministry leaders toward Muslims in the context of their daily engagement of Muslims through their helps-based ministry.

PART III: Future Directions for American Evangelical Relationships with Muslims. Chapter 8 offers a discussion of a theology of religions that Christians must espouse toward all religions in general and toward Islam in particular. It does so by summarizing the works of several scholars regarding theology of other religions including Islam, and by drawing from their work brief principles to guide how Christians should view other religions in general and Islam in particular. In Chapter 9 I offer some general observations of the qualitative data gathered through the one-on-interviews of American evangelicals and the COMM focus group study. This chapter also presents an analysis of this information as well as explicit connections between the qualitative data (Chapters 5-7) and literature discussed in Chapters 2-4 and 8. Finally, in Chapter 10 I present helpful insights and pertinent missiological recommendations for evangelicals regarding Islam and Muslims in the US. These ideas emerged from the analysis of the responses by lay evangelicals and pastors, the ministry of the COMM staff, and the intersection of their responses with the literature on theology of religions.

PART I

The Past Experience of Americans with Religious Others

CHAPTER 2

GROWTH OF RELIGIOUS DIVERSITY IN THE U.S.

As I began my initial reflection on the perspectives, attitudes, and practices of American evangelicals toward Muslims in the US, I began to wonder whether these were new phenomena that had emerged only in the last couple of decades, or if this was something that could be traced back further. And if it could indeed be traced back further, then how far back and what did that look like? This chapter, setting the broader context of the engagement of American evangelicals with Islam and Muslims in the US, offers a brief discussion about this growth as well as ways in which American Christians have responded to religious others in their midst.

Religious Diversity In The US Before 1965

The United States has always been a land characterized by religious diversity. Hutchison (2004) asserts that over the course of the roughly two hundred years of the existence of British colonies in North America, American society came to be increasingly recognized for its diversity (p. 11), but we can go back further. To begin with, this religious diversity included the plethora of Native American religions among the original inhabitants of America (Marger, 2012, p. 137), followed by the arrival of European settlers in the sixteenth century whose religious practices ranged from Christians of a variety of stripes—Catholics from Spain and France, Anglicans and Quakers from Britain, and the Dutch Reformed—to Sephardic Jews. When the slave trade began in the early seventeenth century, many of the enslaved Africans also brought Islam with them. This was followed by immigrants from Japan and China, who came to work in the fields and mines of the West, bringing with them Confucian, Taoist, and Buddhist traditions. Later waves included Jews from Eastern Europe, Catholics from Italy and Ireland, Christians and Muslims from the Middle East, and Sikhs from India (Eck, 2002, p. 3). However, with the passage of the Immigration and Naturalization Acts of 1924 and 1952, immigration from Southern and Eastern Europe, the Middle East, East Asia, and India was severely restricted for several decades.

Wuthnow (2007) offers an insightful analysis of the pre-1965 history of religious diversity in the US (p. 34). He sees a common theme weaving through the approximately 500 year long history of engagement that American Christians had with other religions which included the shaping of Christians' "perceptions of themselves and of their place in the world" (Wuthnow, 2007, p. 35). Regardless of how big the Christian community was during these encounters—in the early period of their encounters as settlers and explorers when they were a "small minority," or much later during the 19th century when Christianity had become a majority religion—American Christians viewed themselves as the "reigning power" and the prevailing "cultural influence" (Wuthnow, 2007, p. 35). This mindset allowed the American Christians to view the adherents of non-Christian religions in a variety of different ways: ignore them and let their presence go unacknowledged, or view them as "proto-Christians, potential converts, degenerate heathen," or in some other fashion that did not give full weight to the intricacy of the "beliefs and practices" of these non-Christian religions (Wuthnow, 2007, p. 35).

For instance, note Columbus' views that were reflective of responses of the early settlers and explorers when they encountered

Native Americans. Columbus described the Indians as "lacking in evil," "naked as their mothers bore them," "credulous," "very gentle," and "very timid" (Wuthnow, 2007, p. 12). Observations such as these led Columbus to think that the Indians had "the qualities of young children who, according to the teachings of his own church, remained innocent and in a special relationship with God" (Wuthnow 2007, p. 12). European settlers who came later would frequently repeat these observations. It was also commonly thought that the religious practices of the Indians were just "superstitions and magic" and "meaningless rituals performed by ignorant people rather than being regarded as evidence of full-fledged religions" (Wuthnow, 2007, p. 13), although thoughtful people gradually did come to see as mistaken the notion that the inhabitants of the New World did not have a religion of their own.

Another excellent example is the 1893 World's Parliament of Religions, a seminal event in America's experience with religious diversity and quite revelatory of American sentiments. This event gave the adherents of various religions the opportunity to stand alongside Christianity, even though they were not on equal grounds. This was the first time in the nation's history that adherents of Hinduism, Buddhism, Zoroastrianism, Confucianism, Shintoism, Islam, and other faiths were able to talk about their faith and their practices themselves instead of being "interpreted by Christian missionaries or travelers" (Wuthnow, 2007, p. 28). Wuthnow remarks that even though the representation of the various religions at the convention was quite significant, the representatives of these religions together comprised only one-sixth of the program, while Christian speakers encompassed five-sixths of the program. Even though some scholars viewed the Parliament as an important achievement, many of the leaders representing the other religions had some reservations, asserting that "they had not been heard or understood," that Christians responded to them with weakening interest or with "polite concern" over the propagation of "religious universalism" or with calls for more fervent proselytization (Wuthnow, 2007, p. 29). These reactions were evident when this event was reported nationwide in newspapers. In small towns and cities, while there was a lot of discussion in church meetings and in the sermons, newspapers did not devote a lot of space to report this event. In some of the bigger cities the papers praised this event as an occasion that affirmed unity and tolerance – characteristics reflective of an advanced civilization. For example, the New-York Tribune reported that Western civilization was the only one that had in it "any hope of progress, enlightenment and happiness," that it was "worth propagating," that it was superior to all other civilizations, and that Christianity held a "place of supremacy" in it (Wuthnow, 2007, p. 29).

American missionaries living overseas also had a response to their encounter with religious others, expressing similar sentiments. The missionaries' experience with people of other religions put them in a place where they could offer interpretations of other civilizations and their religions. Via their reports Americans came to see that other societies and their religions were "corrupt" and their decay in the near future was easy to foresee. For example, an 1861 report by R. G. Wilder asserted that Hinduism, with its practices of suttee, widow celibacy, and polygamy was "breaking up," and that "Hinduism has no elements which can stand before science and Christianity" (p. 12). American Christians consistently treated adherents of non-Christian religions as though they were "almost invisible, ignoring their presence, lumping them into broad categories, and perceiving them through an interpretive lens that minimized the value of their traditions and culture" (Wuthnow, 2007, p. 36).

Through these encounters, and the various responses that came to the fore as a result, the American government's democratic structure operated quite well in facilitating the preservation of accord in American civic life as well as restricting "the worst excesses of religious intolerance within the United States itself" (Wuthnow, 2007, p. 35). The particular characteristics of this time were the battles that were fought among the various Christian denominations, out of which emerged case law that dealt specifically with civil rights of the adherents rather than focusing on the particular teachings of the different Christian groups. One of the ways in which the courts influenced American individuals at the grass-roots level was by encouraging them to behave in a civil manner and to be respectful of their neighbors, irrespective of religious differences. This created a culture where individuals could practice their religion within their own separate communities without having to think much about how others around them were practicing their faith. The net effect of this was that tolerance carried on without the adherents of the different religious groups needing to bear the weight of engaging in deep understanding of and interaction with each other (Wuthnow, 2007, p. 35).

By the time the 20th century came to a close, this engagement, and the culture of tolerance that emerged out of it, prepared American Christians to adjust to the broader religious diversity that was fast becoming a reality (Wuthnow, 2007, p. 35). There were two different ways in which American Christians approached the increasing religious diversity in the US, asserts Wuthnow (2007). On the one hand, they addressed the new differences that they were experiencing with a tolerant spirit, using the same legal standards that had aided them in the past to forge out the practicalities of having to live together. On the other hand, this new religious diversity came with a more formidable challenge of needing to alter the commonly held notion that the

American religious landscape was fundamentally Christian, or Judeo-Christian, in its orientation. For the most part in the past Americans had been able to draw a dividing line between their civic life and their religious practices and convictions—a mindset which allowed them to view America as a Christian country all the while fully cognizant that this was not constitutionally true. Furthermore, they were easily able to believe that their own religion was in fact true without putting very much thought into the fact that other religions were present in their midst. This response was characteristic of American Christians throughout their engagement with adherents of non-Christian religions.

Wuthnow (2007) concludes his brief summary of this broad span of history of the American Christians' response to religious diversity by asking some pertinent questions: "Would Americans now continue to ignore other religions, even when adherents of these religions were living in their own neighborhoods? ... Or would they come to a deeper understanding of their own traditions as they compared it with others?" (p. 36). These questions become all the more pertinent given the current religious landscape.

Religious Diversity In The US After 1965

The Immigration and Naturalization Act of 1965 once again opened doors for immigrants from non-European countries to migrate to the United States, which they did in far greater numbers than ever before, resulting in a rapid increase in this already prevalent religious diversity. When the law took effect, it gave rise to mass migration from a plethora of Asian, African, and Latin countries (Williams, 2004, p. 14), and the Caribbean and Middle East (Warner, 2005, p. 232). While prior to 1965 80% of the migrants were from Europe, now 18% are from Europe, 32% from Asia, 44% from Latin America and the Caribbean Islands, and 6% from Africa. Today's immigrants are far more diverse than the earlier immigrants, come from far more varied countries, and speak a greater variety of languages. They bring not only their languages, foods, music, and customs but also their religions, with the result that religions such as Hinduism, Buddhism, Islam, and others can now be found virtually all over the US. The American landscape now includes mosques, temples, and gurdwaras (Ebaugh & Saltzman Chafetz, 2000, p. 13) besides churches and synagogues. Furthermore, the already existing churches, both Catholic and Protestant, are also becoming more diverse, because many of the new immigrants come from Christian backgrounds (Warner, 2005, p. 257).

While the most recent study conducted by The Pew Forum (2008) on American religious affiliation shows that the United States is still predominantly Christian, the increase in the number of adherents of Eastern religions indicates that religious diversity in the United States is on the rise. In their examination of American religious diversity, scholars have come to different conclusions regarding the religious makeup of America. For instance, from Eck's (2002) perspective, the US has moved from being a "Christian country" to becoming, in the words of his subtitle, "the world's most religiously diverse nation." On the other hand, while he acknowledges the fact of increasing religious diversity due to immigration, Warner (2004) observes that because many of these immigrants are Christian to begin with, "immigration is creating not so much new diversity in American religion as new diversity within American Christianity" (p. 20). That is, what is apparently happening is not the "de-Christianization of American society but de-Europeanization of American Christianity" (Warner, 2004, p. 20). Be that as it may, Eck (2002) points out that Americans are responding in different ways to this diversity, from disliking it to being fearful or suspicious because of "American xenophobia" (Eck, 2002, p. 295) to acknowledging that this diversity has inherent benefits.

This growth in religious diversity has also given rise to a qualitative change in how Americans perceive themselves, bringing to the forefront the issue of the relationship between Christianity and other religions. In light of this new religious pluralism, the issue of how Christians should respond to religious others in the US in the 21st century has taken on increasing salience. Netland (1991) writes that Americans, increasingly aware of religious diversity, are grappling with the presence of non-Christian religions and their truth-claims and are asking questions that bring to the foreground the challenge that religious diversity poses to Christian theology. This "host of disconcerting questions" includes:

> Why are there so many diverse religions? If Christianity is the true religion, why is it that so much of the world rejects it in favor of diametrically opposing religious traditions? Is it theologically and morally acceptable to maintain that one religion is uniquely true and that the others are at best incomplete or even false? Is Jesus Christ really unique after all? (Netland, 1991, p. 8)

Scholars have offered divergent assessments and responses to this growth in religious diversity. Muck (1990) asserts that while religious diversity in the US is increasing, the growth of the non-Christian religions has gone unnoticed by Americans. He gives four reasons for this. First, immigrants settle in urban areas, and the tendency of the American urban dweller is to pay attention to the "most essential issues," such as "poverty, homelessness, crime, drugs" (Muck, 1990, p. 19), etc. rather than to the influx of non-Christian religions. Second, non-Christian religions are still a minority and lack political and economic clout. Third, Americans do not show too much concern for these religions because of the general ethos of tolerance for those who practice non-Christian religions. Fourth, Americans have equated these world religions with cults and then disregarded them as they have "crystals, pyramids, astrology, talismans" (Muck, 1990, p. 19). Muck's assessment led him to lament that a robust "philosophy or theology" to deal properly with these religions has not been developed (p. 19).

Peter Brimelow's (1995) response to this growing diversity is to advocate closing the borders to immigrants because "the 1965 Immigration Act, and its amplifications in 1986 and 1990, have been a disaster and must be repealed" (p. 258). Arthur Schlesinger (1998) laments that multiculturalists fail to recognize the "beauty of e pluribus unum," exalting the pluribus while dismissing the unum. In his view multiculturalism in its "militant form … opposes the idea of a common culture" (pp. 150-151). He asserts that the growing heterogeneity of the American population must be coupled with a renewed pursuit of common American culture and "unifying ideals" (Schlesinger, 1998, p. 24). Wuthnow (2007) states that as more and more Hindus, Muslims, Buddhists, and other immigrants enter the US, Americans increasingly face the challenge of how they as individuals and as a nation should respond to this change in religious and cultural diversity. Issues pertaining to ethnicity, race, people's beliefs, convictions, and "how to live together," etc., are becoming increasingly salient, and responses have ranged from committing "hate crimes" to adopting a "live-and-let-live approach" to coexisting rather than actively engaging to espousing the attitude that it is better to get along than to get acquainted (Wuthnow, 2007, pp. 286-87).

Responses To The Increase In Diversity

As is evident from the brief and selective discussion above, Americans have responded to this increase in religious diversity in a number of ways. It would be instructive at this point to examine in detail some contemporary responses by Christians (churches and individuals) to the religious others in the US, because these responses foreground the discussion that exists among Christians over what constitutes a proper response to religious others. It will become evident that these responses are influenced by Christians' theological convictions, ranging from liberal to conservative Christians to pluralists. In the following paragraphs I draw from the research of five scholars—Paul Numrich, Diana Eck, Robert Wuthnow, Martin Marty and Terry Muck—on the different ways in which Christians have responded to religious others in the US.

Paul H. Numrich

Paul H. Numrich (2009) in The Faith Next Door: American Christians and Their New Religious Neighbors documents the different ways Christians of various stripes have responded to the presence of Hindus and Muslims in their communities. He classifies their responses into two groups: those who respond to religious others keeping in mind Christian truth-claims and doctrine, and those for whom other issues take priority over religious truth-claims in their interactions with religious others.

In the first group, with responses centered on truth-claims, the interactions were varied, ranging from exclusivistic, inclusivistic, and pluralistic responses to religious others. For example, in one instance in the same congregation two leaders had two different responses to Islam. One leader contrasted the claims of Christianity with those of Islam, labeling the former as true and the latter as false, thus falling within the exclusivist group; and the second leader took an inclusivistic stance and sought to emphasize features of Islamic theology that he saw as "partial perceptions of the full divine revelation found in Jesus Christ" (Numrich, 2009, p. 158). This inclusivism was also elucidated in the responses of a Catholic church and an Episcopal church: the

Catholic parish regarded other religions as reflecting rays of "that Truth" that enlightens all people, while the leader of the Episcopal church asserted that most, if not all, religions of the world have in them parts of the truth that Christianity has in its fullness (Numrich, 2009, p. 159). In the pluralistic camp fell two congregations: One church, part of the American Baptist Churches USA, sees no distinction between Christianity and other religions, as is elucidated by its annual interfaith service. Representatives from the Aztec faith, Judaism, Islam, Hinduism, San Mat, and Buddhism participate in this service, with some people praying and others reading passages from their respective scriptures (Numrich, 2009, p. 80). Another church, part of the United Church of Christ, recognizes and respects the teachings of other religions—the pastor even draws from the teachings of the Bhagavad Gita, the Tao-te Ching, and the Qur'an in his preaching (Numrich, 2009, p. 147).

In Numrich's (2009) second group, where the interaction was based on issues that made the Christian truth-claim secondary, Christians responded in a number of different ways (p. 161). In the case of African-American Christians, their shared status with African-American Muslims as minorities was the driving force that made them join efforts to deal with significant community issues. Another Christian exclusivist, while in no way endorsing the theological claims of other religions, affirmed in contradiction to other Christian exclusivists a sort of "civic pluralism" that gave Hindus, Muslims, and adherents of any other non-Christian religion the "constitutional right" (Numrich, 2001, p. 162) to practice their religion in freedom. Yet other exclusivists focused on evangelism and emphasized the friendship aspect of evangelism, and, while not affirming that salvation may be found in other religions, put the truth-claims of the religion second in the order of importance. These Christians, who would first seek to demonstrate their love to the stranger and the neighbor in need, in some cases may never present the message of the gospel and in other cases would continue their friendship with a non-Christian even if the person never became inclined to accepting the gospel (Numrich, 2009, p. 162). Finally, Orthodox Christians, while emphasizing the necessity to guard Christian truths, in their encounter with Islam have shown a proclivity for "dialogue" and "cooperation" and a move away from conflicts to stress "potential mutual redemption as peoples of a shared destiny" (Numrich, 2009, p. 162).

In essence, what Numrich (2009) demonstrates through his research is that Christians may be divided into two groups: those who focus on others' and their own truth-claims, and those who emphasize others' "human needs and social needs" (p. 163) over and above religious truth. In either case, he advises that relationships with religious others must be characterized by respect, humility, meekness, and reverence for God that leads them to live respectful lives among religious others (Numrich, 2009, pp.164-65).

Diana Eck

Eck (2002) defines pluralism as "the dynamic process through which we engage with one another in and through our very deepest differences" (p. 70). Her definition suggests that a Christian response to religious others means participating fully in this experiment of pluralism, a participation that is comprised of four components. First, pluralism is not just a synonym for diversity. It is the act of engaging the plurality or diversity of American life. Without an active engagement of religious others, the religious structures we see around us—churches, temples, mosques, etc.—remain examples of diversity and nothing else. We may "study," "complain about," or "celebrate" diversity, but diversity in and of itself is not pluralism. "Pluralism is not a given but must be created," and for one to create pluralism, it is necessary to participate in and attune oneself to "the life and energies of one another" (Eck, 2002, p. 70).

Second, Christians' participation in American pluralism means moving beyond tolerating others and includes taking initiative to understand religious others. Tolerance by itself, although moving beyond intolerance, does not create the space for one neighbor to learn about the other(s). Eck (2002) laments that American society does not have a good grasp of religious differences; that not many school systems have robust programs to instruct students "about the world's religions in the context of social studies or history" (p. 70) and that while departments of religion in colleges and universities are thriving, not many theological institutions that are preparing students for service in churches provide students with adequate knowledge of the world religions. Our attempts to understand the other must include dispelling the stereotypes and images that color our view of others. To elucidate this component, she cites an example in Milwaukee on the eve of Thanksgiving 2000, when representatives from the Muslim and Christian communities signed a pledge that affirmed mutual love and support and made a commitment to participate in "the exercise of understanding, cooperation, and growth in unity through faith" (Eck, 2002, p. 69). Taking constructive steps to understand religious others is crucial, according to Eck (2002, p. 70), in a highly religious society as ours where almost half the US population participates in religious services on a monthly basis (Koenig, 2009, p. 311).

Third, Christians' participation in American pluralism is the encounter of our commitments to our faith; it is not just relativism in which our "religious commitments" or "secular commitments" are displaced or eliminated (Eck, 2002, p. 71). Pluralism, rather than being a "valueless relativism" that does away with commitment to our faith and as a result eradicates "particularity" to achieve "universality," means actively engaging "differences and particularities" (Eck, 2002, p. 71) one effect of which may be a broader view of one's own faith. Eck (2002) suggests that this encounter of our religious commitments with those of others in the context of "the public school," or "the city council," or "the interfaith council" includes dialogue with people of other faiths, where the goal is to come not to agreement but rather to "achieving relationship" (p. 72). She adds that space has been created, and continues to expand, in the "American civic life" to achieve this relationship as new religious groups are continually added to the mix and "many new religious voices are heard" (Eck, 2002, p. 72).

Fourth, Eck (2002) argues that we need to think of Christians' participation in American pluralism as a process that is never complete but something that is ongoing in which each successive generation participates. In fact, she says that when we take part in this process of pluralism, we are actually "participating in the 'idea of America'" (p. 72). That is to say, when we claim the statements in the Declaration of Independence are self-evident, it is necessary to keep them "alive" in the present by continuing "argument and dialogue" (Eck, 2002, p. 72). In other words, the statements are given fresh meaning by continual engagement of each new generation with the new religious participants recurrently added to the already existing diverse community. Eck (2002) gives the example of California Board of Education's statement that also affirms this process as an "unfinished struggle" (p. 72). The same document, asserting that "study about religion in America is fundamental to understanding and appreciating the American heritage," encourages the teaching of the major religions of the world (California State Department of Education 1991, 23), which is one way in which Christians can participate in this ongoing process.

Having laid out the four components of what it means for Christians to participate in the pluralism project in America, Eck

44

(2002) gives examples of "new beginnings and new bridges of understanding and cooperation built across the lines of religious differences" (p. 340). For instance, when a mosque in Springfield, Massachusetts, was pelted with stones and had its windows broken, and on another occasion when one of the Muslim leaders arriving for prayers during the month of Ramadan had stones thrown at him, the president of the Springfield Council of Churches responded to these incidents by contacting the mosque, calling a television station, and organizing a group of people from a number of churches to visit the mosque. These incidents led the Christians, Muslims, and Jews in this town to generate a "climate of concern" for each other and foster "interfaith relationships" (Eck, 2002, p. 342), ultimately increasing civic awareness in the town of Springfield. From Eck's (2002) perspective, one way Christians engage religious others in the American pluralism project is by showing support for them when they are treated badly.

Other responses that are important to Eck (2002), and that fit in well with her perspective of Christian engagement of religious others, include interfaith dialogues. For instance, when there were open displays of anti-Semitism in Billings, MT, the response of Margaret MacDonald of the Montana Association of Churches led to a number of actions by the people in that town. She persuaded her church to display a menorah in its window; this was followed by the local newspaper printing cutout menorahs that its readers could display in their windows at home. As other displays of anti-Semitism were followed by other shows of solidarity, dialogue between Christians and Jews flourished: the United Church of Christ sponsored a summer family camp devoted to Christian-Jewish dialogue, and the Montana Synod of the Evangelical Lutheran Church of America and the Montana Association of Jewish Communities collaborated for the purpose of intentionally dialoguing and building relationships and have also travelled together to Israel. Furthermore, the Montana Association of Churches has started a statewide program called Christian Witness for Humanity with the sole purpose of informing Christians of the insidious nature of the "white supremacist 'theology'" that underlies the hate movement (Eck, 2002, p. 347). From Eck's (2002) perspective interfaith dialogue, developing interfaith relationships, and providing appropriate education are concrete ways in which Christians should respond to religious others in the US.

Robert Wuthnow

Robert Wuthnow (2007) narrates a number of ways in which Christians have responded to the increasing religious diversity in the US. His research shows that in order to engage religious pluralism, churches have sponsored interfaith programs to promote understanding among the different religions, and some churches are less likely to sponsor these programs than other churches. The highest involvement was seen by Catholic churches at 48%; mainline Protestants, 47%; black Protestant churches, 42%; and evangelical Protestants, 35% (Wuthnow, 2007, p. 234). Information about the variety of ways in which congregations have responded to religious diversity was gathered through "in-depth qualitative interviews with more than fifty pastors from around the country" (Wuthnow, 2007, p. 235), who talked in detail about their churches' programs.

Wuthnow (2007) describes what Faith Lutheran Church in California does to promote religious understanding (p. 235). Comprised of three hundred members and located in a predominantly Jewish upper-middle-class suburb, the church is in close proximity to four Jewish congregations, two mosques, two Buddhist temples, and a Hindu temple. The pastor believes that it is his congregation's responsibility to live harmoniously with other religious groups in his town. He has built upon a foundation laid by his predecessor, who would post a sign during the Jewish holidays, reading, "Happy Holidays to Our Jewish Neighbors." The current pastor teaches the church members that Jews do not need to become Christians because they already have a covenant relationship with God; that Christianity has its roots in Judaism; and that Jews and Christians serve the same God. The pastor is also on the board of an organization whose main purpose is to bring Jewish and Christian clergy together to combat anti-Semitism by donating copies of The Diary of Anne Frank to school libraries and classrooms. This church has also adopted a Holocaust survivor who periodically gives lectures at the church and organizes tours for the members of this congregation to visit the Museum of Tolerance in Los Angeles. Occasionally they sponsor joint projects with a synagogue in the area to bring the members of both groups together to do service projects in the wider community (Wuthnow, 2007).

In order to engage the other religious groups in their town, this church organizes an annual "service of tolerance" (Wuthnow, 2007, p. 236) to which all the religious groups are invited, with approximately two hundred Hindus, Muslims, Jews, and Christians attending. At the end of the service adherents of the different religions recite in their respective language, "God is love and we should love one another." The pastor is deeply interested in reconciliation between the different religious groups not only because of his understanding of the Christian gospel but also because of personal experience with hate crime when someone fire-bombed his church. Working to increase tolerance between different groups is a way in which he demonstrates that "love is more powerful than hate" (Wuthnow, 2007, p. 236).

Other churches are also involved in interfaith activities to develop mutual understanding, which include hosting Middle Eastern dinners where Jews and Muslims are invited to join in and speak;

inviting international students, including Hindus and Muslims, to share meals with members of the church; participating with Muslims in an organization to promote social justice; and inviting Jewish and Muslim leaders to speak in their church. In this wide mix of responses to religious others, Wuthnow (2007) highlights two other ways, from the extreme ends of the spectrum, of responding to the increased religious pluralism: one, "strategies of avoidance" (p. 244), where they neither talk about how to relate to religious others nor organize activities that would bring them into contact with adherents of other religions; and two, downplaying interfaith activities as a means of engaging adherents of other religions in any meaningful way, teaching instead their congregants to develop relationships with people of other faiths on an individual level and win them to the Lord (p. 240).

While Wuthnow (2007) narrates a variety of responses by Christians to the increase in religious diversity, he advocates that we move "beyond shallow responses to diversity" and engage in what he calls "reflective pluralism" (p. 289). Reflective pluralism includes recognizing that people are different and why they are different, and having "good reasons for engaging" with adherents of other religions (Wuthnow, 2007, pp. 289-292). From his perspective, reflective pluralism is comprised of six salient characteristics. First, it includes an interest in the "substantive aspects of pluralism" (p. 290). This includes caring about "specific issues, teachings, or practices" rather than seeking to rise above them. They are not only able to grapple with "broad comparisons" of the various religions but also focus on narrower issues that bring to the foreground larger agreements and disagreements among the religions. This grappling about narrower issues, such as the various understandings of the afterlife, or the identity of Jesus, etc., includes not only thinking about them on an intellectual level but also exploring the various implications these issues have "for personal and social conduct" (Wuthnow, 2007, p. 290).

Second, reflective pluralism means that a person becomes a "studier" (Wuthnow, 2007, p. 290) of other religions in order to understand the divergent truth-claims of the various religions. Rather than assuming that cultural and religious differences are not worthy of our attention, we assume the posture of "inquiry" (Wuthnow, 2007, p. 291). This means having the understanding that while mastery of religious pluralism is not easy, and that it may take a long time to come to a satisfactory view on the deeper questions regarding religious beliefs and values, an endeavor which may never end, this exercise is interesting and worth the effort.

Third, reflective pluralism means "carefully consider[ing] what it means to have a 'view'" (Wuthnow, 2007, p. 291). This includes walking a fine line between recognizing that the things we believe and know depend on our viewpoint, which is shaped by our culture, and that our point of view is not arrived at arbitrarily or disconnected from truth. It also includes the recognition that our viewpoints need to be "examined and compared ... and truth needs to be sought as well" (Wuthnow, 2007, p. 291). That is, in some sense this is an ongoing exercise.

Fourth, engaging in reflective pluralism includes deliberate attempts to defuse any objections raised to pluralism. This includes having awareness that not everyone has positive views about pluralism, trying to understand the root causes of the opposition to pluralism, and not considering our own position as being superior to the position of others.

Fifth, it means respecting others. It includes going beyond making statements such as "I respect you even though I know you are wrong." to recognizing that a person's religious beliefs are closely interwoven with their identity and that it is not easy to separate them. The implication of this is that it is important to consider the other person's religious beliefs differently than just reading about them in a book or thinking about them abstractly.

Sixth, there is willingness to compromise. By this Wuthnow (2007) means that rather than thinking that our religious beliefs and values are insignificant or that we can "simply" replace one belief with another, we deliberately make the decision to give something up in order to develop a working relationship with the adherent(s) of other religions. This may include interacting at a level that moves them out of their comfort zone to a place where differences become more prominent or giving up "the companionship and security" (Wuthnow, 2007, p. 292) that we experience when we live in surroundings that are familiar to us.

Martin Marty

Martin Marty (2005) in When Faiths Collide argues that in a pluralistic context with shared "space and resources," when a variety of faith communities "which are strangers to each other" collide with each other, such a situation is adequately dealt with not through the "conventional plea for tolerance among them" but by being hospitable towards each other, including receiving the stranger, followed by "conversation" and "interplay" (p. 1).

Citing Neusner, Marty (2005) says tolerance is a "notion" that grants that the views of the outsider are "right for the other but not for me"; that does not think about the other religious believers and does not invest in the hard task of determining how the other fits into one's own "theological framework and religious system"; and that regards the others as an "unavoidable inconvenience or an evil that cannot be eliminated" (Marty, 2005, p. 65). For these reasons he considers tolerance by itself to be inadequate to help one deal with the challenge posed by the presence of the stranger. Quoting Niebuhr, he suggests that the solution that makes religious diversity possible must include a "very high form of religious commitment" by the adherents of the faith, meaning that each religion asserts its "highest insights" and at the same time continues to espouse humility and contrition and recognize that "all actual expressions of religious faith are historically conditioned." This will keep any religion from claiming for itself "official validity" or "official monopoly," and will engender a "spirit of tolerance" by each religion toward the stranger (Marty, 2005, p. 66). For Marty (2005), expressing hospitality toward the stranger is the way to deal adequately with the challenge posed by their presence.

He formulates his argument for hospitality by juxtaposing two groups: belongers and strangers. When the stranger enters the space of a group that belongs to that space, the belongers experience fear because of the presence of the stranger. This fear—that their values may be subverted or that their members may be proselytized by the stranger—results in hostility toward the stranger (Marty, 2005, p. 13). He goes on to define the stranger along a continuum that begins with the self as stranger and stretches to the national and international level. One's fear of the stranger can be experienced even in the belonger's fear of the self and the ensuing alienation, which results in estrangement that is characterized by "aloneness, resentment, and hostility over against others" (Marty, 2005, p. 19). In order to deal meaningfully with the stranger in the neighborhood, it is imperative that belongers begin by seeking to understand themselves in order to overcome their alienation with themselves. This introspection includes asking oneself questions such as,

> Why have I been fearful, paralyzed, immobilized, or rendered
> apathetic? Why have I been unable to find perspective, to
> look at the other person or group in open ways? Further,

what commitments have I made that lead me to have to be
distanced from or suspicious of the religious stranger?
(Marty 2005, p. 19)

Asking such questions will help us understand ourselves and overcome
our self-estrangement. And it is this kind of understanding the stranger
in the self that will help us understand those around us whom we
characterize as strangers.

Having said this Marty (2005) goes on to present "a simple
entrée to the concept of hospitality" (p. 128). Hospitality includes many
components, beginning with self- criticism of one's own religious
tradition and expressing in fullness my religious faith along with the
many symbols that reflect my faith. Symbols that are integral to one's
faith must not be obscured or removed so that we may not misinform
the guest—the religious other—about who we are, thereby creating
"confusion and deception" (Marty, 2005, p. 128). At the same time, the
symbols that I display must not offend the guest; i.e., I must display a
level of understanding of the other and his religious sensitivities.
Conversely, when I am the guest receiving hospitality, I must also
expect the religious other to not "hide the symbols and forego the
rituals" (Marty, 2005, p. 129). It is when we are open about who we are
and show sensitivity to the other that we are able to learn about each
other. In other words, the goal of self-criticism is mutual education.
And Marty (2005) goes on to assert that one of the ways in which our
hospitality becomes evident is "when groups begin to regard each other
with civility" (p. 142).

Civility is the first of four principles that characterize
hospitality. Civility itself includes four essential components (Marty,
2005, pp. 144-45). First, "welcome the diversity of beliefs and opinions"
(p. 144). Voices are not to be suppressed or ignored but rather
articulated. Second, recognize that civil discourse is not a product but

rather a process. We must not expect that groups who are experiencing conflict will come to "complete settlement" (Marty, 2005, p. 144), but that dialogue will lead to outcomes for the subsequent stage(s) and we will experience both advancement and setback. Third, "realize and teach that profound social issues have religious dimensions" (p. 144). Marty (2005) admits this may seem like an unnecessary reminder, but in fact this understanding is quite rare in communities that are addressing divisive issues. Fourth, "understand that religious belief frequently calls for some form of civil discourse" (Marty, 2005, p. 145). That is, space must be created where the stranger is made to feel welcome to dialogue with other participants so that new voices may join the conversation.

"Covenants of conversation" (Marty, 2005, p. 145) represent a second principle that characterizes hospitality. This principle involves creating an atmosphere where the participants speak and act with integrity and consider others as doing the same; the participants express their faith; engage others respectfully, keeping in mind the fact that because of our own religious limits we may not have a full grasp on "non-religious knowledge"; and participants must speak when they observe "the failures and mistakes" of their co-believers (Marty, 2005, p. 145).

The third principle characterizing hospitality is "engaging the others" (Marty, 2005, p. 145) in situations where strangers meet to confer with each other. This includes engaging the other on a personal level rather than just through group meetings that generate "reports of task forces, formal documents, and statements of position" (Marty, 2005, p. 145). One way this personal engagement may occur is through telling one's stories, which makes the other a "person." It also includes acting on the basis of agreements, whether partial or relative. This is possible considering that civil discourse is a process. Further, Marty

(2005) asserts that we must listen to the voices of those who have in the past experienced exclusion, and we must act on plans that emerge from our dialogue—i.e., "put words into actions" (p. 146).

The fourth principle that characterizes hospitality is called "living with conflict during and after conversation and argument" (Marty, 2005, p. 146). We must recognize that conflict is to be expected and take steps so that the process does not cease with the conflict but provides the impetus to move beyond it. A part of this process is to take stock of and utilize the religious resources available to us to accomplish this goal.

Terry Muck

Terry Muck's (1990) approach toward American religious pluralism is theological in nature (p. 55). His response to a "religiously diverse, legally endorsed pluralism," attempting to draw from the "unique and unchanging" (Muck, 1990, p. 56) message of the gospel and applying it to the continually changing religious landscape, is threefold: First, we should "love our neighbors unconditionally"; second, we should glorify God through our institutions, where the institution may be a tribe, or temple, or monarchy, or the church; and third, we should preach the gospel (p. 63).

The command to love our neighbor is lived out at two "levels." The first level, with regard to the differences—socioeconomic, employment, etc.—includes sharing with the family next door that is different from us the "common courtesies of life" (Muck, 1990, p. 67), whether that means speaking with them in a pleasant manner, lending them our lawnmower, watching their house when they are away, or not speaking evil of them even when there is opportunity to do so (p. 67). The second level, based on Jesus' story of the Good Samaritan and Paul's teaching on love in Rom 13:8, Lev 19:8, and Exod 23, goes even further and includes loving our enemies. In his attempt to elucidate the story of the Good Samaritan and make a contemporary application, Muck (1990) exhorts us to think of ourselves as one of the three people who had the opportunity to help the "injured man" (p. 68) and to think of the injured man as one of those groups of people that we dislike. Jesus calls us to love the very people that we dislike, Muck says, including in his list groups pertinent to our discussion in this book—the "Hindu, Buddhist, or Muslim" (p. 68). We are called to love them—experiencing inconveniences for their sake, putting their needs ahead of our own, lending them money when they need it—in spite of the fact that these groups are growing in power and have the potential of threatening "the stability and traditions of our communities and churches" (Muck, 1990, p. 69). Furthermore, loving our neighbors means not judging them: While "our understanding of God and the universe may be better than theirs," it does not necessarily mean that we are morally better than them; in fact, our "common sinful" condition puts us on the same plane as them (Muck, 1990, p. 72). It also means that we should remove any barriers in ourselves or in our culture that would impede our relationships with them. We should also treat each person as the unique individuals they are, eradicating any stereotypes that might cause us to treat them as though they are all the same (Muck, 1990, p. 72).

Our love for those who are different and those whom we dislike, in keeping with the teaching of the two greatest commandments, must emanate from our love of the God of the Bible because that is the only accurate "standard" of love we have. The stronger our relationship with God, the better we will be able to love the Hindu, the Buddhist, and the Muslim. Additionally, this love must be expressed in the context of the family, and it must not only include loving with our hearts, souls, and minds, i.e., the "total person," but it must also be "careful love" where we discern how much of the other religions' teaching we expose our children to so that we are able to "insure the transmission of the [Christian] faith to future generations" (Muck, 1990, p. 74).

The second component of Muck's (1990) approach, that of glorifying God through our institutions, is applied to the church with the purpose of transforming the society in cooperation with institutions—temples, mosques—of other religions, while making sure that false teaching does not creep into the church—"its theologians, denominations, pastors, and lay workers" (p. 79)—and it does not become syncretistic. Cooperation with other religious institutions includes "cooperative competition, neutral competition, and hostile competition" (Muck, 1990, p. 80). Describing cooperative competition Muck (1990) suggests that just as in the Old Testament David and Hiram, the king of Tyre, cooperated to build each other's kingdom and helped each other prosper so also we can have friendly relationships with institutions of other religions, fundamental ideological differences notwithstanding. Speaking of neutral cooperation Muck suggests that just as in the Old Testament we read of Joseph's role as administrator in Egypt, we can develop a spirit of neutral cooperation with other religions' institutions, including an exchange of services and goods that are mutually beneficial to all parties involved without the compromise of religious beliefs. And while conflict may not be absent but exists due to misperceptions, the relationship is not hostile in tenor. Explaining hostile competition Muck suggests that just as in the Old Testament the Israelites were called to destroy the Canaanites to keep the nation of Israel pure, so also we in the church need to "rebuff" anyone or anything that may be a threat to the purity of the church. In essence, at the heart of Muck's exhortation about developing friendly relationships with institutions of other religions is not only the significance of loving our neighbors but also recognizing that "friendly cooperation" (p.86) is far more effective when we seek to implement moral reforms in this secular nation to transform our world. Furthermore, it is this sort of cooperation that offers a better witness to the non-Christian world (Muck, 1990, pp. 80-86).

Muck's (1990) third component has to do with proclaiming the truth of the gospel in our cultural context where religious pluralism is affirmed and espousing the "unique truthfulness" (p. 97) of Christianity is considered passé and shunned. At the heart of his nine-fold principle of proclaiming the truth in the climate of American religious pluralism is the necessity to learn about other religions so that we can gain insights about "evangelism and apologetics," not so that we can destroy their influence (Muck, 1990, p. 97). In fact, Muck (1990) asserts that the presence of Hindus, Buddhists, Muslims, their temples and mosques, and their thoughts are not a source of danger for us but opportunities to proclaim the truth to them. Muck's nine principles (pp. 100-04) that undergird the proclamation of the truth in our pluralistic culture include: being intimate with our faith so we can articulate it well; expecting conflict in dialogue with religious others; acknowledging that there is some truth in other religions; recognizing that all the dialogue partners believe and proclaim what they perceive as absolute truth but do so with only a partial understanding of the truth; making sure our motives are right—wrong motives could include trying to gain converts, manipulating others to believe, or arrogantly believing that we are better than others; keeping as the goal of the discussion the clear communicating of the gospel and understanding of the other; not creating our own ideas but rather sticking with God's theology—knowing our faith, being firmly established in the love of our faith, and being committed to transform our world; rather than trying to disprove other religions, focusing on proving Christianity; and adopting an attitude of humility (Muck, 1990).

Some Pertinent Themes

From the review of these responses to religious diversity, a diversity that has always characterized the American religious landscape, three broad themes emerge that are salient to Christian engagement with and perception of Islam and Muslims. First, Christians must adhere to their own faith without compromising biblical truth. Similarly, we must expect and encourage the followers of other religions to adhere to their own faith as well. Second, Christians must proactively engage religious others. This may happen in a variety of ways, including developing friendships, helping them when they have needs, dialoguing with them, entering their world and inviting them into our own by sharing and hearing each other's stories, dispelling myths and stereotypes of religious others, understanding their religion, helping them understand Christianity, defending them when they face challenges from the wider American culture, engaging in collaborative efforts to address mutual problems in society, giving them space to speak from their perspective and listening to them, etc. Our engagement with religious others must be done in a spirit of respect, humility, meekness, and reverence for God. Third, Christians must proclaim the gospel. The imperative of preaching the good news of Jesus Christ to every human being is very clear in the New Testament. A few examples will suffice: Matt 28:16-20, the Great Commission, highlights the significance of making disciples of Jesus from people of all nations; Mark 16:15-16 and Luke 24:46-48 highlight the importance of preaching to all nations the repentance and forgiveness of sins in the name of Jesus; Acts 1:8 highlights Jesus' statement calling the disciples to be witnesses of Jesus to the ends of the earth; and John 20:21 highlights the disciples of Jesus being sent into the world the same way in which Jesus was sent into the world.

The obligation to preach the good news of Jesus Christ is laid upon the shoulders of every disciple of Jesus.

Having explored religious diversity in the United States and American Christians' engagement with it, we now proceed to understand the growth of Islam in this social context.

CHAPTER 3

GROWTH OF ISLAM IN THE US

Since moving to the United States in 1987, I have encountered Muslims on numerous occasions, both as a student as well as professionally. The most memorable encounter occurred in the late 1990s when I was a Master of Divinity student at Trinity Evangelical Divinity School. Studying in the library one day, I noticed a woman wearing a hijab studying there as well. From her dress I gathered that she was from an Islamic background. Mustering up the courage one evening to talk to her, I found out she was an Indian Muslim who had married an Indian-American and had just immigrated to the US. She liked coming to Trinity's library to study to prepare for her medical board exams. A few days later I noticed a man talking to her, and I thought that man might be her husband. Although we made eye contact that evening, we did not engage in any conversation. A few days later I was walking past one of the study rooms in the library, and I caught sight of something through the glass pane that took a few seconds to register in my brain. Not sure that I had actually seen what I thought I saw, I walked back to peek through the window to take another look. Sure enough, I observed this Muslim man facing East, standing on his prayer rug and going through the Islamic prayer ritual. I was quite shocked to see a Muslim praying in the library of an evangelical Christian institution. Over the next few days, as I reflected on what I had seen, I decided that the next time I saw this man in the library I would engage him in conversation. It was not long after that that I was able to meet him, and we talked at length about matters pertaining to spirituality and religion. I took the opportunity to explain the gospel to him, and he in turn shared the challenges that Muslims face in the US. He communicated to me that he wanted Christians to have the proper understanding of Islam and even asked if he could come to my church to explain to my congregants the fundamentals of Islam and share with my congregation that Muslims are peaceful people.

Since that occasion I have been observing as well as reading about the growth of Islam in the religiously diverse American context. In this chapter we will briefly discuss this growth of Islam, touching upon the following: American Christians' views of Muslims, Muslims immigration to the US, formation of Muslim communities, challenges that Muslims face, and the impact of these challenges upon Muslims in the US.

American Christians' Views of Muslims

In Islam in America Jane I. Smith (2010) writes that some scholars believe that, for about two centuries before the arrival of Columbus, Muslims had been coming to the Americas from Spain and from the northwest coast of Africa, and in fact some of the members of Columbus' crew practiced Islam. These aforementioned scholars think that African Muslim explorers may have penetrated many areas of the Americas, set up trading posts, developed relationships with, and even intermarried with Native Americans (Smith, 2010, p. 51). While these suggestions are not accepted by all scholars, it is certain that large numbers of Muslims were part of the forced resettlement of Africans to the Americas during the slave trade. Between 1451 and 1870 almost two million enslaved Africans were brought to North America (Curtin, 1969, p. 268). Although there are no official records specifying how many Muslims were represented in this number, Austin (1984) estimates that nearly 30,000 enslaved Africans brought to antebellum America were Muslim (pp. 29-36).

In his 2000 book, The Crescent Obscured, Allison asserts that Americans' encounter with Muslims began before the United States even came into existence; in fact, he suggests that contact may have happened "almost before" the Europeans' awareness of the existence of America (p. xiv). The very first encounter of an American with Muslims may have been when Capt. John Smith, a New England settler, was fighting the Turks in Eastern Europe. Other contacts came when an American ship was captured off the coast of Morocco in 1625. This was followed twenty years later when a ship manned by settlers from the Cambridge, Massachusetts, colony engaged and defeated an Algerian ship in battle. In another incident, in 1673, an American ship from New York was captured by Algerians, and its sailors were held captive by the Muslims. Similarly, toward the end of the 17th century another American sailor, Joshua Gee, was held captive in Morocco. These episodes are significant because they contributed to early impressions of Muslims as barbarians and of clashes with them as a struggle between Christians and Muslims, indeed as a struggle between "civilization and what the newly civilized world would define as barbarism" (Allison, 2000, p. xv). These views, so common today, not only predate Muslim immigration to the US but also predate the country itself.

Perusal of the significant literature authored over the next 200 years shows that Americans continued to have less than flattering views of Muslims. Novels and poems about Muslims included stories of captivities, history, and biographies of Muhammad. An American edition of the legendary book Arabian Nights was first published in the 1790s (Allison, 2000, p. 74). This literature presented a consistently negative image of the Muslim world, showing Americans the consequences of "wrong choices" (Allison, 2000, p. xvii). For example, while Muhammad had given the people a chance to change by "adopting a new religion, building states and empires, re- organizing family life" (Allison, 2000, p. xvii), these changes had been grave mistakes. As a result, countries like Egypt, Syria, Turkey, and Mauritania, which had once been prosperous nations, had now become impoverished because of bad government, and their once-fertile lands had become desert. Thriving ports like Tunis, Algiers, and Tripoli, which had once engaged in honest trade, now engaged in piracy. Everywhere in the Muslim world women were degraded by being kept in "harems and seraglios," and had become victims of "unrestrained sexual power" (Allison, 2000, p. xvii). The Muslim world was despotic, characterized by the suppression of public debate and "tyranny and anarchy" (p. 35). For Americans, the Muslim world had become a cautionary lesson in how not to build a country or a family and how not to engage in commerce (Allison, 2000, p. xvii).

The American image of the Islamic world was well-illustrated in 1802 in an anonymous biographical account of Muhammad, entitled: The Life of Mahomet; or, the History of that Imposture which was begun, carried on, and finally established by him in Arabia: and which has Subjugated a Larger Portion of the Globe, than the Religion of Jesus has yet set at Liberty. The author laments that rational people have been degraded by Muhammad's wicked and insincere behavior; that Muslims have been so degraded because of violent and fraudulent actions and enslaved by such an iniquitous and blasphemous system that the only way to free them of this is through their conquest by the West; that it was not possible to enlighten Muslims through the work of missionaries or teachers because they were ruled by despots who would not be persuaded by arguments but only force; and that it would be easier to convert "heathens and savages" (Allison, 2000, p. 36) than the

Muslims. Through his writing the author asserted that Islam creates a tyranny over the minds of people, which leads to political tyranny just as bad as Muhammad's religious pretenses (Allison, 2000, pp. 35-36). Humphrey Prideaux (1698), in his biography of Muhammad, asserted that Muhammad was a liar and a cheat who attempted to "delude" his hearers (p. 26). He viewed Muhammad as a religious fraud and a false prophet driven to tyranny by his lust and ambition (p. 55).

The 18th-century Western impression of the Islamic world was that it was characterized by a "wicked mix of political tyranny and wild sex" (Allison, 2000, p. 61). For example, Penelope Aubin in her 1797 book, The Noble Slaves, wrote:

> The Monarch gives a loose to his passions, and thinks it no crime to keep as many women for his use, as his lustful appetite excited him to like; and his Favorites, Ministers of State, and Governance, who always follow their Master's Example, imitate his way of living. (Preface)

The perception among Americans was that this sexually deviant behavior existed because Islam taught that "women had no souls" (Allison, 2000, p. 63). John Foss, an American who had been held captive in the Algiers, wrote that for Muslims, women were created for the purpose of bearing children, were not allowed to enter mosques, and were not able to go to heaven, "yet the women say their prayers secretly at home" (Foss, 1798, p. 65). In other words, women were not seen as spiritually equal to men but merely as "objects of male lust ... and desire" (Allison, 2000, p. 63). Thus, the only way that men and women could associate was in a sexual way.

Lady Mary Wortley Montagu, who lived in Constantinople between 1717 and 1718, disputed this perception. While in Constantinople, she wore Turkish attire and "visited women in their homes, in the harems, and even in the bath" (Allison, 2000, p. 65). Her experience and observations were a challenge to the Western perceptions of "Muslim sexual confinement and depravity" (Allison, 2000, p. 65). According to her, other accounts of women in the Levant were inaccurate and absurd, having been written by individuals who had not had the opportunity to make actual observations of the lives of women or what happens in mosques (Wharncliffe et al, 1893, p. 334). She wrote that the Turkish women described as living in "miserable confinement" are actually freer than any other women in the world, living lives of pleasure, without any cares, spending their time "visiting, bathing, or the agreeable amusement of spending money, and inventing new fashions" (Wharncliffe et al, 1893, p. 361). While the only public places that these women are able to go to are the "bagnios" or public baths where they have contact only with women, her perhaps unconsciously biased perception was that these women "take great pleasure" in this "diversion" (Wharncliffe et al, 1893, p. 361).

These differing observations indicate that the perceptions of the Americans about Muslim women were influenced by biases and misinformation. It is helpful to situate the growth of Islam in the US against this background of a general negative view of Islam and Muslims espoused by Americans, an outlook which defined the American context and impacted the life of Muslims as they immigrated to the US.

Muslim Immigration to the US

In her 2010 book, Islam in America, Smith reviews several historical waves of Muslim immigration to the United States. The first wave came to the US between 1875 and 1912 from the Levant—what is today Syria, Jordan, Palestine, and Lebanon (Smith, 2010, p. 52). The second wave came to the United States at the end of World War I when the Ottoman Empire dissolved. Many of these immigrants were related to Muslims who had immigrated earlier and had established themselves in the United States. The next wave of immigration started in 1945 after World War II and extended up to the 1960s.

While past waves of immigration brought in a small number of Muslims, this changed when President Lyndon Johnson signed the Immigration and Nationality Act of 1965, abolishing the quota system that had based immigration on ethnic or national background. This change reduced European immigration and brought in a wave of Asian, Middle Eastern, and African immigrants from a variety of different religious backgrounds, including larger numbers of Muslims. In 2010 the largest percentage of the Muslim population in the US was from Pakistan, India, and Bangladesh, with estimates of over a million people. After a few Muslim immigrants had arrived toward the end of the 19th century, the numbers of immigrants greatly increased in the 1970s and 1980s. A large number of Muslim immigrants had come from Indonesia and Malaysia. An estimated one million Iranians had immigrated, including Jews, Zoroastrians, Baha'is, Eastern Christians, as well as Muslims. Close behind were Muslims from the Arab countries in the Middle East, Turkey, and Eastern Europe. Also present were Muslims from many African countries, including Ghana, Kenya, Senegal, Uganda, Cameroon, Guinea, Sierra Leone, Liberia, and Tanzania (Smith, 2010, p. 54).

In its 2015 study, "America's Changing Religious Landscape," the Pew Research Center reported that in 2014, 0.9% of the American population—approximately 2.85 million people identified themselves as Muslims. Estimates of the total number of Muslims in the US range from 2.75 million in 2011 (Pew Research Center, 2011), to 3.3 million in 2015 (Mohamed, 2016). In 2011, 63% of Muslims in the US were immigrants and of this number 45% came into the US after 1990. These first-generation Muslims have come from a wide variety of countries: 41% from the Middle East or North Africa; 26% from South Asian countries, including 14% from Pakistan, 5% from Bangladesh, and 3% from India; 11% from Sub-Saharan Africa; 7% from Europe; 5% from Iran; and 9% from other countries (Pew Research Center, 2011). Furthermore, from October 1, 2015, to September 30, 2016, the US admitted 38,901 Muslim refugees—45.77% of the total number of 84,995 refugees admitted from all nations. This is the highest number of Muslim refugees admitted into the US since 2002 when information on self-reported religious affiliation first became accessible to the public. In the last 15 years, 279,339 Muslim refugees have entered the US, which is 32% of the total refugees admitted during this time period (Connor, 2016).

What are the characteristics that define these Muslims immigrating to America toward the end of the 19th century? They display diversity in terms of "languages, cultures, movements, and ideologies" (Smith 2010, p. 54). Some of them are Shiites, others are Sunnis, and some are "Sufis and members of sectarian groups" (Smith, 2010, p. 54). Some of them are religious, others secular, some highly political, and others do not have a political or religious agenda. Some come from countries where Islam is the majority religion, while others were a minority in their country of origin. The former group faces many challenges as they adjust to their "minority status" in the US; the latter group comes with well-developed "coping skills."

Smith (2010) describes what the life of Muslim immigrants in America toward the end of the 19th century looked like (p. 55). Some of them were young, unskilled men and came primarily from Lebanon and Syria, immigrating to America for a variety of reasons; others had fled because they were afraid of conscription into the Turkish army; and still others, seeing Christians from their countries that had immigrated to the US and had returned after accumulating significant amount of wealth, decided at times even reluctantly to seek their fortune in a predominantly non-Muslim country. Some Muslim immigrants were single and others traveled without their wives, but both groups looked at their sojourn in America as temporary and came with the hope of earning money and then returning to their homelands to establish themselves and their families (Smith, 2010, p. 55). However, jobs were not always easy to find, and procuring them was complicated by the immigrants' lack of education and English proficiency. Many resorted to unskilled work "such as migrant labor, petty merchandising, or mining" (Smith, 2010, p. 55); joined work-gangs building railroads; or engaged in peddling because it did not require much capital, strong language skills, or vocational training. Starting out from the Atlantic Coast they traveled south and west across the country in spite of harsh weather, theft, and hostility from the locals.

Eventually women started to arrive, married these men, and found work in factories and mills with long hours and very harsh conditions. Doumato (1985) recounts the story of one 12-year-old immigrant girl, Jameila, who was indentured to the owners of a garment factory in New York who had paid for her passage to America. Being too young to work, when the inspectors came to tour the plant she would hide in a box, sometimes for hours, in order to escape their notice (Doumato, 1985, p. 103). Early Muslim immigrants often felt isolated and unhappy because of their poor "language skills, poverty, loneliness, and the absence of coreligionists" (Smith, 2010, p. 55). Life was made even more difficult for them because Americans in those days were not very welcoming of foreigners with strange customs who practiced a non-Christian religion (Smith, 2010, p. 55). One Syrian immigrant shared her experience of being called a "dago" or "sheeny" (Naff, 1985, p. 249). In another instance, Congressman Burnett, who was in support of excluding Asians from the US, referred to Syrian immigrants as the "most undesirable of the undesirable peoples of Asia

Minor" (Naff, 1985, p. 250). Muslim children were scorned by their classmates because they were non-Christian and had different cultural practices (Naff, 1985, p. 252).

The community life Muslim immigrants tried to maintain in a foreign context had to be done without any form of "institutional support" (Smith, 2010, p. 55). There were very few opportunities available to their children and grandchildren for religious training. In their home countries there were opportunities constantly available for young people to grow up celebrating Muslim holidays and religious observances, but the American context was completely different, and it was very difficult for them to maintain an awareness and regular observances of the Muslim faith. The schools and businesses the Muslim immigrants were part of had no interest in making facilities available to them for daily prayers. No special accommodations were made in their workplaces for devout Muslims who wanted to observe the feast of Ramadan and fast daily for a month. They did not have extended families to provide support and religious instruction and were not yet economically well-off enough to travel back home "for reinforcement of the larger familiar context" (Smith, 2010, p. 55). Islam is a communal religion, not simply a personal faith. Thus, because communities were not as yet well- established, observing holidays, daily prayers, and other Islamic traditions was quite difficult and a significant challenge to maintaining their faith. Even though they were living in a society built by immigrants, because they were living in a context that did not show much appreciation for the cultural differences of these immigrants, these newcomers had a hard time maintaining their identity and their religion (Smith, 2010, p. 56).

In time their hopes of accumulating wealth quickly and returning home faded, and they had to adapt to life in America in a number of different significant ways (Smith, 2010, p. 56). Young men could not find young Muslim women of marriageable age, so some of them returned home for a brief trip to get married, while others had their marriages arranged with women in their home countries through the help of relatives. In both instances traditional courtship patterns gave way to expediency. In other cases, Arab Muslim men married Arab Christian women in spite of the negative pressure they experienced from the Muslim community for such marriages, an issue that is still quite prevalent in the 21st century in the American Islamic community. Other changes that influenced the Islamic community in the early 20th century had to do with their faith and/or their ethnic identity. Some families, especially the younger generation, began moving away from their faith and began to conceal or eradicate the cultural markers that set them apart from the American people. Those whose skin color was darker than the average American found that local populations, especially in the southern states, treated them as "colored" and they were not allowed to use public facilities that were reserved for the white population. People had negative stereotypes about Arab Muslims as "people with large black eyes, big noses and mustaches, and ill-fitting clothes" (Smith, 2010, p. 57). The younger generation began moving away from speaking Arabic, a language that sounded "strange" to American youth. This decision was especially hard for Arab families because Arabic was not only their cultural language but also their liturgical language. Parents began to give American names to their children or allowed them to use nicknames: Muslim names like Muhammad, or Ya'qub, or Nasreen became Mike, or Jack, or Nancy, respectively. As the younger generations sought to assimilate to the majority American culture rather than to maintain the heritage of their home country, Arab identity, and even to some extent the Islamic identity, began to erode and was regarded as something to be left in the past. The younger generations began increasingly to consider non-

Muslims as possible marriage partners, with the result that intermarriage rates for the subsequent generations greatly increased. Across the nation, the Muslim community's apprehension about the secularization and Americanization of the younger generation led to a movement to organize themselves into communities to affirm and maintain their identities.

Formation of Muslim Communities

Surprisingly, the first community to organize itself was located in thinly populated North Dakota. In the early 1900s a Lebanese Muslim group living in the small town of Ross began meeting together for prayer, eventually building a mosque around 1930. By the 1940s, however, very few people were actually using the mosque, as many of them had converted to the Christian faith. By the 1970s the children of this early community decided to tear down the mosque, though another was built on its site later. In Michigan City, Indiana, Syrian and Lebanese Muslims established an Islamic center in early 1914. As other Muslims from the surrounding area were attracted to the Islamic center, it was restructured in 1924 as the Modern Age Arabic Islamic Society. In Cedar Rapids, Iowa, a Muslim community of shopkeepers, traders, and farmers began meeting as a group in a rented hall in 1920 and then built a mosque in 1934. This mosque, proclaimed as the "Mother Mosque of America" (http://mothermosque.org), was "the first permanent structure to be built specifically to serve as a mosque in the United States" (Smith, 2010, p. 58).

Muslims have lived in New York City since the late 19th century, coming from various different racial and ethnic groups and working as businessmen, traveling tradesmen, and shipmen. In 1907 immigrants from Russia, Lithuania, and Poland established the American Mohammedan Society in Brooklyn, and in the early 1930s they bought a building and began using it as a mosque. Also in the

1930s a Moroccan immigrant founded a second mosque in New York, the Islamic Mission of America for the Propagation of Islam and the Defense of the Faith and the Faithful. Mosque construction has continued over the past several decades as the Muslim population in New York has increased. Motivated to live as observant Muslims in a "hostile environment," immigrants have made great effort to make sure that Islam becomes a "significant social force within the five boroughs" (Ferris, 1994, pp. 226-227).

The large number of Muslims and the diversity of the population in New York City has created space not only for the formation of Islamic associations for the various ethnic groups but also for the establishment of associations that focus on bringing together various Muslim groups, including Sunnis and Shiites. For example, the Islamic Cultural Center of New York, the first mosque built in Manhattan, has worked to attract not only various immigrant groups but African-American Muslims as well. This diversity has also created space for national Islamic organizations to work among these diverse groups of Muslims. For example, the Muslim Community Network seeks to meet a variety of needs of the Islamic community in New York City (http://mcnny.org), and the Majlis Ash Shura, comprised of representatives from over sixty mosques and organizations, seeks to unite the various Muslim communities in New York (http://www.shuranewyork.org/).

Chicago has attracted numerous Muslim immigrants as well, many of whom arrived from Syria and Palestine before the end of the 19th century. Chicago has the country's largest Indian Muslim population, coming chiefly from Gujarat, Hyderabad, and Maharashtra. Like New York, Chicago and its suburbs host a great variety of Islamic centers and mosques for different Muslim groups. An interesting example of a Muslim agency established in Chicago is the Inner-City

Muslim Action Network (IMAN, an acronym that corresponds to the Arabic iman, meaning "faith"), a nonprofit community-based organization that provides a wide range of services, including health services, career development, services to the youth to deal with issues related to drugs and gangs, activities related to the cultivation of arts, etc. (https://www.imancentral.org). Although IMAN is an Islamic organization, its efforts include working for and with "community residents of all ethnic, cultural, and religious backgrounds" (Smith, 2010, p. 60).

Dearborn, Michigan, which had only a small number of Sunni Muslims at the beginning of the 20th century, has grown considerably and today has one of the largest concentrations of Muslims in the United States, with large groups from Yemen, Lebanon, and Palestine, and is home to The Islamic Center of America, the largest mosque in the country. Dearborn also boasts an Arab-American Museum, the very first of its kind in the United States, making Dearborn a center for Islamic and Arabic studies (Smith, 2010, p. 62).

Challenges Faced By Muslims

While the Muslim population in the US continues to grow and plant roots in America, they also face numerous challenges. Wuthnow (2007) documents a number of these. First, while Muslims are encouraged by the teachings of the Qur'an to pray daily in the mosque and also at home, American Muslims do not attend mosques as frequently as Christians go to church. In part this is due to the fact that in a mosque the main service is held on Fridays, which often conflicts with work and school schedules. Second, while there are aspects of Islamic practices that are constant, changes are occurring in Islam because of the American context in which it is practiced. For example, even though prayers continue to be recited in Arabic, it is becoming more common for the teachings in the mosques to be done in both

English and Arabic, and in some cases only in English. Changes are also occurring in the gender roles in Islam as practiced in America. While women still experience marginalization in mosques (Abusharaf, 1988, pp. 247-48), an increasing number of them are permitted to serve on mosque boards (Bagby, Perl, & Froehle, 2001, p. 56). Third, first generation immigrants experience "generational strains" (Wuthnow, 2007, p. 62) with their children because their children are more assimilated into the American culture, a common experience among other immigrant groups as well. Typically, in their native countries children show a very high reverence for the parents, whereas upon immigrating to the US and earning higher salaries than their parents, they tend not to show them much respect beyond participating in ceremonial functions a couple of times a year (Wuthnow, 2007, p. 62).

According to Wuthnow (2007) the most significant change is that Muslims who have immigrated to the US practice Islam with greater intentionality than they did in their country of origin, which stems from the fourth challenge Muslims face: the onslaught of the American culture around them. Islamic leaders explain the Muslim community's response to this challenge in several ways. Some leaders say that back home in a Muslim-majority environment people tended to take their faith for granted, but in America as a minority Muslim immigrants feel that they have to "guard Islam." Others feel that Muslim immigrants in America become more religious because they are fearful that they will lose their faith and their families to the pressures and attractions of a non-Muslim culture. Finally, some leaders think the people's desire to be more religious results less from a desire to defend Islam than from the realization that it is a valuable tool regarding the challenges that come from living in America, including drugs, alcohol, and the temptations of economic success, all of which require deeper religious commitment. The lack of emphasis on God in

American culture is a great challenge, which increases the sense of vigilance in the minds of the Muslim immigrants. More fervent observance of their faith gives some Muslims a sense of security as a way to keep divided families together even when they are physically separated by a great distance (Wuthnow, 2007, pp. 62-63).

In her 2002 book, A New Religious America, Eck narrates other challenges that Muslims experience in the religiously diverse American culture. Americans tend to be "misinformed" about Islam, and American culture is by and large characterized by "sheer ignorance of Islam" (Eck, 2002, p. 222). Even though American Muslims are actively involved in the American cultural and political life—groups of Muslims all over the country have been coming together to form "congregations" and build mosques and Islamic centers, registering to vote, etc.—and engaging in positive, democratic, community-building activities, the media consistently presents negative images of Islam to the American people. They are portrayed as people engaged in a jihad, as terrorists with leaders toting rifles and hiding out, and Islam is seen as "dangerous, subversive, highly political, and anti-American" (Eck, 2002, p. 222). One of the direct effects of this perception is that when a terrorist attack linked to Islam occurs in another part of the world, even though American Muslims condemn these attacks and try to communicate that Islam does not advocate, engage in, or condone terrorism, their voice is not heard. They also suffer direct discrimination, such as having their mosques pelted with stones, defaced with graffiti, or desecrated with pork products. The solution, asserts Ali Asani, Eck's colleague at Harvard University, is to educate those around them and to "get to know one another" (Eck, 2002, p. 223). This is very crucial. While in terms of its history and theology Islam is closer to both Judaism and Christianity than to other Eastern religions, it is also one of the most misunderstood religions (Eck, 2002,

p. 233), certainly in part due to the way in which radical Muslims live out their Islamic faith, thus linking Islam directly with terrorism. It is because of this lack of understanding that the experience of Muslims in their engagement of religious diversity in the US is consistently characterized by proactive steps to educate others.

The Pew Research Center's 2011 study found that 10 years after the 9/11 attacks 55% of American Muslims say that living as a Muslim in the US has become more difficult and the biggest challenges they face include "negative views about Muslims, discrimination and prejudice, or public misconceptions about Islam." At the same time 66% also stated that for Muslims the quality of life in the US is better than in most Muslim countries, and 48% assert that Americans are friendly toward them as compared to 16% who say that American people are unfriendly.

Other negative experiences of Muslim Americans included the following: 28% thought that in the last twelve months people have treated them with suspicion because they were Muslim, and 22% said that Americans had called them offensive names; approximately 21% felt that they had been singled out by security officials at airports because they were Muslim; 52% thought that they have been singled out for increased monitoring and surveillance by the government's anti-terrorism policies; 14% asserted that in the last few years there has been opposition to building a mosque in their neighborhood and 15% said that in the last 12 months an Islamic center or mosque in their neighborhood has experienced hostility or vandalism; and 55% of Muslim Americans felt that American news organizations present Muslims and Islam unfairly (Pew Research Center, 2011).

Impact of Challenges

Smith (2010) asserts that the issues Muslims face as they seek to make themselves resident in this religiously diverse culture lead them to make Islam more visible in the American religious landscape, one result of which has been the acceptance by the American society of their right to freely practice Islam (p. 104). The face of Islam is becoming visible in four different ways, the first of which is through the building of mosques. The failure of one Muslim architect, an immigrant from Pakistan, to find a mosque to worship in led him to dedicate himself to designing mosques for the Western context. In 1979 the Islamic Society of North America commissioned him to design a mosque at its headquarters in Plainfield, Indiana. In general, though, when Muslim immigrants were unable to find other Muslim groups with whom they could share their experiences, they began Islamic-based activities, such as common worship, Qur'an study groups, and other meetings that allowed them to emphasize their faith. Subsequent generations, upon reaching the age to marry and have families, saw the need to create space to educate their children in the "social, cultural, and religious" (Smith, 2010, p. 105) aspects of their heritage. This led to the formation of Muslim communities without trained leaders to teach them the fundamentals of the faith or to lead the prayer (Smith, 2010, p. 105). Quite often lay leaders with minimal education in the Qur'an were called on to teach, while others with virtually no training were commissioned to serve as prayer leaders or imams. Over time Muslim communities all over the US that met in each other's homes, rented buildings, or shared space in local churches began to think about more structured ways in which they could practice their faith, which eventually led to building mosques. As of 2011, Bagby (2012) asserts that the count of the number of mosques in the US was up to 2,106, with 257 in New York, 246 in California, 166 in Texas, and at least one mosque in every state (pp. 5-6). These mosques and Islamic centers serve as visible institutional structures that make it easier for Muslims to congregate and worship together, develop their pride as they identify with Islam, and legitimate Islam as one of the religions in the religiously diverse American landscape. Islam is also gaining visibility in the US by creating space in major airports to serve as Muslim chapels, with Denver's international airport being the first to build a mosque. And the interfaith chapel at JFK in New York boasts a flag with the Muslim crescent and star on it. These visible structures serve as "one more tool in the effort to foster the faith and its better understanding" (Smith, 2010, p. 110).

A second way in which Islam is becoming more public and visible is through the development of Muslim organizations that support and guide Islamic life in the US, the most influential of which is the Muslim Student Association (MSA). Although the MSA was started before the 1965 influx of immigrants and organized its first national conference in 1963 with the aim of uniting Muslim student groups on college campuses across the US, it made space for the later creation of "subsidiary organizations" that have lent support to Muslim life in the US in a number of ways (Smith, 2010, p. 123). For example, the North American Islamic Trust deals with financial issues, such as investments, loans, mutual funds, book services, etc.; and the Islamic Teaching Center supports the education of Muslims by developing publications and promotional literature, and providing material for proselytization (Smith, 2010, p. 123). Other examples include: the Islamic Medical Association, the Association of Muslim Social Scientists, the Association of Muslim Businessmen and Professionals, and the Islamic Society of North America (ISNA). All of these together serve as avenues to support the Muslim community in the US, giving them a "sense of strength and power" (Smith, 2010, p. 124) and helping the development of Islamic values.

A number of organizations have arisen to provide support to Muslim women in the US (Smith, 2010, p. 125). For example,

KARAMAH: Muslim Women Lawyers for Human Rights is an organization that helps Muslim women understand and exercise their legal rights. The North American Council for Muslim Women works for Muslim women's welfare, hosting annual conferences to address issues pertaining to women that include violence, law, politics, concerns of the youth, etc.

Muslims in America have also organized local and national level organizations that serve as avenues through which they can increase their political power (Smith, 2010; Kumar, 2006, p. 308). For instance, AMC—the American Muslim Council in Washington, D.C.— was established to educate Muslims about the American electoral process. The AMC is engaged in efforts to obtain official recognition of two Islamic feasts as American national holidays: 'eid al-fitr (ending the fast of Ramadan) and 'eid al-adha (a feast commemorating Abraham's response to Allah's command to offer Ishmael as a sacrifice). The AMC's efforts resulted in the 2002 creation of 'eid stamps by the US Postal Service (Smith, 2010, p. 127).

Some Pertinent Themes

From this brief discussion of the growth of Islam in the US, two themes become readily apparent: First, while much has changed for the Muslim community in America, their experience of doing life in the religiously diverse American context is replete with challenges, quite like the challenges experienced by other non-Christian groups right from the time Columbus set foot on this land. Second and connected to the first, Muslims, not unlike other non-Christian religious groups, have been viewed negatively, with the negativity arising from the lack of knowledge and understanding that American Christians have regarding Islam and Muslims. Both these themes will become readily apparent from the discussion in Chapter 4. It is within this context of the growth of Islam in the US, and all that that includes, that Christian-Muslim relations in the US need to be situated and understood.

CHAPTER 4

CHRISTIAN-MUSLIM RELATIONSHIPS IN THE US

On December 5, 2015, the news broke of a terrorist attack in San Bernardino, California, by two American Muslims, a husband and wife, that took the life of fourteen people and seriously injured twenty-two more. In response to this event, Jerry Falwell, Jr., President of Liberty University in Lynchburg, VA, commented during a university convocation, "I've always thought that if more good people had concealed-carry permits, then we could end those Muslims before they walked in ... [loud applause] ... let's teach them a lesson if they ever show here" (Bailey, 2015). Are Falwell's views on an extreme fringe or characteristic of the views of American Christians?

Much has been written about Christian-Muslim relationships in the US, including perspectives, attitudes, and practices of Christians toward Muslims. In this chapter I offer a brief sampling of some of this literature, which not only reveals American Christians' perspectives and practices but also reinforces and shapes them. The discussion, situated within the broader context of religious diversity in the US and the growth of Islam in the US, is broken up into two parts: American non-evangelical sources and American evangelical sources.

Non-Evangelical American Writings On Islam And Muslims In The U.S.

A number of works have informed Americans about relationships between Christians and Muslims in the US and, by virtue of bringing this discourse to the forefront, have influenced Christian-Muslim relationships. One such seminal work is Edward Said's 1979 book Orientalism, which has been translated into some thirty-six languages (Said, 2003, p. xv) and has been quite influential in informing Western ideas and perspectives about non-Westerners and Islam in particular. Said (1979) begins his discussion by asserting that what made European culture, inside and outside Europe, hegemonic was the ethnocentric idea that European identity is superior to "all non-European peoples and cultures" (p. 7). Said tries to justify this assertion by demonstrating how in a systematic manner "European culture was able to manage – and even produce – [the concept of] 'the Orient' politically, sociologically, militarily, ideologically, scientifically, and imaginatively during the post-Enlightenment period" (p. 3). Said further justifies his assertion by demonstrating that "European culture gained in strength and identity by setting itself off against the Orient as a sort of surrogate and even underground self" (p. 3). The European mindset regarding the Orient is evident in the following remarks made by Lord Balfour, Prime Minister of the UK from July 1902 to December 1905, who never denies the "fact" of the superiority of the British and the inferiority of Egypt but simply takes it for granted:

> First of all, look at the facts of the case. Western nations as soon as they emerge into history show the beginnings of those capacities for self-government ... having merits of their own... You may look through the whole history of the Orientals in what is called, broadly speaking, the East, and you never find traces of self-government. All their great centuries – and they have been very great – have been passed under despotisms, under absolute government. All their great contributions to civilization – and they have been great – have been made under that form of government. Conqueror

has succeeded conqueror; one domination has followed another; but never in all the revolutions of fate and fortune have you seen one of those nations of its own motion establish what we, from a Western point of view, called self-government. That is the fact. It is not a question of superiority and inferiority. I suppose a true Eastern sage would say that the working government which we have taken upon ourselves in Egypt and elsewhere is not a work worthy of a philosopher – that it is the dirty work, the inferior work, of carrying on the necessary labour. (Said, 1979, pp. 32-33)

Said's (1979) stated goal is to demonstrate that the American mindset is pervaded by the "traditional European Orientalism" of the late 18th century—a mindset he calls "American Orientalism" (pp. 2-3, 285). Said cites Harold W. Glidden's essay, "The Arab World," which appeared in the February 1972 issue of the American Journal of Psychiatry, as a prime example of this American Orientalism. To Said, the tone and the content of this article are very similar to the perspective and mindset of the Orientalists. Glidden's four-page-long essay offers a psychological sketch of more than 100 million people, spanning a history of 1,300 years, but bases his perspective on only four sources. His sources include a recently authored book on Tripoli; one issue of Al-Ahram, an Egyptian newspaper; a periodical entitled Oriente Moderno; and a book authored by the well-known Orientalist Majid Khadduri. Glidden's (1972) article begins with the claim that his goal is to reveal the underlying mindset of the behavior of the Arabs, which while from the perspective of the Arabs may be "normative," from the perspective of the West is "aberrant" (p. 984). Glidden then goes on to describe the Arabs in unflattering terms: Arab culture has a tendency to require "a high degree of conformity and therefore imparts a strong authoritarian tone to Arab culture and society"; it is a "shame-oriented culture," meaning that Arabs are intensely concerned about "catering to outward appearances and public opinion" (p. 985); Glidden remarks that the only situations in which Arabs can function are ones that involve conflict; the only way a person can gain prestige is by their ability to dominate others. While from the Western perspective, making peace is the only rational thing to do, the Arabs do not value "objectivity" and thus are not "governed by this kind of logic" (p. 986). He opines that one of the virtues of a shame culture is that of revenge (Glidden, 1972, pp. 984-986). To justify his conclusion, Glidden quotes from the June 29, 1970, issue of Al-Ahram, which says,

> In Egypt in 1969, in 1,070 cases of murder where the perpetrators were apprehended, it was found that 20 percent of the murders were based on a desire to "wipe out shame" (mahw al-'ār), 30 percent on a desire to satisfy real or imaginary wrongs (intiqām), and 31 percent on a desire for blood revenge (akhdh al-tha'r). In addition, revenge was a major motive in cases of kidnapping. (Glidden, 1972, p. 987)

Glidden (1979) continues to describe Arab culture as follows: From the Arab view the only thing that matters is success and "the end justifies the means"; the way in which Arabs live in the world is "characterized by anxiety expressed in generalized suspicion and distrust, which has been labeled 'free-floating hostility'"; both Arab life and Islam are characterized by a well- developed "art of subterfuge"; Arabs are primarily driven with a desire for vengeance, which supersedes everything else, without which the shame that the Arabs would experience would destroy their ego (pp. 986-987). Glidden further asserts that because in Arab tribal society going on raids was one of the two main ways in which the economy was supported, the "normal state of affairs" (p. 987) was characterized by strife rather than peace. Said (1979) summarizes that the views of Balfour and Glidden, and indeed Orientalism in general, are very similar to each other in their binary division of the world as well as the descriptions of the Western world and the Orient: Westerners are "rational, peaceful, liberal, logical, capable of holding real values, without natural suspicion," and the Arab-Orientals, on the other hand, "are none of these" (p. 49).

Said takes this broad understanding of Orientalism and connects it specifically to Islam in his 1997 book Covering Islam. Summarizing his broad discussion in Orientalism, Said (1997) asserts that even though the Orient has by and large been regarded as inferior, the West has always had the perspective that it has "greater potential power (usually destructive) than the West" (p. 4). Regarding Islam, Said remarks that because Islam has always been viewed as part of the Orient, it is regarded, firstly, as one monolithic entity, and, secondly, as a power filled with a special kind of "hostility and fear" (p. 4). While there are many reasons for this attitude, including "religious, psychological, and political," from a Western standpoint these myriad reasons stem from the perception that Islam is a "formidable competitor" as well as a recently arrived "challenge to Christianity" (Said, 1997, p. 5)

Viewing Islam as a recently arrived challenge, argues Said (1997), is not something new; indeed, negative perspectives of Islam, as well as viewing it as a threat, were quite prevalent in the preceding centuries (p. 5). In fact, for a large part of the Middle Ages up until the early years of the Renaissance in Europe, Islam was considered to be a "demonic religion," characterized by "apostasy, blasphemy, and obscurity" (Said, 1997, p. 5). It made no difference to the Christians that Muslims did not consider Muhammad as a God, only a prophet. The only thing that was of significance for the Christians was that he was a false prophet, someone who sowed dissension, enjoyed sensual pleasures, was hypocritical, and a representative of the devil. These understandings about Muhammad were not "doctrinal" but were derived through current events in the real world, which made Islam a significant political force to be reckoned with. For centuries, Islamic military forces had been a threat to Europe, disrupting its trade, demolishing its colonies, and occupying parts of Europe itself. In Said's (1997) words: "It was as if a younger, more virile and energetic version of Christianity had arisen in the East, equipped itself with the learning of the ancient Greeks, invigorated itself with a simple, fearless, and warlike creed, and set about destroying Christianity" (p. 5). The Christian fear of "Mohammedanism" continued even when Islam began to weaken and Europe began to grow in power. Because Islam was geographically closer to Europe than the other non-Christian religions, it never ceased to remind the West of its previous intrusions on Europe and of its dormant powers. While the other cultures of the East, e.g., China and India, were regarded by the West as having been defeated and distant enough not to be a continuous source of worry, Islam was never viewed as an entity that had been completely subdued by the West. This perspective carried forward into the early 1970s when the oil prices rose sharply as a result of the Arab oil embargo—it seemed that the Islamic world once again posed an existential threat to the West. This "shock," asserts Said, has been further intensified by the Islamic terrorism that began in the 1980s and 1990s (Said, 1997, p. 5).

A factor that further compounds the way Islam is misunderstood and misrepresented: Many of the experts who write about the Islamic world do not have a command of the pertinent languages (Said, 1997, p. 22). For this reason they are forced to rely on information presented by the press or other Western writers. The conventional or official ways in which this information is presented impact media coverage. During the frenzy of attention focused on

"Islamic 'fundamentalism' and 'terrorism'" in the late 20th century, the press reported on a narrow range of topics: "elites, modernization programs, the role of the military, greatly visible leaders, sensational crises, jihad networks, geopolitical strategy (from the American point of view), and 'Islamic' inroads" (Said, 1997, p. 23). Supporting this view, James Bill (1978-79) of the University of Texas noted that coverage of the Iranian crisis of 1978 was largely "superficial" and biased toward the Pahlavis (the Iranian royal family) and that the US did not make an adequate effort to get an in-depth understanding of the country or to have any dialogue with the opposition (p. 23). Said (1997) remarks that "these failures" are in general indicative of the attitude of the United States toward the Islamic world (p. 23). His research could not uncover any time period during the course of American history in which Islam was not "generally discussed or thought about outside a framework created by passion, prejudice, and political interests" (p. 24). Said includes in this discussion every area of scholarly and scientific discipline in the field of Orientalism which has focused its study on the Orient since the early part of the 19th century. American scholars of Islam and the Middle East at prestigious institutions such as Princeton, Harvard, and the University of Chicago have not been "unbiased and free of special pleading in what they do" (Said, 1997, p. 25). In fact, Said goes so far as to assert that these Orientalist scholars have used their position as experts "to deny their deep-seated feelings about Islam" while using language that purports to authenticate their "objectivity" and "scientific impartiality" (Said, 1997, p. 25).

These kinds of channels—the media, the government, and academia—frequently disseminate information that negatively characterizes the Islamic world and Muslims. All these notions and ideas contribute to developing a certain image of Islam in the West that is then used particularly in the United States (Said, 1997, p. 4) to give the impression that the Islamic world in general is characterized by violence. These images negatively influence the perspectives and behaviors of Americans toward the Islamic world as a socio-religious entity as well as toward Muslims as individuals.

Thomas Kidd's 2009 book American Christians and Islam is another seminal work that has informed Americans about relationships between Christians and Muslims in the US and by virtue of bringing this discourse to the forefront has influenced Christian-Muslim relationships. Kidd, writing as a non-evangelical American, makes a number of pertinent points. He asserts that one important indicator of the presence of Muslims in the US was the 1957 establishment of the Islamic Center in Washington DC. In his speech at the dedication of the Islamic Center, President Eisenhower assured the American Muslim community that they were welcome here because freedom of religion was a value for Americans. While the Muslim community in America grew slowly before 1965, after the enactment of the United States' Immigration and Nationality Act of 1965 the Muslim community in America has grown significantly. Kidd observes that as the Muslim immigrant population grew, American Christians became increasingly anxious about "Muslims' aggressive evangelism, lack of assimilation, or their possible association with terrorist plots" (p. 96). American Christians responded to the growing Muslim community by evangelizing them (Kidd, 2009, p. 113).

Among American Christians the Southern Baptist Convention took the leadership in proselytizing Muslims. In 1967 the Home Mission Board published a booklet entitled A Baptist Look at Islam that discussed some of the basic traditional beliefs of Islam. The author, Joseph R. Estes, asserted, "despite its rigid legalism and fervent religious practices, Islam offers its adherents nothing like the assurance of salvation which is in Christ" (Kidd, 2009, p. 113).

The call by the Southern Baptist Convention to evangelize Muslims reflected an awareness by American Christians of the growing presence of Islam in America, an awareness that in the 1970s led other evangelical groups to begin putting programs in place to evangelize Muslims. A natural place to begin was on college campuses because many evangelical groups had already established campus ministries that could connect with non-Christian international students (Kidd, 2009, p. 113). For example, in 1975 a Southern Baptist missionary named Ray Register began an outreach program to Muslim students on the campus of North Carolina State University. Other parachurch organizations, such as InterVarsity, the Navigators, and Campus Crusade for Christ (now Cru), working among college students on campuses across the United States have also developed outreach ministries to Muslims. And International Students, Inc., an evangelical organization, focuses its ministry exclusively on international students, including Muslims (Kidd, 2009, p. 114).

Kidd (2009) goes on to point out that as the Muslim community in America grew, American Christians increasingly wanted more understanding and organization in their efforts to evangelize Muslims, one example of which was the 1999 conference on the evangelization of Muslims in America organized by the Billy Graham Center. One topic of discussion at the conference was the various ways in which Christians had been involved in mission work among Muslims who have come to the US as refugees, as immigrants, or as college students (Kidd, 2009, p. 115). For example, David Philip (Philip, Stewart, Jr., & Blincoe, 2001), who does campus ministry among Muslim students at a state university, asserted that he sought to meet the "felt needs" (p. 134) of the new students by welcoming them and familiarizing them with the campus community. Philip also attended functions hosted by the Muslim Student Association and organized debates about Christianity and Islam that were open to the public but asserted that the best way to work among Muslims was by contacting them individually. Hence, in order to do that he perused the student phone book for names that sounded Islamic, such as "Ali, Hassan, Khadijah, Mohammad," etc. (Philip et al., 2001, p. 137). He then contacted them, asking if they had any interest in talking about issues related to faith. Philip's goal was that "every Muslim student in the United States is prayed for by name and then has the opportunity to receive a Bible, Jesus video, a chance to study the Bible, and a chance to interact with the body of Christ and see Christians in action" (2001, pp. 134-39). Even though many Muslim students are cognizant of these kinds of approaches, because of the freedom of expression on the campuses and the fact that international students are often lonely, college campuses are idyllic settings for evangelization (Kidd, 2009, p. 115).

This burgeoning interest in reaching out to Muslims is reflected by the interest of American evangelicals in so-called "insider" literature on Islam, especially material authored by Muslims who have converted to Christianity. This kind of material falls into two categories. Some of it assumes that American Christian readers would be interested in sharing their faith with their Muslim neighbors and hence provides teaching on how Muslims can be engaged in dialogue. Shirin Taber's Muslims Next Door: Uncovering Myths and Creating Friendships (2004) is an example of this kind of literature. Other literature—for example William Wagner's (2004) How Islam Plans to Change the World—is authored with the goal of divulging or revealing "the ostensibly hidden truth about Muslims' beliefs," material which was published in great abundance after 2001 (Kidd, 2009, p. 116). According to Kidd (2009) another seminal event in the Middle East that influenced as well as brought to light the views that American

Christians held regarding Muslims and Islam was the question of the Jewish people and the formation of the land of Israel as their home. This event gave rise to a plethora of literature by American Christians in which Muslims and Islam for the most part were presented in a negative light. Kidd asserts that for American Christians their sense of urgency regarding mission work may have been invigorated by the news that was coming out of the Middle East (p. 83). Kidd completed a survey of this literature regarding the relationship between Judaism and Islam starting from the 1940s and into the 1990s, the majority of which would be considered prophetic literature (pp. 83-95). For instance, in relation to the Arab opposition to the return of the Jewish people to the land of Israel, A. H. Carter contended that this opposition was demonic: "Whatever Satan and his instruments may attempt to do, they can never succeed in frustrating God's purposes regarding the children of Israel. The Arabs' present efforts ... will never be successful" (Carter quoted in Kidd, 2009, p. 84). The evangelist Charles Price asserted that the removal of the Arab people from the land of Palestine was ordained in the Bible. He was also convinced that eventually the Jewish people would tear down the Dome of the Rock in order to rebuild the Temple, and "then the Moslem world would gnash its teeth in rage," but to no avail because there was no way to preempt the prophetic timetable (Kidd, 2009, p. 85). Pastor Dean Bedford of Rochester, New York, held the conviction that all anti-Semitism, including the anti-Semitism stemming from the Arabs, had its roots in the biblical enmity between Isaac and Ishmael. Bedford thought that Ishmael was "Satan's substitute for Isaac" (Kidd, 2009, p. 85). And, in fact, this hostility gave rise through Ishmael to not only a "competing racial group," which Kidd (2009) presumes to be the Arabs, but also a "competing religion," which Kidd presumes to be Islam (p. 86). Kidd remarks that the view that the conflict between the Arabs and Israelis stemmed from the conflict between Ishmael and Isaac became a commonly held view among conservative Christians toward the end of the 20th century. This was coupled with the conviction that it was the "unlimited obligation" of Christians to give support to Israel against Arab Muslims (Kidd, 2009, p. 86).

J. Christy Wilson, on the other hand, while asserting that Islam did not have any fundamental spiritual characteristics of the forgiveness of sin and of eternal life, with reference to the conflict in the Middle East seemed not to favor one side or the other. So, while he lauded Israel for gaining its independence and asserted that it was necessary for the Jews to have their own homeland where they could enjoy their own freedom and peace from the enemies, he also asserted "we must not lose sight of the Arab side of the question" (Wilson, 1950, p. 28). Arabs had lived in Palestine for a long time, but when the nation of Israel was established, over a million Muslim and Christian Arabs were made homeless. With reference to the prophetic understanding of their rightful residents of the land of Israel, Martin DeHaan asserted that "the present day Arabs are direct descendants of Ishmael" (DeHaan, 1950, p. 61) and the land of Israel was promised by God to Isaac and not Ishmael. According to DeHaan it would not be possible to find a solution to the current conflict between the Arabs and Israelis "until, in obedience to God, the sons of the bondwoman [Arabs] are put out to make way for the sons of promise" (DeHaan, 1950, p. 61). DeHaan also thought that the land that was promised to Israel in the Bible was much larger than even the present "undivided Palestine," which meant that many more Middle Eastern Muslims from Jordan, Syria, and even Iraq, and Egypt would be displaced by the "restored nation of Israel" (Kidd, 2009, p. 87). This understanding would go on to "make many American Christians sympathetic to Israel's desire to expand beyond its 1948 boundaries" (Kidd, 2009, pp. 87-88). DeHaan was convinced that any nation that tried to intervene in the prophetic right that Israel had to the land was asking for God's judgment. In other words, viewing the conflict between the Arab Muslims and Israelis from this "biblical" prophetic perspective created space for American Christians to view Israel's enemies, and in this instance the Muslim nations, as God's enemies who opposed God's prophetic plan (Kidd, 2009, p. 88).

As these end-times debates continued, other American Christians also made statements from a variety of perspectives directly relating to Muslims in the Middle East. William Culbertson, President of the Moody Bible Institute in Chicago, while acknowledging the complaints of the Arabs in their conflict with Israel also asserted that Israel's military actions and handling of Arab refugees was acceptable because Israel had the right to defend itself (Culbertson, 1968, p. 8). James Kelso, a leader in the United Presbyterian Church, on the other hand, in a June 1968 editorial in Christianity Today pointed out that Israel had a long history of abusing the Arab people and whatever friendliness the Arab Muslims had shown towards the United States since World War I had been lost because of the United States' support for Zionism (Kelso, 1968, p. 7, 9). This unquestioning support by the United States for Israel hampered missionary work among Arab Muslims in the Middle East and made the conversion of Muslims to Christianity unimaginable (Kidd, 2009, p. 92).

Other American evangelicals contributing to these prophetic narratives from different perspectives included Charles Feinberg of Biblical Theological Seminary in Los Angeles; Frank Epp, a Canadian Mennonite; Charles Ryrie of Dallas Theological Seminary; Hal Lindsey; Tim LaHaye; Milton Lindberg; etc. Kidd (2009) writes that in spite of influential Christian leaders—Samuel Zwemer, J. Christry Wilson, and Kenneth Cragg— encouraging American Christians to show "deeper sympathy and understanding of Islam" (p. 95), the perpetually tense situation in the Middle East has resulted in American Christians having a less than lenient view of Islam. And the fear that American Christians harbored regarding Islam was further exacerbated by the growing presence of Muslims in the United States itself (Kidd, 2009, p. 95). Kidd (2009) concludes the argument of his book by asserting that it is not as yet clear what effect the 9/11 attacks have had on American Christians, but he thinks that the two themes of Muslims converting to Christianity and Islam's role in the end times have been "re-energized" (p. xvi). It is Kidd's assessment that the fact that the events of 9/11 have given rise to "a new kind of dispensationalist literature" that puts Islam at the heart of end-time events with an Islamic Antichrist rising up against Israel reveals that Christian theology tends to get shaped by "latest crises" presented by the media (Kidd, 2009, pp. xvi-xvii).

Jane I. Smith's 2007 book Muslims, Christians, and the Challenge of Interfaith Dialogue is another important work that considers Christian-Muslim relations in the US. Smith presents a number of ways in which Christians and Muslims can dialogue with each other (p. 63), developed through her own and others' experience of participating in efforts to converse with each other. These models serve as examples of ways in which Christians and Muslims have related to each other in the US. Christian-Muslim relations have taken the form of: persuading each other of one's own faith and of the falsehood of the other's faith; participating in sessions where both religious groups try to get to know each other better; dialoging with each other in a classroom setting to gain understanding of each other; having a deeper theological conversation about "elements of faith" in Christianity and Islam; talking together about common problems of youth—e.g., drugs, alcohol—that are of concern to both Christian and Muslim parents; imparting ethical values to their children; inviting adherents of the other faith to "observe and learn" what their religion looks like "in practice" or even having a joint worship service; dialoguing about elements of spirituality that are common to both religions, deemphasizing differences and reemphasizing "sharing and mutuality"; and cooperating together to address "pragmatic concerns," such as participating in Habitat for Humanity projects (p. 81). Smith remarks that of the ways in which Christians and Muslims have related to each other the most common way has been participating in sessions where both groups try to get to know each other. She adds that while this is the first step in any kind of mutual relations, this also usually ends up being the last step (Smith, 2007, p. 68).

Kimball (1991) lists a number of groups in the US who have, under the influence of the Vatican and the WCC, engaged in interfaith work. These organizations include National Council of Churches in the U.S.A.; the Secretariat for Interreligious and Ecumenical Affairs of the National Conference of Catholic Bishops; and denominations such as the Presbyterians, Methodists, Lutherans, Episcopalians, the United Churches of Christ, and others. Among mainline denominations the Presbyterian Church (USA) has an Interfaith Relations Office and has produced numerous resources such as a document entitled A Study on Islam (Interfaith Relations 2016). The Evangelical Lutheran Church in America's Inter-Religious Relations department engages in Lutheran-Muslim relations, including promoting awareness of Islam and developing numerous resources such as Talking Points: Topics in Christian-Muslim Relations and the six-disc DVD series Discover Islam (Evangelical Lutheran Church 2016). The Roman Catholic Church's Pontifical Council for Inter-religious Dialogue helps foster relationships among Catholics and adherents of other faiths. The PCID has developed a special commission for Islamic relations and sponsors studies on Christian-Muslim relations (PCID 2016). Most programs of interfaith work include educational programs, literature, and dialogue sessions, which Kimball (1991) suggests are examples of concrete ways we can move forward in Christian-Muslim relations (p. 103). New interfaith organizations and outreaches are being formed on a regular basis.

This sampling of literature on Christian-Muslim relations in the US discussed in non-evangelical American sources illustrates a tendency in the US toward a negative presentation of Islam. The information disseminated as well as the volatile nature of some of the issues discussed has the propensity to stir up animosity between Christians and Muslims. It is within this broader discourse that information presented in American evangelicals' writings on Islam and Muslims in the US needs to be situated and understood.

American Evangelical Writings On Islam And Muslims In The US

American evangelical writings on Islam and Muslims vary from negative to positive in tone and cover a variety of topics. For example, Ruth Frances Woodsmall, who served in the Middle East with the YWCA, wrote Moslem Women Enter a New World in 1936. She asserted that a defining characteristic of a Muslim woman's religion was her "complete acquiescence to fate" (p. 402). While Islam may have stripped her of any privileges, she still had responsibilities, the most important of which was to accept her fate as Allah's will. This "spirit of fatalism" (p. 402) has kept Muslim women in an oppressed status for centuries. Even though most Muslim women continued to espouse a similar attitude toward Islam, "a small minority of women has begun to question the relationship between the accepted teaching of Islam and the demands of the modern world" (p. 402). And education, asserts Woodsmall (1936), undermines the prevailing "attitude of fatalism toward religion and life" (p. 402):

A renaissance in education is stirring Baghdad from a long Rip Van Winkle sleep, giving it new vitality and power. No change in the

Eastern world, in this twentieth-century era of change, has more far-reaching or fundamental significance, not only for Eastern women but for Eastern society, than the growth in girls' education. (p. 133) Woodsmall's book also contains a discussion about education as central to progress in other countries such as Iran, India, Egypt, Palestine and Trans-Jordan, Syria, and Turkey.

The views that American Christians held about Muslims were also reflected in the writings of missionaries serving in Africa with the Sudan Interior Mission (SIM) at the beginning of the 20th century. Merryweather described Islam as a religion that was deceitful and "Satan's masterpiece," designed to trap its followers (Cooper 2006, p. 102). In these missionaries' perception, Muslims were religiously nominal followers of a pagan religion that caused social problems and corrupted family life (Cooper, 2006, p. 106).

Other missionaries' writings that influenced American Christians included Eric Fisk's The Prickly Pear, published in 1951, in which he said that mission work among the Muslims was extremely difficult because it was an attack on the stronghold of the devil. He proclaimed that "Islam is the devil's reply to Calvary and Pentecost" (p. 20). Because Islam appeared to be honoring God but denied the lordship and deity of Christ, it was a "masterpiece of delusion" (Fisk, 1951, p. 21). Elwyn Lee Means in her 1955 book World Within a World had the following to say about Muslims: They need "to be saved, not because they are Moslems or the devotees of any other faith, but because they need Christ" (pp. 5-6); each and every Muslim "is of great worth in the sight of God" (p. 115). And Finlay Graham, in his 1969 book Sons of Ishmael, commented that a "divided Palestine" and "extreme Zionism" are both hurdles to developing peaceful relationships and effective witnessing of Christ in the Middle East (p. 13).

In 1950, J. Christy Wilson published Introducing Islam, a pamphlet published in five editions between 1950 and the 1980s. While Wilson asserted that Christianity was superior in its spirituality, Islam did have "great truths and high accomplishments" (p. 3). Wilson was also convinced that Islam would see a "dramatic and new era" of change as Islamic regions came under the influence of the West (p. 18). Michael Youssef, an evangelist born in Egypt, warned in his 1991 book America, Oil, and the Islamic Mind that the Islamic OPEC nations were planning an economic jihad to bring the West under the submission of Islam. According to him, the United States needed to tighten its foreign investment laws and seek alternate sources of energy so that they could be independent of OPEC (Youssef, 1991, pp. 38-40, 129-33). In 1992 Robert Morey's The Islamic Invasion charged that the millions of Muslims living in America were not interested in assimilating into American culture. To him, Islam was essentially a religion of intolerance and a "form of cultural imperialism" (Morey, 1992, p. 19). Michael Fortner in The Scarlet Beast worried that the "many millions of Muslims that have immigrated to Europe and the U.S. is [sic] part of a planned invasion" (Kidd, 2009, p. 117).

Cimino's (2005) research shows that American evangelicals' writings have taken a notable shift after 9/11, sharpening the boundaries between Christianity and Islam and labeling Islam as a religion of violence. He also concludes that as diversity becomes more prevalent in the US, new "boundary markers" are being set up between evangelicalism and other religions, which strengthen evangelical identity but also "strain interfaith relations" (p. 162). For example, Caner and Caner (2009), writing from the perspective of former insiders while seeking to help evangelicals become more effective in their witness to Muslims, contribute to the propagation of a negative image of Islam. They assert: Muhammad was not a hero—he expressed doubt that the messages he got were revelations and sometimes thought that he was demon possessed (p. 62); with the exception of the Crusades, over the course of 1,400 years of Christian-Muslim history, "due largely to the philosophy of jihad," most wars have been initiated by Muslims (p. 77); war is Islam's main instrument for its expansion (p. 77); they teach Allah does not love the unbeliever and his "heart is set against the infidel (kafir)" (p. 118); etc.

William Wagner (2004), a Southern Baptist expert on missions, in his book How Islam Plans to Change the World makes the argument that Muslims have a plan to take over the world and bring it under submission to Islam. Wagner writes:

> The continuing wars and acts of terrorism are a result of the unfolding conflict between Islam and the West. Many Muslim leaders feel that it is Allah's will that the whole world accept Islam... I see the situation being so acute that we could easily be living in the last days. (pp. 13-15)

Wagner thought the United States "was being infiltrated by aggressive Saudi-funded Wahabbist Muslims," who, instead of assimilating into American culture, wanted to "evangelize and conquer" (pp. 36-38).

Unlike American Christians who recommend engaging Muslims in friendships and dialogue, Wagner (2004), based on his experience, had a negative view of dialogue as a model for evangelism, arguing that neither Muslims nor "conservative Christians" were ready to "cede anything" to each other, and hence dialoging would not produce any fruit (p. 140). He asserted that the better way to evangelize Muslims was through "spiritual power encounters" (p. 144), where Christianity comes into conflict with Islam and through this encounter Christianity is demonstrated to be the true religion. The reason for this was that the most effective way of converting Muslims to Christianity was through non-human means, such as through people seeing visions

and dreams and receiving healing and prophetic messages (pp. 144-
152). Wagner expects that in the last days the world will see an increase
in violence by Muslims, especially toward Christians, culminating in the
return of Christ. Wagner asserts:

> Ultimately there will be one large conflict before Jesus Christ
> does return, not to proclaim the merits of Muhammad but
> rather to establish his [Christ's] kingdom. The ultimate victor
> in this process will not be the Christians but rather Jesus
> Christ. (2004, pp. 216-17).

Negative perspectives espoused by American evangelicals were
further reinforced by the events of 9/11, which gave rise to rash
comments by a number of influential evangelicals. A few examples
suffice to illustrate. As previously noted, Pat Robertson (2002)
commented, "Somehow I wish the Jews in America would wake up,
open their eyes and read what is being said about them. This is worse
than the Nazis. Adolf Hitler was bad, but what the Muslims want to do
to the Jews is worse." (para. 2)

Jerry Falwell was interviewed by Bob Simon on CBS' 60
Minutes on October 6, 2002. The following excerpt of that interview is
noteworthy:

> [Simon]: "A lot of Muslims feel these days that Christians and
> Jews are getting together and ganging up on them."
>
> [Falwell]: "That's true. I'm sorry, that's true. I hope it will
> cease to be so. But I think that is the fact right now."
>
> [Simon]: "You wrote an approving piece recently about a
> book called 'Unveiling Islam.' ... The authors of that book
> wrote, 'The Muslim who commits acts of violence in jihad

does so with the approval of Mohammed.' Do you believe that?"

[Falwell]: "I do... I think Mohammed was a terrorist. I read enough of the history of his life, written by both Muslims and non-Muslims, [to know] that he was a violent man, a man of war."

[Simon]: "So, in the same way that Moses provided the ultimate example for the Jews and same way that Jesus provided the ultimate example for Christians, Mohammed provided the ultimate example for Muslims and he was a terrorist."

[Falwell]: "In my opinion... And I do believe that – Jesus set the example for love, as did Moses. And I think that Mohammed set an opposite example." (McKay, 2002)

Franklin Graham described the God of Islam as "a different God" and Islam as "a very evil and wicked religion" (Cox, 2001, p. 30). And Jerry Vines, pastor of the First Baptist Church of Jacksonville, Florida, asserted that Muhammad was "a demon-possessed pedophile" and Islam promotes "the destruction of all non-Muslims" (Falwell, 2002). Jerry Falwell quoted these statements at the Southern Baptist Convention's annual meeting in reference to the Caner brothers' 2009 book Unveiling Islam: An Insider's Look at Muslim Life and Beliefs. With over 100,000 copies in print (Kidd, 2009, p. 148), this book was authored with the goal of helping Christians get a better understanding of Islam and "to present Christ more effectively" (Caner & Caner, 2009, p. 20). To help the reader get a better understanding of Islam, these former Muslims discuss topics such as Muslim attitudes toward non-Muslims, the revelation of the Qur'an, the life of Muhammad, etc. The

Caners (2009) assert that Muslim views of non-Muslims are connected with their sense of salvation:

> Eternal security is further based on a Muslim's hatred toward enemies of Allah. Muhammad gave the above command as future guidance to all believers, and it still applies. Muslims must not trust others who seek to harm the cause of Allah. The worst thing the enemies of Allah can do is persuade Muslims to "reject the Truth" (sura 60:2). (pp. 34-35)

In order to have a greater hope of achieving Paradise, Muslims are commanded to hate the enemies of Islam. They cannot love other people in secret while giving the appearance of hating them "outwardly"; if they do, they will be judged by Allah. In other words, Muslims are commanded to hate with great passion those who oppose the expansion of the cause of Allah (Caner & Caner, 2009, p. 35). Regarding Muhammad the Caner brothers (2009) assert that at one point during the course of receiving revelations he thought that he was "possessed by an evil spirit, or jinn" (p. 41); that he claimed to be speaking to the dead as well as offered prayers for the dead at a cemetery; that he alternated between receiving revelations from Satan and Allah; and that he married a girl who was six years old and consummated his marriage with her when she was nine years old (pp. 41-58). This last fact "has provided salacious evidence used [by Christians] to denigrate the Prophet's character" (Kidd, 2009, p. 148), as evident in the comments made by Vines quoted above.

Finally, regarding the "final choice for a 'canon'" of the Qur'an, the Caners explain that Uthman, the third caliph who ruled from 644 CE to 656 CE, picked one version from the various versions available to Muslims, accepted it as the authoritative text, and burned all other extant manuscripts, "some twenty-four variants" (Caner & Caner, 2009, pp. 85), a point which calls into question the Islamic claim that the Qur'an has always existed in heaven alongside Allah.

Another influential American evangelical, John MacArthur, like the Caners, also presents the violent side of Muhammad and Islam in his 2001 book Terrorism, Jihad, and the Bible: A Response to the Terrorist Attacks. MacArthur examines the reasons why the 9/11 attacks took place and presents his arguments within the framework of "biblical history, going all the way back to Old Testament times" (p. 5). He asserts that the reasons for this include the sinfulness of human beings; the age-old enmity between Isaac and Ishmael; the birth of Islam as a religion; etc. (pp. 12-54). MacArthur asserts that the revelations received by Muhammad were demonic in nature, upon which he "built his whole system of religion" (p. 44).

It is apparent from the discussion above that while some evangelicals have presented some aspects of Islam in a positive light, such as Kenneth Cragg (2000) who describes Islam as a faith that teaches the "oneness of believers"; the repudiation of "class consciousness"; hospitality; and the responsibility of the Muslim towards family, community, and God (p. 60); for the most part the perception of American evangelicals has been consistently negative. This should be of grave concern, as Timothy George, Dean of Beeson Divinity School at Samford University, makes apparent in his response to Falwell's comments:

> To use highly charged language as such as he did in referring to Muhammad as a terrorist is unhelpful to present the good news of Jesus Christ to Muslims," George said. "Those Christian leaders who have spoken with such passion and lack of caution about Islam will maybe step back for thoughtful concern of 'How can we Christians who are called

to share the gospel of Jesus Christ conduct ourselves so that there will be a warm, winsome witness?'" (Hertz, 2002)

A group of Southern Baptist missionaries expressed great concern over the comments made by Vines that Muhammad was a "demon-possessed pedophile" (Falwell, 2002). They asserted that comments of this nature increase Muslim animosity toward evangelical Christians serving as missionaries in Muslim countries. They go on to urge the readers to focus on the need that Muslims have for salvation that is available only through faith in Jesus Christ and to communicate and live in a way that will facilitate the preaching of the gospel to the world's more than one billion Muslims. They further exhort American Christians with the following words:

> We have found it more beneficial with our Muslim friends to concentrate on sharing Christ in love and concentrating on the message of the gospel, instead of speaking in a degrading manner about their religion or prophet. We encourage you all to reach out to the people of Islam in love and in a fashion that is consistent with the life of our Lord Jesus Christ. (Baptist Standard, 2003)

Their concern and their prayers are much needed advice for American evangelicals.

Given these assessments and perspectives and the general tendency of American evangelicals to be cognizant predominantly of the "dark side" of Islam (Poston & Ellis, 2000, p. 18), perhaps viewing Muslims from the perspective of Poston and Ellis' (2000) two-group classification becomes increasingly salient (pp. 22-29). The two groups are: "defensive-pacifist Muslims" (p. 22) and "offensive-activist" Muslims (p. 25). Defensive-pacifist Muslims have come to the US for economic opportunity and social or political freedom and have very little desire to seek converts to Islam. They "vehemently oppose media stereotypes which portray Muslims as terrorists or as backward camel-riders" (Poston & Ellis, 2000, p. 25), a message that needs to be heard in the midst of the often quite loud negative portrayal of Islam and Muslims in the media. Offensive-activist Muslims do not seek to offend Americans but are simply eager to spread their faith and seek converts to Islam. They refuse assimilation into American society, and as they grow in size, so does their influence. For example, Muslims in Chicago would like to have Fridays declared as a weekend for Muslims and want Islamic holy days to be declared "official holidays" (Poston & Ellis, 2000, p. 28). Understanding that the majority of American Muslims comprise these two groups will go a long way toward creating space for American evangelicals to develop relationships with American Muslims and dispel their negative perceptions instead of contributing to them and propagating a "type of medieval crusader mentality that only serves to alienate the very people we are seeking to win to Christ" (Parshall, 2002, p. 17).

Writings of American evangelicals include numerous examples in which Muslims are not viewed so negatively and that recommend outreach to Muslims be done in ways that will help foster friendly relationships. Ray Register, a Southern Baptist evangelist who does outreach ministry to Muslim students on the campus of North Carolina State University, focuses his ministry on dialoguing with Muslims, including understanding Islam at a deeper level, developing friendships with Muslims, and engaging them in conversations about religion and faith. He explicitly suggests that Christians avoid trying to defend US foreign policy in the Middle East because that is one of the biggest obstacles to engaging Muslims in dialogue. In Register's perspective, the objective of Christian-Muslim friendships is to understand each other and to witness to each other. He believes that even in the context of evangelism, a responsibility inherent in both Christianity and Islam, it is still possible to understand each other and engage in friendly conversation (Register, 1979, pp. 7-10, 17).

Shirin Taber's 2004 book, entitled Muslims Next Door: Uncovering Myths and Creating Friendships, recommends ways to evangelize Muslims in America successfully. Taber, an Iranian-American evangelical Christian and former Muslim, asserts that "learning to empathize with Muslims and to understand the issues that trouble them can help smother the flames of suspicion and the fear of terrorism" (p. 16). It is also her hope that people in the West would get a better grasp of the Muslim perspective and "learn how to take steps to establish friendships which can point to Christ" (Taber, 2004, pp. 16-17). She wants to help facilitate understanding and respect between both groups so that people in the West will see Muslims as approachable. She would like Westerners to "identify with their Muslim neighbors in a way that reveals the love and compassion of Christ" (Taber, 2004, pp. 16-17). Taber (2004) gives numerous practical suggestions for how Christians can develop relationships with Muslims through the cultural values that both groups share, such as the significance of raising children and their misgivings about the moral values of Western pop-culture. She shares her experience of how she was harassed as a student in American schools during the Iranian hostage crisis and appeals to American Christians not to treat Muslims in the same way because of the 9/11 attacks. Taber asserts that even though Muslims and Christians have theological differences that will always remain, these two groups do share similarities in terms of culture and morality. For some American Christians, supporting Israel politically seems more important than witnessing to Muslims in an endearing manner, but unquestioning support for Israel is a hindrance to understanding why Muslims are angry over the Arab-Israeli conflict.

Taber shares the story of how she led her Iranian Muslim friend, Sarah, to Christ after sharing with her the forgiveness offered by Christ and goes on to assert that if American Christians were more sympathetic toward Muslims, many more Muslims would come to faith in Christ (Taber, 2004).

Like Taber, other American Christians also highlight the significance of inculcating an attitude of understanding rather than suspicion and stressing the importance of proselytizing Muslims in spite of the fact that American evangelicals tend to be hostile toward them (Kidd, 2009, p. 116). For example, two Presbyterian ministers, McDowell and Zaka (1999), criticize American "media and literature" for its stereotypes of Islam's "militancy, harshness, view of women, and oil wealth" (p. xviii), and assert that this practice has a negative impact on the evangelization of Muslims. In their view, Muslims are "in many ways ... just like each of us" (p. xviii). Muslims are not "all militants seeking to destroy everything that Western civilization holds dear... Our enemy is Satan, not Muslims" (p. xviii). They encourage American Christians to develop evangelistically fruitful friendships with their Muslim neighbors (pp. 171-98). Among the numerous models and methods that they discuss regarding evangelizing Muslims, the ministry model that they especially recommend they call "Meetings for Better Understanding" (p. 182). These meetings will be places where Christians and Muslims can meet in order to talk about and compare their faiths without any theological compromise and would be a very effective way of evangelizing Muslims because "the gospel has its own power to change their minds and open their hearts to say 'yes' to Jesus" (McDowell & Zaka, 1999, pp. 219). McDowell and Zaka (1999) go on to say that since 1999 these kinds of meetings were being held in some of the major cities and on numerous college campuses all over the country. Even though some people may be tempted to view Christian attempts to convert Muslims through discussions and dialogue as duplicitous or violating the culture of Muslims (Kidd, 2009, p. 117), there is a general consensus that this methodology is advantageous because it involves voluntary engagement in peaceful conversation by believers on both sides. In fact, because both Christians and Muslims desire to convert the other, this is the context in which any attempts to understand each other must take place (McDowell & Zaka, 1999, pp. 229-32).

The Internet is another avenue via which American Muslims are being evangelized. Jochen Katz, developer and webmaster of the website Answering Islam (http://answering-islam.org), asserts that approximately 50,000 people visit the site every month, half of which may be from an Islamic background. This website provides material on evangelism for Muslims, apologetic material to help Christians seeking to evangelize Muslims, and testimonies of Muslims who have converted to Christianity (Morton & Katz, 2001, pp. 155-64). Other sites provide helpful resources to equip Christians to evangelize Muslims. COMMA (A Coalition of Ministries to Muslims in America, http://www.commanetwork.com) claims that at the current rate of growth, by 2030 Muslims will account for a quarter of the world's population. The number of US Muslims will double and Americans will be as likely to know a Muslim as they are a Jewish person or an Episcopalian (2016). In light of this demographic growth, COMMA works to network with organizations that are engaged in ministry to Muslims in order to motivate, teach, and equip local churches and individual Christians to reach out evangelistically to Muslims. Still another example is the Crescent Project (https://www.crescentproject.org), which offers DVDs, books, and online resources as well as organizes conferences devoted to friendship-based approaches to evangelism of Muslims. One such conference is specifically designed to train Christian women to foster friendships with Muslim women.

Although not an American, Kenneth Cragg has had enormous influence on American evangelicals. In his 1956 book The Call of the Minaret, which has been reprinted numerous times, he offers valid criticisms of the ways in which Western missionaries have engaged in missions in the Middle East as well as some helpful lessons for those engaging in ministry to Muslims. For Cragg, continued proclamation of the gospel is not an option but a necessity, and it must continue in spite of the paucity of positive response from Muslims. His advice to future missionaries is that they "should remember to think before they start to count" (Cragg, 2000, p. 313). Cragg (2000) asserts that when Christian missionaries work among Muslims, they should work with the expectation that they are going to face challenges as they serve, quite often without seeing any apparent fruit of their labor. Cragg also suggests that when Muslims convert to Christianity, it might be better to deemphasize the significance of being baptized, so that others in their community may not infer that the converts are leaving Islam, their culture, and their families (pp. 316-318). Cragg (2000) also adamantly maintains that a "Christian mission that renounces the making of Christians has forsaken both its genius and its duty. Christ did not serve the world with good advice, and no more shall we" p. 325).

Another topic that is of great concern to American evangelicals is evangelistic activity carried on by Muslims. For example, Charles Colson (2002), an American evangelical leader, had much to say after 9/11 about Muslim clerics reaching out to prisoners. Colson writes: According to published reports, radical Islamists—Muslims who follow a rigid interpretation of the Qur'an called Wahhabism—have put a high priority on reaching disaffected inmates around the world and recruiting them for their own deadly purposes. The Washington Times quotes an al-Qaeda training manual that identifies as "candidates" for recruitment those who are "disenchanted with their country's policies," including convicted criminals. The article quotes a U.S. corrections official who acknowledges that Americans behind bars are "literally a captive audience, and many inmates are anxious to hear how they can attack the institutions of America." (p. 19)

Colson believes the growing influence of Islam among prison inmates is "no accident," given that

> The National Islamic Prison Foundation (NIPF) was specifically organized to convert American inmates to Wahhabism ... [and] the NIPF is one of more than two dozen interlocking groups that together form a huge, nationwide network of outreach programs, funded with hundreds of millions in Saudi Arabian money. (p. 20)

In the conversion process, these prisoners, here referring to blacks who believe they are "being oppressed by the white power structure" (Colson, 2002, p. 20), are invited to join the brotherhood and avail themselves of the opportunity to strike back at their oppressors. They are taught that "the more aggressive they are, the more favor they gain with Allah" (Colson, 2002, p. 20). The solution to all of this, asserts Colson (2002), is preaching the gospel to these prisoners and telling them that through faith in Christ their sins are forgiven—i.e., converting them to Christianity, because "when the gospel is preached, and the men embrace Christ, they eschew violence" (p. 20). This, says Colson, is "the long- term answer; the short-term one is keeping the promoters of terror out of our prisons and away from the inmates they would exploit" (p. 21).

In 1978, Max Kershaw developed an International Students, Inc. booklet entitled How to Share the Good News with your Muslim Friend in which he asserted that Muslims living in America present a "unique challenge and opportunity" (p. i). His intent through this booklet was to help Christians obtain a basic understanding of Muslims and how to share the gospel with them (Kershaw, 1978, p. i). He suggested that people read Christy Wilson's book Introducing Islam in order to gain understanding of Muslims and that Christians should engage Muslims in dialogue in order to evangelize (Kershaw, 1978, p. 4). Kershaw (1978) cautioned that Christians should avoid talking about the Palestinian crisis because Arab Muslims had the perception that Israel had been unfairly supported by the United States, and talking about the rightful ownership of Palestine would not be a very sensitive way in which to develop relationships with Arab Muslims (pp. 23-24).

Oksnevad (2001) writes that in his exploration of work being done among Muslims in America, it became evident that there was a lack of communication between groups and individuals reaching out to Muslims, which resulted in a duplication of efforts by the different parties, and that Christian leaders working among Muslims in America have become increasingly dissatisfied over the lack of concerted evangelization of the Islamic community. In order to address this problem, the Billy Graham Center organized a conference in 1999 to discuss the evangelization of Muslims in America, from which emerged the book The Gospel for Islam: Reaching Muslims in North America (pp. v-vi). At the conference, Larry Poston (2001), an evangelical scholar on Islam, asserted that a theology that diminishes the authority of the Bible as the "sole source of revelation from God to humankind about Himself and his activity in human history" will result in a "weakening of the Bible's clear message that men and women without Christ are lost in sin, are unrighteous before God, and will be eternally punished in a 'lake of fire'," which according to Poston is "one of the greatest – if not the greatest – of the issues facing the Church in coming decades" and will greatly compromise ministry to Muslims (p. 15). A second issue that will be detrimental to ministry among Muslims is the "moral and ethical lifestyle" of Christians, an area in which, asserts Poston (2001), "it often appears that it is not Christians, but rather Muslims, who have 'the edge'" (p. 16). In comparison to Muslims, Christians show a lack in terms of knowledge of the teachings of the Bible, whereas Muslims may memorize the Qur'an in its entirety; Christians pray "perhaps only once per day," while Muslims all over the world are devoted to praying five times every day; not many Christians fast "for any length of time," while Muslims fast every year for an entire month; and not many Christians live "notably moral" lives, while Muslims "live strict lives" (Poston, 2001, pp. 16-17). For Muslims, Christianity as a viable alternative is not a very attractive option (Poston, 2001).

Some Pertinent Themes

The discussion in this chapter shows that American evangelicals have both positive and negative perspectives, attitudes, and practices toward Muslims in the US; that they are interested in ministry to Muslims; and that they are influenced by the information presented in a wide variety of sources—American evangelical and non-evangelical Christian as well as non-Christian sources—discussing Christian-Muslim relations in the US. In all the information that is disseminated by Christian as well as secular sources particularly noteworthy are the negative assertions that American evangelical leaders make about Islam, the Qur'an, Muhammad, etc. Assertions of this nature are inflammatory and have immense negative influence on American evangelicals. This highlights the need to develop a robust evangelical theology of religions in general, and Islam in particular, as a proper framework for thinking about and interacting with Muslims. I will focus on this subject in Chapter 8. Now, however, we will consider qualitative information about the perspectives, attitudes, and practices of American evangelicals as viewed through their own eyes in a series of research interviews.

PART II:

The 21st–Century Experience of American Evangelicals with Muslims

CHAPTER 5

PERSPECTIVES, ATTITUDES, AND PRACTICES

As I reflected on what scholars—both non-Christian and Christian of various stripes— evangelists, missionaries, and other evangelical leaders have said and what journalists have reported, I wanted to find out for myself what ordinary American evangelicals today think and say about Islam, and how they act toward Muslims. I contacted four evangelical churches in different suburbs of Chicago to interview the pastors and 40 members of the congregation. Over a period of four months, from April through August 2013, I interviewed participants in 30-60 minute sessions, listening to them speak openly and honestly from their heart. You, the reader, may find that in some cases you share some of these perspectives, attitudes, and practices, and in other cases not. In either case, my hope is that in reading what others have so openly shared, you will be prompted to do some healthy soul-searching.

Respondents answered ten open-ended questions during the course of the individual interviews to gather the qualitative information to answer my first research question: "What perspectives, attitudes, and practices toward Muslims and Islam are found among evangelical laypeople and pastors? The summary or direct quotes of comments made by the American evangelical respondents presented below, selectively drawn from their responses, help illustrate the general gist of the perspectives, attitudes, and practices found among the interviewees. Names and identifying details of the respondents have been altered to protect their anonymity.

Q1: When you hear the word Islam, what immediately comes to your mind?

Respondents expressed a variety of views. Some of them thought about Islam theologically, discussing its differences with Christianity in the doctrines of the Trinity, Muhammad, the five pillars of Islam, monotheism, or the understanding of Jesus. Some, such as Gabriel, a professional in the IT industry in his mid-50s, mentioned the history of Christianity and Islam, the "contentious relationship between the two," the Crusades, etc., while others brought up their mental images of the Middle-East: Muslims praying, mosques, parapets, Islamic art and architecture, clothing styles, etc. However, most perspectives were negative, as the following comments made apparent. One respondent described Islam as not only a religion but a culture, a society, and a way of life that began in the late 7th century. "Islam is complex and it's complex because I think there are multiple denominations or lines of thinking in Islam, [such as] the Sunni and the Shiite." It is not "as monolithic as most people like to think it is... There is a lot of information out there that's ... not from an objective source and so you have to be careful as to its conclusions." There are some who are "using Islam for ... worldly ends or political ends, it's really a tool to power... The media have generally speaking treated Islam in a simplistic way... The media talks about the burning of the Qur'an in Florida, and the public face increasingly of Islam has been terrorism."

John, a business executive, went on to say that there have been attempts by some Muslims to say that "that's not true Islam." It makes people think that "everybody thinks the way that the Al Qaeda does or the Taliban does" but this is "a minority of what Islam really thinks."

Along these lines Simon, a retired business executive in his mid-70s and an active youth-worker, asserted that one of the first things he thinks about in relation to Islam is "radical Islam," but at the same time he was "fairly cognizant of the fact that all of Islam is not radical." He also thought that "the need for evangelizing Muslims is great and it's a daunting task because of the sheer numbers and the relative isolation that they put themselves in." Another commented that it is hard to determine how many Muslims are actually radicalized.

Lisa, a retiree, reported feeling "some amount of fear" because of what is reported in the news. It made her think that "all Muslims are radical and [Islam] was something to be afraid of." She did not want mosques in her neighborhood because her fear was that that would ruin property values. But she also said that things had changed for her after she rented out the room in her house to a Muslim, of whom she said: "He was the most gentle, kind person and he was very thoughtful about his wife and his new baby." Her perception in the past had been that Muslim men treated their wives terribly: "that they beat their wives; their wives were very submissive, just like slaves. And if their wives did anything they did not like, they could absolutely have them eliminated, killed." Her perception of Sunni Muslims was that they were very peaceful, whereas Shiite Muslims were "going to try and take over the world. That's their agenda starting with Israel and the Christians in America, probably." And they will "attack," or "slit the throat or cut off the heads of some other who's not a believer." Bill, a mental-health professional in his late 70s, feels "a little bit apprehensive" when he hears about people who plot to blow up trains and other such acts, but at the same time would appreciate the opportunity to sit down and dialogue with a cleric. Carl, a home environment worker in his mid-40s, fearfully asserted that "Islam is ... not always what it seems. Muslims aren't always what they seem." Peter, a financial professional in his late-20s, asserted that his perception of Islam was impacted by the "violence that is reported in the media." Islam is "violent in the name of the religion." We hear that it is the extremists who engage in jihad and martyrdom, "but I get the sense that that's not just the extreme, although the extremes act on it, but it's ingrained more than that into the religion itself."

Mary's "general impression" was that Muslims were religious people, more so than other Americans, and they actually had more interest in talking about religious issues than non-Muslim Americans; they were open, emotional people, they would tell you what they thought, and they wanted to talk to you, but they had beliefs that were going to be hard to overcome because they had wrong ideas about Christianity. For example, she found out early on that Muslims had an "intense dislike of evangelical Christians because they felt that they unfairly took Israel's side all the time and that was creating a big barrier between them and Christians." She also asserted that she liked Muslims and liked talking to them even though she did not feel that she "could become close friends with them." She thought that the Qur'an was "an evil book" and viewed "Muslims as being controlled and manipulated by Islam." She thought that "Islam itself is kind of a tyranny that's kind of pressed down on the people" and that Muslims "don't have freedom of religion." She also thought that Islam had "done a lot of destruction in the world" and that it was promoted "by the sword." In her opinion, violence was "an intricate and innate part of the religion," and radical, fundamentalist Islam was the "pure Islam." On the other hand there were also some good things about Islam such as "a lot of family emphasis [and] ... almsgiving."

For numerous respondents the first word or phrase that came to their mind was: "terrorist" or "terrorism," "jihad", Muslims are "scary people", "enemy, anger," Islam is oppressive and that it persecutes "Christians, Hindus, [and] Buddhists," etc. And Rebecca, a woman in her 50s with a daughter who has studied at a Christian college, as well as a personal friend whose daughter is a Muslim asserted that "I do not believe that there is peaceful Islam."

The perspectives of the pastors interviewed were similar to those of lay evangelicals. Pastor Justin, who is in his mid-60s and has been a pastor all his life, asserted that he was confused as to how to "engage with these fellow citizens when I don't really understand them very well. A part of me feels this huge tinge [sic] that I don't trust these people because of the violence." Theologically he thought that Islam was a "works based thing that ... really drives people in bad directions." Pastor Tim, who is in his early 60s and who was in the business world prior to becoming a pastor, asserted that Islam is "not a religion of peace." At the same time he is quick to remind himself that "there is a fundamentalist bent to Islam, 15%, maybe 17%." There are also many Muslims who have a "very unorthodox understanding of Islam, especially in the US there are many moderate Muslims." Pastor Sawyer, a former accountant in his mid-60s, thought that Islam means "submission to God." And Pastor Seth, who used to practice law and is now in his early 60s, described it as a "significant religious force in America ... a very powerful force and influence in the world." He described the phrase "powerful force and influence in the world" in terms of Islam's cultural impact. He thought of Islam as a "more restrictive culture in some senses ... certain moralities that are accepted and some that are definitely not accepted within certain Islamic cultures." He also thought that Muslims display "tremendous amount of devotion or commitment to their faith" and "have an influence to world politics through their religious positions." Finally, he mentioned that living in the modern world today it is hard to not think of "acts of violence that have been attributed to 'Islamists, terrorists'."

Q2: How would you describe Islam as a religion?

Paul, a semi-retired IT professional in his 70s, contrasted Islam and Christianity: Christianity is a religion of love and has a "God of love"; Allah "demands things and if you pass the test you get to go to some sort of heaven." In Islam "there is very little mercy, there is very little love." "Allah is nearly capricious." Luke, an office worker in his early 60s, thought of Islam as a "theocracy" which in its "full-blown" form is at odds with "democracy." While religion, no matter which religion it is, is good for society because there is a moral basis that "allows people to understand the right from wrong," Islam is not good for society because it makes threats through "jihad or holy war" and has forced "the majority, the good people, to keep their mouth shut." For this respondent it was hard to understand how people could give up their lives "to destroy other human beings." Numerous respondents described Islam in the following terms: it is a "very male-dominated" religion and women are kept "under their thumb" and "have no say"; it is an "archaic religion dictating that women have no rights"; it is "sexist, ... female infanticide is okay"; it is a "satanic religion." Some noted that no matter which country you look at, for example Pakistan or Sudan, wherever Islam has "really become commonplace" that place has become "cruel," "backward," and "oppressive towards people"; it is the "opposite of what God wanted to have for us." Karen, a homemaker in her 60s and former editor, also asserted that Islam is satanic and that if Satan was going to establish a religion with himself as God it would have a book like the Bible, which is the Qur'an, and he would have a messenger, who is Muhammad. According to her, Islam is Satan's attempt to replace God and to be god. Islam has taken many parts of the Bible and distorted it "by putting their own characters into it," such as by replacing Isaac with Ishmael. Islam is "the antithesis of Christianity." Lisa thought that Muhammad was a false prophet, and

Hannah called him a "disturbed individual." Peter asserted that a Muslim is not allowed to leave Islam. His understanding was that if a Muslim tries to leave they are either "disowned by their families" or in some cases they get "the death penalty for being an apostate."

Some respondents had a few positive things to say about Islam. Harry, a middle class professional in his late-50s, described it as "a pretty well put religion" because it has the Qur'an, prophets, and mosques, and "it has all the pieces of a religion." The only thing that is missing is the "true, the right God. You put the right God in there, it can be great." Steve, a business executive who has worked internationally, was very impressed with the "intensity in [Muslims'] religious beliefs and practice," for example praying five times a day, however he was explicit in stating that he was "not talking about religious extremism." Joshua, a leader in his congregation in his late 30s, thought that Muslims have a holistic view of "community and culture." Muslims care about other Muslims, which means that "when there is a conflict and Muslims are hurt, there is an appeal to the whole world Muslim community that we need to take care of these people because they are Muslims and they are one of us," a mindset that is lacking in Christianity, he asserted. At the same time this respondent was troubled, because he thought that Muslims have a dichotomous view of religion. For example, "their insistence that God is one really conflicts with how they say that they appreciate the Bible." This respondent also thought that when the media portrays Muslims as "ignorant and poor and impoverished, ... that's [not] always a fair view." Just because Muslims have a "naïve consciousness" about their religion does not make them inferior to followers of another religion. Hilda, a homemaker in her late 40s who has lived overseas in an Islamic context, asserted that the Muslims that she has met in the US, from a "cultural and ... religious standpoint," are "lovely people, they are gentle, they are kind, they are very hospitable."

The perspectives of the pastors were somewhat similar to that of the laity. Pastor Justin asserted that Islam is a works-based religion, where some works are good such as "helping the poor" and others are "just religious farce." Because of all the religious rituals in Islam, such as "bowing to Mecca five times a day," it did not seem to him that Muslims "have much freedom or joy." To him Muslims were "devout" because they engaged in religious activities "to set themselves apart at some cost, ... wearing certain garments or ... praying in a certain way." He went on to say that, like Christianity, Islam is framed by its followers in numerous ways, and hence it is complex and "not the same religion to everybody." He also thought that it was an "acquisitive religion" and that it was "out to gain" not so much by "conversion" but by "overpowering." Pastor Justin could not conceive of Muslims "standing on the street corner witnessing to somebody and winning them over by the strength of logic, of spiritual influence." Islam takes over either by "birthrate" or by "combat."

Pastor Tim described it as "one of the global, superpower religions" and "a big tent" because "there is a militant side to it; there is a very uneducated, oppressive, but uneducated side to it; [and] there is a moderate side to it."

Pastor Seth described Islam as "monotheistic [and] rejecting all other religions"; having commonalities with Judaism"; certainly in the patriarchs"; and accepting Christ as a human, historical figure and a prophet but rejecting him as Messiah. He also described it as a "religion of good works for salvation" that promotes the idea of God who is more arbitrary than moved by grace, love, mercy... The essence of their salvation is good works: you have [to do] more in your life that's good than bad therefore you have salvation... So, there is an arbitrary aspect,

. . . maybe God thinks that's enough good works, maybe God doesn't think that's enough good works... [In their system] it differs according to the individual.

Pastor Sawyer had questions about how much of the content of the Qur'an actually came from Muhammad. First, because his wife was influential, he wondered if some of the content actually came from her. Second, "there was a significant period of time where he and other people were convinced he was demonized." As to the question whether the Qur'an was a demonic revelation, he asserted that he did not know but thought that "history doesn't line up very well to be recognizing him as God's prophet or ultimate prophet." He also went on to say that the media shows "a very narrow band of what historically would be considered a quite extremist version of Islam, which isn't necessarily the way it is." For example, Islam in Saudi Arabia "represents a very particular minority sect of relatively recent vintage," and Islam would be seen differently in other places such as Egypt. For the last 1500 years or so "we know much of Islam has been a lot more tolerant and a lot more soft-edged in its actual practice than what we hear about or see right now."

In summary, while respondents described Muslims using words like "gentle," "kind," "thoughtful," "peaceful," "open," and "fairly easy to talk to," all of which were used in contexts of relationships with Muslim individuals, most perspectives that respondents had of Islam and Muslims were negative: Islam is a tyranny; they are fearful of Muslims because of what they hear on the media about Islam; they do not want mosques in their neighborhoods because that would ruin property values; Shiite Muslims were going to take over the world, Israel, and the Christians in America and slit the throats of anyone who is not a believer; there is no such thing as a peaceful Islam; Islam is the source of future conflicts; Islam is the source of the greatest amount of persecution of Christians; Islam subjugates women; etc. The respondents displayed a deep sense of fear of Islam and Muslims. The two respondents who used positive words to describe Muslims also used strong negative words and phrases to describe Islam, which indicates that they were conflicted in their perspectives. One male respondent actually wept at the end of the interview because of his conflicted views that while in actual fact he hated the leaders of Islam and harbored a great deal of animosity toward Islam, based on the teaching of the Bible as a Christian he is not supposed to feel this way. Another respondent also expressed conflicted sentiments towards Muslims in that although she knows that she is supposed to love Muslims, she harbors feelings of hostility toward them. But most respondents did not seem troubled by their espousal of negative feelings toward Muslims and did not question whether their negative perspectives and attitudes toward Muslims were warranted.

Q3: Some people think Islam is basically a good and peaceful religion that some radicals have hijacked; others think it is an evil religion. What do you think about Islam?

When asked what the lay respondents thought of Islam, the responses described Islam in positive as well as negative terms, with the overwhelming descriptions being negative in tenor. Positive descriptions included statements such as: Muslims have a holistic view of community and culture, they care about each other and are willing to meet the needs of other Muslims, Muslims are God-fearing and peace-loving, etc. Negative descriptions of Islam included statements such as Islam is not good for society because it makes threats of jihad; it is a male-dominated, sexist religion; Muslims are proud and difficult to understand, lack freedom or joy, and Islamic people are unsafe; Christianity is a religion of love and has a God of love, but Allah, who is very capricious, demands obedience, and if you pass the test you get to go to heaven; there is very little love and mercy in Islam; Islam is a theocracy, which in its full-blown form is at odds with democracy; while the intensity of Islam, such as praying five times a day is impressive, it is also a prescriptive religion of rote rituals; it is works-oriented; etc. One way to look at this question was through a theological lens. John asserted that Scripture is inspired by God and that the only way to get to the Father is through Jesus. To say that other paths—Hinduism, Confucianism, Mormonism, etc.—are evil is "probably a bit of a reaching," yet he believed that one could make this theological argument because the Bible is clear about what it says about "anything that is opposed to ... God's word." Another respondent made this theological argument in a more categorical way, asserting that Islam is evil because it does not "preach Christ." John and Natalie both felt that Islam is, at its core, good and peaceful. John went on to say that Islam "has been hijacked by a minority for political purposes, political and economic purposes... What was the Taliban benefiting from in Afghanistan? The poppy fields, right? Pure and simple." But, he added that Christians are also "vulnerable to the same dynamic." And Sam asserted that "Islam started out as a warring religion. First thing they did was go to war."

Mike, an IT professional in his mid-50s, said that Muslims believe "when everyone is subjected to Islam then peace will come," thus, "to me it's a religion of violence." Most Muslims do not necessarily see it this way because they are not being asked to do anything to "subjugate everyone else to Islam." This respondent also saw it as a "religion of the devil" because God had chosen Abraham who had "two seeds, Ishmael and Isaac." God wanted his blessings to come through Isaac, while the devil has taken "hold of Ishmael's seed and has caused them to worship him." In his own paraphrase of Matthew (Matt 7:21-

23), Mike said "many have done things in my name, you know, Lord, Lord, I have done these things, you know, depart from me, I never knew you, you workers of iniquity." To Mike, this concept applies to Muslims who think that they are worshiping God in the right way but will then "have the shock of their eternal lives to realize that they were totally wrong."

Lisa asserted that even though there are "good and gentle people who are Muslims," their agenda is "to make the world a Muslim world." Even the Sunnis, when they have gained enough control and find that there are people who are not going to convert to Islam, will become more forceful and become "ready to maybe slit somebody's throat or threaten their life if they don't convert." Islam is "basically an evil religion, "something to be watched carefully, feared." Limits need to be set in this country on admitting Muslim immigrants, because countries like France, England, and Germany have let them in, and now they regret "having welcomed them as much as they did." They were welcomed in the hope that friendly relationships would develop, but Islam has a different agenda: "The agenda is to take over and to have sharia law and to turn that country into a Muslim country... So, it is actually evil at that point." According to David, an engineer in his mid-60s, people who think that Islam is a "faith of love and friendship" need to "take that back." "When you have these clerics who can demand people to kill , ... the whole religion [is] inherently suspect." Stuart, an American of European background, expressed similar sentiments. Giving the example of Iran, he asserted that "regular people in Iran are actually fairly pro-American... But, it is the leadership that isn't." The "extreme element of Islam does not get corrected by the leadership." You see and hear from radical imams who applaud "all kinds of terrorist attacks" but "don't hear a lot of peaceful Muslim people speaking out against it." He went on to say that Muslims should not come to the US with their "sharia law." He gave the example of Joel Rosenberg, who does not believe "it is a peaceful religion," and asserted that if it is "accurate" that Muslims are "waiting for the twelfth Imam ... [who] will kill the small devil which is Israel and the big devil which is the US," then it is "not a peaceful religion."

Karen asserted that she had learned that when the early parts of the Qur'an were written, Muslims were encouraged "to live at peace with people" because they were small in number and vulnerable in a non-Muslim majority. But this changed as the Muslim community grew and they were to "kill the unbelievers," Jews in particular. The law of abrogation allows Muslims to do away with the early parts of the Qur'an, which were peaceful, and live by the later parts of the Qur'an, which teach that they should kill their unbelieving friends or neighbors and not have Christians as friends. If somebody wanted to convert to Islam, they could live, but if not, then Muslims could "kill them or take them and sell them as slaves or keep them as sex slaves if they are women—or men, I suppose, for that matter." Karen cited a verse she attributed to the Qur'an but that is actually a paraphrase of the Hadith (Sahih Muslim Book 041, No. 6985): "'A Muslim ... tree says, O Muslim, there is a Jew behind me, come and kill him.' Well, that's not very peaceful." If there are Muslims who are living peacefully it is because they know what the Qur'an teaches but they "are gentle-natured people and they want to get along," which has nothing to do with them being Muslims, or they are obeying a Muslim teaching "called maruna," where they are taught to lie in order to "fit in and get along" with the ultimate goal of "complete world domination." Hazel, a corporate accountant in her 40s, chuckling with embarrassment, admitted "that when things like terrorism happen, whether that was 9/11 or the Boston Marathon bombings, my first thought is it's an Islamic terrorist."

Rebecca stated something very different from every other interviewee: "I think it's an evil religion that some have hijacked into a peaceful theology ... and those who think they are Islamists peacefully, they're not Islamists. They're something else because true fundamental Islam is violent and intolerant." She also characterized the Qur'an as "extremely hateful, violent, unethical. I mean, Muhammad was married to a nine-year-old, had many wives, you know, kill the infidel, you know, search behind every rock, I think that was about the Jews. It's intolerant if you follow their holy book ... this was certainly not a peaceful religion."

The pastors' perspectives were sometimes similar, sometimes different from their parishioners. Pastor Justin asserted that any religion that denies "the Lordship of Jesus Christ" is an evil religion, and it is "diabolical" because it teaches that Muslims have to please Allah by their actions. Culturally speaking most Muslims are peaceful people, but there is also a mindset that says, "we are going to conquer the world." Pastor Tim said that Islam is a "misguided religion" and that there are "many victims in Islam." Victims include not only women or those "hijacked by and forced to live under sharia law," but also those "who are misinformed and don't know of the grace of God extended through Christ ... [or] about God's love and grace and mercy and the free gift of forgiveness and eternal life." Victims also include "political prisoners," people "subject to Islamic law" living in societies that do not "recognize the value of human life... life in many fundamentalist corners of the Islamic world is small and mean and ugly and oppressive."

Pastor Sawyer thought that these statements are "too simple to be either really very accurate to be true. It's a lot more complex than that:"

On the one hand Islam is a peaceful religion because it certainly calls for certain morals, has a moral standard, it encourages respect towards other people and even religions, especially religions that are sort of people of the book, people who are theologically descendants of Abraham who are monotheists, but on the other hand, it could also be argued that "Islam has always been a militant religion in the sense that it is expansionist, it makes sort of militant claims... in the ancient world both Christianity and Islam expanded or tried to expand by military force... Christians have given up the militant aspect because it is counterproductive, but I'm not sure that all Muslims have.

Pastor Seth asserted that he did not think that Islam was "fundamentally a violent religion, [but] essentially was one of peace." Any religion according to him is "capable at least for a while of being hijacked by something that is very public and very loud." As to whether Islam is evil, he asserted that because it denies "the exclusivity ... of Christ, it's wrong." It can be used for evil because "Satan can use it to blind the hearts and minds of billions, ... therefore by guilt by association I guess you could call it evil ... by what it can accomplish, but I don't know if I would characterize it as evil in and of itself." In summary, for the most part the respondents espoused negative perspectives about Islam. Islam was viewed negatively from a biblical perspective in that it opposes God and what He says in the Bible, and it is evil because it does not preach about Christ; it is a demonic religion because while God wanted His blessings to come through Isaac, the devil has taken hold of Ishmael and has caused Muslims to worship him; Muslims want to make the whole world Islamic; Islam is to be feared and watched; etc. Islam was also viewed negatively from a political and societal perspective in that it is basically a violent religion and has an agenda to take over the world; Muslims have a psyche of militancy; Muslims have tried to impose their faith on society and because people do things in the name of jihad; if Muslims do things that destroy other people's lives then it does become evil; it is evil because they want to impose sharia law on everybody; they train children to engage in terrorist activities; Muslims are the main perpetrators of terrorism; etc. Many respondents viewed Islam negatively from an Islamic theological perspective: the Qur'an is extremely hateful, violent, and unethical; it is not a peaceful book, and since Islam is based on that, it is not a peaceful religion; the Qur'an teaches to kill Jews and to lie in the name of Islam; etc. While a few respondents viewed Islam positively, for example asserting that it has some good principles such as prayer, living a clean lifestyle, not drinking, etc., these respondents also shared their negative perceptions, such as that it condones the killing of people who refuse to convert or who are not Muslim. That is, the respondents, in addition to espousing negative perspectives about Islam and Muslims, were also conflicted in their views about Islam. Furthermore, the responses also make clear that the respondents were influenced by the violence associated with Islam.

Q4: Do you think that Christians should look at Islam differently than other religions, such as Buddhism or Hinduism? Or should we look at them basically the same way?

Joshua asserted that Christians are "nervous about Islam and Muslims" because they have a hard time separating "the events of 9/11 and the conflict of the last twelve years" from what it means to be a Muslim and understanding that engaging in jihad or being an "Arab terrorist" is not the "identity of the vast majority of Muslims." Our fears can often dominate "our trust that God will take care of us and will guide us as we try to engage people." He went on to say that Christians also view Muslims through "insufficient theological lenses." Muslims are seen through the lens of "Ishmael and Hagar," where "Isaac is a child of promise," but Ishmael is not. For Christians this translates to "everything for Isaac, nothing for Ishmael, which is not really how Genesis presents it or what the whole scope of Scriptures ask us to do." This theological lens makes the engagement of Christians with Muslims awkward as they learn to figure out how to do this well:

> They want to do better at reaching everybody but they just don't know how to, ... you know, "Can I invite my Muslim friend over for a barbeque?" You know, "what can or can't I serve him?" "Would he want to go to a movie with me?" "Would he play golf with me?" "Can I have my child play with the Muslim neighbor's kids?" You know, those kinds of things I think are questions and concerns that a lot of evangelicals have, and they're trying to get over their awkwardness in saying, "OK, these are normal people who just hold different beliefs than I hold, and, yes, those beliefs aren't about saving faith in Jesus, but they are people who God loves and God cares about, and I could at least get started in presenting the true Jesus by just starting a relationship." And I think that's the scary thing [for] most evangelicals.

A view that was shared by many respondents, such as John, was that Islam should not be "singled out or be viewed differently." While it is a different "line of religious thinking," and one that I do not agree with, "it's also important that we respect the multicultural reality in which we live today." Jesus said that we should love our neighbors as ourselves, which is not limited to just loving Christian neighbors, but loving your "Hindu, Islam, Atheist, Mormon, Confucian, whatever, agnostic" neighbor. "And so in that light I don't see how Islam should be treated any differently than anybody else who has a different worldview than I do. I should love them like I love myself." James, a banker in his 50s, asserted that we also "need to be knowledgeable about where the differences are and within the context of evangelism know where the pressure points are."

This view was shared by numerous respondents, which highlighted the significance of reaching out to Muslims with the gospel espoused by American evangelicals: "I think in one sense that we should look at everyone who has not had the opportunity to get to know Jesus, to get to know the idea of the Christian religion, that we should try to do what we could to let other people see no matter what they are" (Darryl); "well, as souls that need Christ we look at them all the same way because we are winning souls for the kingdom" (Peter); we should "try to convince them in love that they are on the wrong pathway" (Stuart); "we need to look at all the world's religions as false religions and in that sense have compassion for the people that are lost in those false religions" (James); "in order to reach people in each of those religions, you need to look at those religions differently in order to meet those people where you are to be able to present the gospel [in terms of the] different tenets, different items of the faith they are following" (Hazel).

Paul, thinking theologically, commented that because each of these religions has a different understanding of the nature of God, and Buddhism does not have the concept of God at all, they "should all be dealt with differently." Moreover, Islam requires a different approach, because in Islam, "if you leave the Muslim faith, your family will disown you," so "yes, we should deal with them differently." Paul went on to say that Islam is also "politically ... quite different." In every part of the world Christians are in danger from Muslims. "I can be in Boston trying to run a marathon and get killed by Muslims." Something like this would not "happen from a Hindu." I do not have the sense that the "Hindu religion wants to take over the United States." One branch of Islam wants everyone to come under "sharia law. Another branch wants to have so many children that pretty soon the majority of the population is Muslim in a sort of quiet takeover. Another branch wants to fly planes into the World Trade Center." Luke asserted that Islam is "more than a religion," it is an intolerant religion, and "if you are not a Muslim, then you are depicted as evil." A view shared by a number of respondents was that because of the persecution that Christians have to face from Islam it needs to be viewed differently.

Lisa feels Islam should be looked at differently because while these other religions try to convert people, they do not use "force," or make "threats," or "go out and bomb people," or "kill people and level the Twin Towers, and all this in an effort to get someone to see their point of view." The other religions do not have to be "feared as much." We have the responsibility "to tell them about Jesus, but we don't have the threat behind it, and we don't have the fear that they are going to annihilate us, or our families, or our towns, or ruin our country." Stacy, a homemaker and ministry volunteer in her 50s, asserted that "Buddhism is actually quite a gentle religion, … [and] the Hindu religion is basically a very peaceful religion. I don't think that Islam is a peaceful religion. Of all the religions that is the one that I fear the most, I fear that it's most aggressive and negative." She also stated that it is Islam itself, not the people, that we should look at differently. Hannah noted, while there are passionate Hindus and Buddhists, their religion does not affect "their life to the extent that it becomes a radical, political kind of thing." But with Islam you have a "branch that is very radical" and that wants to implement sharia law. This would "affect a lot of people [and] … greatly affect my life." This is "to be concerned about for sure."

The pastors interviewed shared some views of their congregants. Pastor Justin said that these three religions are similar in that they do not acknowledge "Christ as Lord." At the same time, "they are really not alike." Because the adherents of each of these religions process life differently and have different ways of thinking about things, "it is better for us to know the distinctive[s] ... and not just theological but actually cultural." It will not be helpful when you communicate or engage with people "if you think of them [as] alike." Pastor Tim asserted, "I think most people are intellectually lazy, and they make broad generalizations, and it's not helpful." Because Islam has a large "market share," and one "that is growing," he was more worried about the impact of Islam politically and culturally than that of Buddhism or Hinduism. "So, [Muslims,] ... they take land, they never give it up, right? So, at one level I do think about Islam differently than other religions." And elaborating on what he meant by politically and culturally, he asserted that he was "thinking of fundamentalist Islam." Pastor Tim was quite impressed by Eboo Patel because as a "moderate Muslim" he was "arguing for peace." He also appreciated Patel's Interfaith Youth Core. In light of these he asserted that "there is a lot of good culture that comes out of Islam." But at the same time there are a lot of "small, uneducated ... people trying to impose sharia law by force one way or the other." According to him this number has grown because of "missteps" by Americans and Christians, "not because we're extending love and grace ...[but] because we are extending hate. And that's not a card we have an option to play, but we play it. [And] ... American foreign policy hasn't helped us."

In summary, when comparing their views regarding Islam and other religions, such as Buddhism or Hinduism, the respondents stated that from a biblical and theological perspective Islam should not be looked at differently than other religions. Jesus said that we should love our neighbors as ourselves, and from that perspective we should love all our neighbors in the same way, irrespective of their religion; in this vein each religion should also be viewed differently because they are theologically different and each requires a unique evangelistic approach. From a political perspective respondents felt that Islam needs to be viewed differently than other religions: other religions do not want to take over the US or impose religious law; other religions make converts without using force or bombing people or making threats; Islam is the most aggressive and negative religion; other religions do not teach their followers to take sex slaves or beat their wives if they are not submissive; Islam is nasty, vile, and satanic because it does these things. Thus, the respondents recognized all non-Christian religious groups as being lost and in need of Christ's salvation, but their impression—drawn for the most part from the media—of Islam as a violent religion gave them a less favorable impression of it than they have of Buddhism, Hinduism, and other faiths that are not portrayed as negatively in the media.

Q5: Have you known personally any Muslims? Tell me about this relationship.

Of the 40 evangelicals interviewed, nine had not known any Muslims personally, although one thought that his dentist might be a Muslim. One female respondent, Stacy, had lived in Detroit and had worked for several years at a school that taught English to Yemeni women and through this had developed relationships with them. She commented that in the beginning these women were "very suspicious" because they had "heard very negative things about Christians." Initially these women kept the Christians at arm's length, and in time some, some but not all, "became more open." They were "questioning, warm, very loving people who [often] didn't want to be in the situation that they were in." These women were living in Muslim households and were not allowed to "leave the house except to go to the mosque." In fact, even the shopping was done by the men. These women were "basically kept prisoners. They stayed in the house bringing up children. So, as I said, very lovely people, very oppressed." Stacy had also worked with Muslims—Yemeni women in the US and Pakistani women in the UK—and found each experience "not too much different." Her work as a nurse in the healthcare industry in the UK took her out into the community. Her experience with Muslim men was that they would not shake her hand, they would not make eye contact, and she was "very low down in the rankings," which she found to be "a little bit difficult." But she found "the women very warm and just very lovely." Another issue that came up in which she was not directly involved but that upset her was that when the Muslim women went to the hospital to have babies "they would literally weep with sorrow if they gave birth to a girl, particularly if they were on their sort of third or fourth child and it was another girl because they knew that when they went back home they could well be beaten." Her experience was "not positive."

Lisa rented out rooms in her house and through that had come to know several Muslims. The first one, Aborga, was an individual "who loved his family, loved his wife, was very concerned about her, wanted the very best for her, was willing to allow her to pick out the house of her choice, which to me was far from what I had heard about Muslims, and he was very gentle and kind." Another individual, Ali, was "very nice too." He had even offered to drive the respondent to the hospital: "If you don't have a ride, I can arrange ... my work schedule, and I will see you there." She commented on her interactions with Muslims, saying, "Yes, I think that they are nice people, but I think their agenda also behind it is to befriend people in order to convert them." She had another Muslim living in her house currently who also, according to her, was "very, very nice." This individual had asked to go to church with her, which led her at first to assume he had an interest in Christianity. As time went on she realized that he actually was interested in converting her and her minister to Islam. "That's what his agenda is. And, it's kind of funny, but he is very adamant about what his goal is. But, he's been very nice to me, very nice. He's generous, he shares his food ... and we talk a lot, and we tell each other what we think." Once he asked her what she thought about Muhammad, to which she replied, "I think he's a false prophet." "He just said, 'okay.' He just wanted to know where I was coming from, I guess." When I asked her how she knew that these individuals had an agenda, she responded by saying that it was her initial response to my question.

Karen talked about two different sets of Muslim friends. The first, a Muslim couple who lived in her neighborhood, was very involved in the mosque. She had seen a photograph of the Muslim man and his imam in their family room taken when they were still building the mosque; they were both standing with shovels in the hands. She thought that "he was sort of high up in the hierarchy of the mosque." She mentioned that the couple was "very, very friendly" and that there was not "anything they wouldn't do for you." At the same time she wondered, "if they are following Islam and the teaching that goes on in their mosque, you know, about hatred towards Christians, towards Jews." She shared an incident where the woman visited her home. The Muslim woman observed the star with a cross that the Christian woman wears, a big gold platter with Hebrew writing on it, a shofar, a kiddish cup, etc. around the dining table and realized that they are all "Jewish related." She said that she tried to witness to this Muslim woman "what it is to be a Christian." On one occasion as the Muslim woman was leaving, she remarked, "Well, of course, we don't see Jesus in the same way that you do... He didn't really die and ended up marrying Mary and they had lots of kids. He's going to come back and he's going to be a prophet for the twelfth imam, ... he was a prophet." Karen said that she knew that Muslims think that Jesus went up on the cross but then he was secretly taken down, and "they've got this whole scenario for Jesus, and so they see him as very different." She went on to say that she could not understand how Muslims cannot accept the story of Jonah being swallowed by a fish or the "parting of the Red Sea for Moses"—"how in the world could they ever believe anything in the Qur'an?" She thought that Muslims probably do not read the Qur'an like Christians read the Bible and said that her neighbor was a "very intelligent woman, ... very nice person, and her religion is there, but she's not beating people over the head trying to proselytize or anything like that."

Karen mentioned that while her neighbors are very friendly, she doesn't know "where it's going to end up with them." When I asked what she meant by that and if they were going to do something, she asserted that "Well, because I know what their religion, the ultimate goal of their religion is." She said that it was "too coincidental" that Muslims were building a "large" mosque in Oostburg, "a little town in Wisconsin ... which is just nothing but farmers ... and there aren't even that many people [who] are Muslims." She said that the reason they are doing that is because they "plan to bring Muslims to that area and fill up the mosque." She sees the same thing happening in Murfreesboro, Tennessee, where they are building "a 54,000 square-foot mosque and community center." Given that, when they only had around 50 families, she wondered where the money came from to build "such a huge mosque" and who would attend it? She speculated, "I think, that their intention is to bring Muslims into this country." There are a lot of people coming in from the Middle East, and "what they are doing is planning on filling up these areas ... and ... if the Lord waits long enough, I think someday we will see these mosques become larger." She also thought that Mahmoud Ahmedinejad, the President of Iran, wanted to "take over the United States right away and annihilate Israel. So, you know, I think that there is a plan." Karen added that she did not mean to sound like a "conspiracy theorist" but thought that "probably someday" in the future there is a plan. Asked whether she imagined the specific Muslim couple she knows would be a part of the plan, she responded, "I suppose. If that's the way their mosque goes, that's what they're going to do. So that I wouldn't be surprised if someday you see that taking place." She went on to say that her Muslim friend mentioned to her that the Muslim community wanted to get a Muslim on the school board and her husband thought that she should seek that position. Karen believes this is a way of Muslims becoming involved politically "through the back door" in order to "have an influence on other people. Draw other people to come to [the] mosque."

Driving past the mosque Karen also saw that while Friday was "their big day," their parking lot was full on Sundays as well, which made her wonder if there was a "church that is meeting there on Sundays ... because every time I drive past there on a Sunday, it's like why are there people here on Sundays? I know it's not ... the people from the mosque. They're there on Fridays." Thinking about this scenario she said, "But, I want to find out. I will probably call and find out."

Karen said, "it bothers me" that "really upstanding Christian theologians have [been] taken into this 'Chrislam' thing"—approaches to Islam that seem to blur the distinctions between it and Christianity. She talked about a letter circulated by Yale "apologizing for some things that were said about Islam." This letter was signed by some of the "big names" in Christianity, including Rick Warren (author of The Purpose Driven Life and The Purpose Driven Church), Bill Hybels (senior pastor of Willow Creek Community Church), and Stuart Briscoe (former senior pastor of Elmbrook Church in Brookfield, Wisconsin). Karen understood the letter to be an apology that said "something to the effect that we are asking Allah to forgive us, or something like that."[3] Karen commented,

> Well, if you're asking another ... quote unquote "deity" to forgive you, are you not in essence praying to that person? There was almost a prayer, because how else do you talk to Allah? You know, if he were to exist, how would you talk to him? Offer prayer. So, you're praying to another deity.

Seeing names of certain Christian leaders on this letter was "very bothersome" to her because she saw who she thought were "strong Christians, people who take a stand and who are well known in Christian circles and outside of Christian circles ... as giving in to this mindset that we have to adapt and accept and be chummy-chummy with [these] people." Karen did not think that Christians should be doing that but that they should be saying,

> You know what, I respect your right to be here, I respect your right to vote, I respect your right to say what you believe, but when you come across with the idea that you're supposed to kill Jews, you're supposed to kill Christians, or anybody else, infidels... I don't believe you're supposed to that here. You want to do that, go back to, go back to the Middle East and do it there.

Karen was "very upset ... not upset, but ... very disappointed" that these pastors would sign this letter.

The other friend Karen talked about was a former Muslim and "a terrorist in Israel." He was born in Bethlehem to a Muslim father and an American Christian mother. When he came to the US he "came right

---

3 A copy of the letter referenced by Karen can be found at http://faith.yale.edu/common-word/common-word-christian-response

to the Bridgeview mosque, started working with the other Muslims—they were planning different attacks here." He came to Christ after meeting his third wife. He treated his first two wives terribly: "If they had a little piece of hair hanging outside the hijab, he would start to beat them, see it being disrespectful... And even his third wife he says that he was very unkind to her." He wanted his third wife to become a Muslim, but she said to him, "Well, you show me the inconsistencies and lies in the Bible, and I'll think about it." This led him to start reading the Bible and the first thing he did was "he prayed to the God of Abraham and he said, 'if you are real, show me the truth'." And then he went on to say that during his reading "somewhere between Genesis and Revelation he realized that this was the true God and not Allah, and this was the God he needed to follow." And he became a Christian, and "he's an outstanding believer" who speaks internationally. When he speaks in churches and shares a story, he always tells Christian girls, "Girls, anybody here in this church, listen to your parents when they say, "don't marry an unbeliever." Whatever you do, don't marry a Muslim. They're going to take you right back to the Middle East, and you'll never come home again." Karen asserted that this was what had happened to his mother: "She was really held against her will there."

Mary, an accountant in her 60s, had met over 20 Muslims over the years in business circumstances and in college. She described an interaction she had with a female clerk a number of years ago. This woman was planning to go back to Afghanistan for the wedding of her son, and she was "really nervous" about going back. She said that if she goes back, she may "not be able to get out." She was from a "backward area of Afghanistan, ... a tribal area that bin Laden was hiding in." These are areas which "are not only kind of Muslim but they were actually kind of lawless, that she could go in there and for some reason her family would not let her leave, something might happen to her, she might be killed or something like this." Mary said hearing this "gave me a somewhat different idea about Islam." When the Muslim woman came back almost four weeks after the scheduled time, she said that she had trouble getting out but would not say anything more. While she was loyal to her country, her people, her Muslim background, "there were things she didn't like about it. There were things that were oppressive and wrong to her in her mind," and she was the first Muslim the respondent had met who expressed that there were problems with Islam. The Muslims that Mary had met in college raved about Islam and did not "express that sense that they had some tension with their own religion [or that] they felt that there were issues there, there were problems there, like she did." They did not doubt "their own faith or express any issues with it. It was a much different political climate at that time, obviously, too." Her first impression of Islam was that "not all Muslims embrace everything about Islam. [They] don't like the facts of Islam in their life, and [find] that it can be very difficult for them."

Hazel, through interactions with Muslims at her workplace, came away with positive impressions. She commented: "My personal experience has all been positive, so the negative that I see is more from the media." Hannah, a musician in her early 40s who studied Islamic culture in college, has known many Muslims and has been able to develop "deeper friendships" with some of them, all of whom "were very respectful" of her and her faith. Some of them, while very secular, "would still consider themselves Muslim in every way." She has found that she has "more in common with them than with a lot of secular friends [for whom] God isn't important in their lives." While the way their faith is expressed is "very different," it is easy to be friends with a Muslim woman "because she knows ... what my values are and respects that. There is just so much common ground there. The things that are important to them are important to me, I think particularly as a woman."

Hannah asserted that she had a number of "deep conversations" with a Muslim woman named Aminah who she worked and travelled with. They came to know each other and their families well. While many of these conversations took place in the car in the presence of the Aminah's husband, on one trip Hannah and Aminah were able to share a hotel room for ten days. This gave them the opportunity to discover how much they had in common: "the things that were important to us, the things that shocked us about the culture that we live in, the things that we see on television." One of the topics they discussed was media bias against both Muslims and Christians. They decided to spend a week watching TV to "just observe how much they say against Christianity and how much they say about Islam." Commenting on her experience Hannah said, "it was shocking to both of us ... almost every commercial, almost everything we watched, 'Jesus' [as] a curse word, Christians portrayed as idiots." Aminah was "really surprised at the end of that and remarked, "I had never noticed that before." They also talked a lot about the Boston Marathon bombings that had happened just a week before. Hannah tried to see it from the perspective of a Muslim, asserting,

> How scary it is for them every time something like this happens because everybody's waiting to find out who it was. Was it a Muslim? All the Muslims are like, "please don't let it be a Muslim." And they find out that it's a Muslim, "oooh." And then they have to go through all this again, the backlash and the shame.

Aminah brought up "so many good points." For example, some people asserted that Timothy McVeigh, the person responsible for the Oklahoma City bombings and who claimed to be an atheist but took last rites before he died, was a Christian, while others said he was not, but "nobody puts all of Christians on the defense for the bombing: 'Oh, that was a Christian thing.'" In addition to politics and culture, they delved into theology: "We talked a lot about the things we have in common with our faith, the differences, we talked a lot about the Trinity and how difficult it is to explain to a Muslim." Hannah described it as "fun" to see "their faiths lived out in the course of the week."

The friendship and trust between these women became strong enough that they even prayed for one another. Aminah has five kids and had arranged for a sitter to pick her children up after school. One day she called to find out that the sitter had not picked her children up from school "and they were stranded and alone and she is, like, absolutely freaking out." They were only five minutes late and she was thinking "they are dead and there's been an accident." So, they said to each other, "we believe that God is in control of our lives, let's just pray about this." Hannah explained that this was a great opportunity "to have all that in common and be able to share that and at the same time discuss the differences with somebody that I felt safe with." They had great discussions without their friendship exploding, and even though things got heated on occasions and "it was really tough," their friendship was "strong enough to go through that."

The experiences of the pastors were different than that of the laity interviewed; all their relationships with Muslims were in personal settings rather than professional settings for the obvious reason that no evangelical churches employ Muslims. Pastor Justin had met a Muslim man from India at a gas station in his neighborhood where he bought gas and a cup of coffee on Sunday mornings and would have a conversation. Eventually the Muslim got his phone number, and sometimes they would chat on the phone. They talked about their professions, their families, raising their kids, what they believed, etc. In time Pastor Justin also learned that if he was not going to be at the gas station, he should let his friend know, so that he would not get worried. Through their discussions they learned a lot about each other. He recalled one discussion right after 9/11. Justin's Muslim friend "was very distressed, and he wanted to make a statement to his fellow employees at the bank where he worked that he did not agree with what had happened." Lacking confidence in his English language skills, he asked Justin's help to "write a statement [that] as a Muslim, this wasn't his view."

Eventually Pastor Justin invited him and his family over to his house for dinner because they "wanted to show them an American home. They had never been in a regular American home." His wife came wearing a head covering and his teenage daughters, teenage son, and an infant daughter were also there. The discussion included the kind of food they ate, the henna patterns on their hands, and much else. "We had a nice time," said Justin. Shortly after that the Muslim family invited Pastor Justin and his wife to a meal "which was delicious." In Justin's words, "We had a great time, I think they trusted us, I think it was fun, it was eye-opening, this was their culture, not their religion, ... the low table and the food, . . there was a big thing on the wall with the names of Allah , ... and prayer rugs and things like that." A few months later the Muslim man asked Pastor Justin for a Bible, and he got him one in Urdu.

As the friendship grew, Pastor Justin invited them to his home for Christmas because he "thought they might like to see an American home on Christmas." This time the wife did not come, but his teenage daughters were there, and they were "intrigued with the Christmas tree, and the stockings, and things like that." Pastor Justin also recalled the discussion over the manger scene in his house: "I said, 'Do you know what this is?' 'Oh, of course. We believe in the story of Jesus and the birth of Jesus. We know the story.' That was interesting to me." On one occasion Pastor Justin helped his son with writing a school assignment on Islam. Pastor Justin remarked that he "learned something from his paper, ... the most memorable was his describing Abraham's sacrifice of Ishmael." One Sunday morning Pastor Justin brought this up and said that Christians and Jews also have the same story, "except it's about Isaac." He then explained to him "how Christians see this as a foreshadowing of what Jesus would do on the cross for us, the Lamb of God." The Muslim man was simply "speechless. I mean, the idea of a symbolic meaning, I don't think he even had a frame of reference for something like that. He didn't disagree with anything."

On another Sunday morning the Muslim man was sharing how proud he was that his wife had become "more conservative" in her faith. Pastor Justin asked the Muslim man why his wife "had to be all covered." The discussion went as follows:

> I said, "Why would God make a woman who is as bright and capable as your wife become a nonperson in public?" "Well, she's not." "Of course she is. You can't even see her face in public. She is like a shadow. Why would God do this?" "Well, you know, I..." And he got kind of blustery. I could see that I was treading on ... I saw ... I backed off and I said, "this seems like it's the men who ought to be dealing with their sin, not this woman." Well, we finished about five or ten minutes later, and I was getting ready to go, and out of the blue he leans over the counter, and he goes, "Well, it just makes the men more curious anyway."

On another occasion they talked about how Islam views loaning money for interest. They had these kinds of discussions on a regular basis. Eventually Justin's Muslim friend died unexpectedly. Pastor

Justin recalled that it was a "shock" to him, that he had "lost a friend," that he "felt sad ... [and] puzzled as a Christian."

> I had been very impressed with the earnestness of his devotion to God. I understood that this man really did believe in God, he really did pray, he wasn't going through the motions. But I also saw this pride in his works—"I fasted, I stayed at the mosque for seven days, I give money to the poor"—[to him], that was the language of pleasing God.

> Justin described this as a "fascinating relationship" that helped him in his own personal growth.

Pastor Tim lives next to a Muslim from Turkey. Tim spends time with him and has him over for dinner every month. The Muslim neighbor has said that when he came to the US, "he was unaware of how much of a Muslim he was. It was only when he saw 'American' America that he realized that he was not just Turkish, he was a Muslim." He visits a Bible study at Tim's house. They have "had some longer conversations," and Tim considers him a "thoughtful guy" and a "friend."

The other two pastors have known Muslims but only as acquaintances. Pastor Sawyer has met several Muslims who have come to his church, "usually looking for help, recent immigrants coming to the food pantry, something like that." Others he has met as he has traveled in the Middle East in countries such as "Turkey, Egypt, Jordan, Israel, Tajikistan." He has had discussions with them but not of a theological nature. He does not believe "most Muslims are thinking theologically, necessarily, ... unless they are a cleric or something like that." His conversations with them have been "getting acquainted kinds of discussions: ... how do you guys do things, where are you from, how do people do things there?"

Pastor Seth has met Muslims "primarily through living in the same neighborhood … [the] kids play together down in the park." He has had four or five Muslim families as neighbors over the years. He describes these relationships as "kind of a polite relationship in the sense of we are not having each other over for dinner or going out for movies or the ball games together." The families "seemed very much into themselves." They are always "very polite, very friendly when encountered on a walk: 'hi, how are you, beautiful day,' but he has never had friendships that have gone to a "different level of relationship."

Evangelicals who were interviewed have known Muslims both professionally and personally; some have been acquaintances, while others began as acquaintances but developed into deeper friendships; they have engaged the Muslims that they have known in a variety of different conversations, some casual and some deeper, discussing a wide variety of topics, including Christian faith, Islamic faith, Islamic cultural life, family life, local and global politics, how the media views Muslims and Christians, etc.

It is notable that all the interactions that the respondents had with Muslims led the Christians to have a positive view of the Muslims that they had interacted with, describing the Muslims using words such as "very congenial and pleasant person," "nice," "very devout," etc. None of the Christians came away with negative impressions of the Muslims with whom they had interacted. It appears that as long as the respondents associated Muslims with Islam, a religion consistently put in the negative category, and thought of Muslims in the abstract, the respondents' perspectives of Muslims were negative, but when they interacted with specific Muslims and had concrete relationships and discussions with them, their perspective of Muslims was positive.

At the same time, some of the comments made by the respondents suggest that in spite of the positive views of individual Muslims with whom they interacted, they remained suspicious of Muslims' agenda: Muslims want to take over the US, which is why they are building very large mosques in small towns; their plan is to bring Muslims into the US; Muslims are neighborly, but they want to get on the school board so that they can maneuver into political power; Muslims are nice, but behind that they have an agenda to convert people; etc. These answers indicate that the respondents are conflicted in their perspectives.

Q6: Do you think Muslims should have the same freedoms to build their mosques in our communities that Christians have for building churches?

John stated that Muslims "should have that right to build mosques" because "that's the Constitution." "That's part of what we espouse in our Constitution. We have to abide by that." They have the same rights as other religious groups do to build their places of worship. "I may not be happy about it because of how I feel about their faith and their infringement on our society, you really can't stop them. So, no, I think that they have the right to build mosques." Regarding building a mosque near the 9/11 site, John thought that "quite honestly, there needs to be wisdom and discernment on the part of anyone thinking about planting ... a mosque." This respondent viewed this particular situation from the perspective of planting a church in "Jeddah, Saudi Arabia. Is that going to happen? Is that the right place to do it? Is that really the right thing to do to further the kingdom from a Christian perspective?" People need to look back at that specific situation and say, "What are their motivations?" Because how many Muslims are there really in downtown Manhattan available to attend there? Really! They can be probably served better by a mosque located closer to their homes."

In this vein Joseph, a business professional in his mid-50s, thought that Muslims have a "concept of territoriality: once an area becomes the Islamic they should not allow it to revert to another control of other religions or whatever or other regimes, even if they are secular." For Muslims building a mosque at Ground Zero "would be a symbolic gesture of in a sense expanding their influence and control in America." Joseph believed that Muslims have a "political agenda," which is to conquer "the great Satan," a term "strict fundamentalist Muslims" use to describe America. This was of concern to Joseph because it would "infringe on freedom of religion" and "I won't be free to practice my faith." At the same time "the federal government should not be involved" because if this was "done lawfully, it should not be prohibited." While their agenda "scares" him, he also thinks that

we have to deal with it on the level of right principle. We can't just shove them or hate them. We have to engage them and we have to allow them to have rights in this country on the same level as other people.

For Joshua this was, among other things, an issue of hospitality. He asserted: "What bothers me about this is that Christians often lead the charge against... 'No, we can't have a mosque in our neighborhood' ... [this attitude is] not particularly hospitable." Stacy, while asserting that there should be no reason why they cannot build mosques since we live in a democratic society, added, "by the same token I'm fearful of that because I've seen what's happened in the UK, for example, where a couple of groups of Muslim people have been praying in a house which has then become a mosque." She did not understand why after praying for a certain while in the house that then becomes a mosque, they are not willing to "give it up." After that they demand that they want to build a mosque on the site of the house where they have been praying.

She has also heard of cases where the mosque was across the church and the church was "burned down mysteriously." There were churches that did not have a large attendance on a Sunday, and they were "removed, and there would be arson attacks on the churches, and then the mosques would go up."

One pastor, Justin, asserted that based on "American principles," as a US citizen he would say yes. But he does not like the idea because he does not "like to see inroads made contrary to the Christian faith." He went on to say that he does not "really fear them" and that the growth of the Islamic community is "inevitable in America." Look at Scandinavia where there are "so many Muslims, but they are second-class citizens in so many ways, and that tension will kill you sooner or later." It is necessary that we "live by American principles, and as Christians that's a different thing"—we have to seek to develop relationships with them.

Pastor Sawyer agreed there should be "freedom for everybody. So, yes, absolutely, they should have as much freedom as we have." And then he added: "If we want to still have freedom, we better make sure they have freedom … otherwise we are next … we're going to be next on the chopping block." Regarding building the mosque on Ground Zero, Pastor Sawyer asserted that "actually it was six blocks away, [but] everyone acted like they were trying to build a mosque on Ground Zero." Regarding this controversy, Pastor Sawyer thought that "it was just a stupid controversy, and my feeling at the time was that their [opponents of the mosque] reaction was uninformed and unhelpful. They were just ignorant. They believe everything they see on Fox News." He also thought that the "whole thing was ridiculous, stupid, and unhelpful."

The negative perceptions that the respondents had of Islam and Muslims did not keep them from asserting that Muslims should have the same freedoms that Christians have, or other religious groups have, to build their places of worship in our communities. The reason they gave for this was that the American Constitution guarantees freedom of religion for everybody, without exception. But, while affirming freedom of religion, some respondents also had reservations about it, and a few even stated outright that Muslims should not have the right to build mosques. They gave numerous reasons for this: the violent behaviors associated with Islam; the fear of Muslims taking over America and implementing sharia law (something that would limit the political and religious freedom of Americans in general and Christians in particular); Muslims who go to Islamic schools do not assimilate into society; not wanting to hear the Muslim call to prayer early in the morning in the communities; mosques are hideouts for plotting violence, to preach violence, and to raise funds for it; Islam is more than a religion, it is a way of life that goes against the country, against the citizens who are not Muslim, etc. One perspective was that Muslims should be allowed to build mosques, but the FBI should investigate them to make sure they are not teaching violence. No one gave any biblical or theological reasons for these views or asserted that Hindus or Buddhists should not be allowed to build their houses of worship.

Q7: Recently we had the Boston Marathon bombings. The younger brother, who survived, had become a US citizen less than a year prior to the event. Can Muslims be good citizens of the US?

A few respondents asked how one would determine what it means to be a good citizen or what it even means to be a citizen. Mike answered by stating that all of us could go "awry." Stuart, considering "that civility lessons, that culture, that [the] unseen element that keeps society together," and that things that were clear 50 years ago—such as what a parent is or what family is—are "fading" and "there is a cultural breakdown," asserted that "absolutely, they can be good US citizens." But if they want their "laws and rules and regulations, then you've got a problem."

John emphatically stated, "Absolutely! No question in my mind. Just like Christians can be good citizens, just like Hindus can be good citizens." Amy, a homemaker in her 50s, said that "the majority probably are." The young man appeared to be a "nice young man, I actually felt bad for him... He must've got poisoned, training to do what he did, but so many opportunities and such potential he had." Their mother also "influenced them a little bit towards the bad ... unfortunately his real mother influenced him more than the motherland. Yes, they can be." Steve thought that all Muslims should not be judged "by the actions of a few individuals." He did not "blame the religion" but "the individuals."

Mike angrily asserted that "some can, some cannot." This is a challenge because we do not "know how to determine which is which, and you can't because it gets down to judging intent, and you really can't judge intent." Mike went on to say that there are "different degrees of following the Islamic codes and traditions." For those Muslims who think that everybody should be a Muslim and the whole world should be Islamic, "no, they cannot be a good American citizen." But the "average Muslim" who is not "engaged" in such "thought processes, "yes, could be a good, typical American citizen." In this vein, David remarked that the "1% or one half of 1% of them that believe that it's okay to run around and slaughter people ... are going to screw things up for the other 99% of them." He also thought that "we've had about enough of this," "the backlash is coming," and "the great majority of the people in this country are going to want to say, 'get out of our country and don't come back. And none of you are coming here again because of this.'"

Mary said she had "certain qualms" about allowing immigrants from "Muslim countries." I'm not sure it's the wisest thing for the US to allow free immigration of Muslims into the US, to allow them to become citizens in the US, ... some people are concerned about immigrants, about Muslim communities developing terrorist cells inside the US.

Allowing Muslims to immigrate creates a way for terrorists with a violent jihad in mind to enter the US and "position themselves to strike the US." The Boston Marathon bombings made apparent that there could definitely be Muslims who are US citizens and "who are going to attack the US." Working in Dearborn, Michigan, "the biggest Muslim town in the country," led her to conclude that "I'm somewhat uncomfortable with big Muslim communities or strong Muslim [communities], honestly, developing in the US because I believe that they might exert pressure to be allowed to practice sharia law, which would subvert US laws." Mary was also afraid that having large "politicized Muslim communities in the US" would mean that "they could possibly exert pressure that would limit Christians' ability to speak out about our faith and to do evangelizing about our faith." According to her there is already "a lot of political pressure aimed at limiting Christian speech." For instance, the pastor in Florida who wanted to burn the Qur'an "as a statement" had the right to do it and should have been able to but was not "because of all the political pressure directed against him."

In response to this question, Stacy shared that she had just seen a documentary in which an Islamic scholar in the UK had "stated categorically that as a Muslim, the laws of the land that you live in are irrelevant [and] Islamic law is superior to any of the laws of the land that you live in." So basically you don't have to adhere to the laws of the land. Muslims will look at this in different ways. Some will be "very law-abiding, good people," but others who are "a little bit more extreme" will do what their leaders tell them to do, thinking that this is acceptable because it is coming from their leaders.

Natalie, whose neighbors are Pakistani Muslims and whose daughter lived briefly with a Muslim family in Morocco, strongly agreed that Muslims can be good citizens of the US but admitted, "I guess there is always this, since September 11th, this undercurrent of mistrust. I fall into it myself. You get on an airplane and there is somebody who looks different and you start thinking about what could happen, who is this person really." Thinking about her Muslim neighbors, she said it is sad, but "I think it sometimes does raise questions. Who are those people and what are they doing here?"

Pastor Justin asserted that he did not "think that [the Boston Marathon bombings] had much to do with him being a Muslim." Christians also "have got their share of people who have done terrible things." He also did not think that "violence is the issue with Islam in a society." What was problematic for him was "this rapid growth of this people by birth and by immigration" and this American idea that "we really have to welcome, we really have to be open-minded. They are more open-minded about Islam than they are about evangelicals." He thought that there was a strong possibility, as has already happened in Europe, of Muslims "becoming really dominant and it's going to affect us. But I don't see how to stop it as an American citizen with the rights we give people."

Pastor Tim thought that Muslims can be good citizens of the US, but "I don't think they all will be." By the same token he added that "there are Christians I would not want to have as neighbors because they are embarrassing to be around because they have very small, ugly views that don't reflect my understanding of Christ and his love." He did think that "Muslims can become good neighbors." At the same time, "there is risk involved with that today" and he did not "know how to put those two together." The reason there is risk involved is that "it is just reality" that "the Boston bomber comes from a Muslim background." He gave the example of his Muslim neighbor for whom he had to "fill out a reference ... to get military clearance as an army doctor." He spent some time thinking about that—"Could I be completely hoodwinked on this guy, right? Is it possible that he is a Muslim terrorist?"—, and he said, "No, I don't see that. I've seen nothing of that. I have seen a nice guy." He described his neighbor whom he has known for five years as someone who "cares for his family, he is a doctor, he's trying to have a relatively good life," etc., and he is a good citizen, and he is a doctor who has been helping our veterans.

Pastor Sawyer responded,

> I would say right now we have about a million-to- one odds
> that Muslims can be good citizens of the US. At least 1
> million, if not 5 or 10 million Muslims in this country who are
> citizens, who are good citizens. And you had one that wasn't.

The consensus view among the respondents was that Muslims can be good citizens of the US, and that the community as a whole should not be judged because of the actions of a few individuals. Some respondents indicated that while Muslims can be good citizens, some will choose not to be. Those who strictly follow Islamic codes and traditions and think that everybody should be a Muslim cannot be good American citizens, but the "average Muslim," who does not think this way, can be. Several respondents also expressed the fear that substantial Muslim communities may exert pressure to be allowed to practice sharia law, which would subvert US law, or that politicized Muslim communities may limit Christians' ability to evangelize freely. Thus, in addition to their concerns about possible violence associated with Islam, the respondents wondered whether Muslims would respect the US

Constitution, including the freedom of choice in religion, and assimilate into American culture. Some had qualms about allowing immigrants from Muslim countries because Muslim communities may develop terrorist cells inside the US or build secret rooms in mosques where they can hide anti-American, jihadist literature that incites violence against Jews and Christians and the destruction of synagogues and churches. These views show that the respondents have significant fears and suspicions about their Muslim neighbors.

Q8: Some people say that, despite our differences on some matters, Christians and Muslims worship the same God. What do you think about this question?

One respondent, John, noted, "By Islam's own teaching , ... according to Islam we worship the same God." From an evangelical perspective it could be argued "that we worship the same God." But "the critical difference" is that "they don't accept Jesus Christ as the way, the truth, the life." Another big difference is that Islam does not have "the concept of grace." Referring to John 3:16, John claimed, "You don't have the notion of an unmerited gift in Islam." Muhammad taught that "It's not Jesus Christ, there is another way, it's my way. And it's his lifestyle and all these practices, what he lays down in the Qur'an." Paul asserted that "ours is a God of love, theirs is a God of works." Allah seems like

> an angry God, a God who is just waiting for you to make a mistake, ... forgiveness of sins I don't think is ever mentioned... Muslims are telling me this: that the God of the Muslim world doesn't seem to care whether you're with him for eternity or not.

Amy asserted that their God is "a lot like our God, ... almost everything about their God seems similar more than dissimilar, even if their motives get mixed up and wrong ... grenades and things are powerful, bombs or something. Our God is a God of peace." While "their God may be [a god of peace], there is more violence in their theology." Thinking about the violence, Bill asserted that Muslims "feel like they're doing God's will if they were to go out and kill different kinds of people, and I think that's wrong, and that isn't the God that I worship." While there were people killed in the Old Testament that God sanctions and wanted them to do it because they believed other things, but some of the other things they believed were that you could go out and slaughter your own children... God was really down on that, I'll tell you.

In describing Islam, Mike commented, "I can't help but think of the analogies of the devil and the description of when the devil was thrown out of heaven." Darryl, in his mid- 50s, said, "No, I don't see that," and then described Allah in the following way: "Allah is not God ... Allah might be a demon ... I see a judging God, I see a judging Allah. So in that sense there are similarities. But I don't see the other side of the coin, I don't see the love and the concern, I don't see that. So I don't think they're the same, no. " Harry asserted, "They call us the great Satan, I think they are the great Satan. I think their Allah is Satan." He also thought that "the Black Stone ... came from an ancient satanic worship temple ... long before Muhammad. So, they worship a stone that came out of an ancient devil worship temple." Furthermore, he asserted, they do not worship the triune God, and "the only other powerful nontriune creature that I know is Satan. So I put those two together."

Hannah said, "I think that we are worshiping the same God, but they don't know him the way we know him," and Mary also had a similar understanding:

> I guess I lean at this point towards feeling that we do worship the same God, although Muslims do not understand what that God requires from them... Muslims do recognize that there is one God ... I think we should give them the benefit of the doubt and say, "Yes, we worship the same God, just not with the same understanding of the nature of that God or what he requires from us"

Along the same lines Natalie admitted, "that's a tough one." She continued, "I guess at the core, probably we do worship the same God. I think it's a different approach to how we see God, to how we see religion." For Islam, actions are the "criteria for getting into heaven, ... whereas with Christians it's all about belief and the relationship with Jesus." Natalie also stated that "I just think that God is big, I think he loves every person he created. It's hard for me to believe that God doesn't love people who are Muslims as much as he loves Christians. And I think that the Muslim person who is earnestly seeking God, that he will find Him." Regarding the "different approach" in Islam, she stated, "Because I believe there is one God, whatever direction they take to get there, I think they're still worshiping the same God." But, several times she admitted, "I don't know."

The responses given by pastors were similar to the responses given by lay evangelicals. Pastor Justin thought that while the God of Islam and the God of Christianity "do have things in common, I don't think they are the same God":

> I think that the gods we speak of have much in common in terms of descriptive things ... all-powerful, all-knowing,

things like that ... but, there is a vast difference when you believe in a personal, loving, redeeming God whose primary man-oriented effort is to save us from our sins as opposed to a God who can be appeased or pleased by good works and things like that.

Pastor Tim had a similar understanding. He did not think that the God they worship with the Islamic creed—"there is one God, Muhammad is his prophet"—and "God the Father-Son-Holy Spirit" are the same God. The God that was described by Muhammad is not the "God who has revealed himself in Christ." He also said that this was not a "completely binary," a "yes or no" question. He thought that all people have "an awareness of God" and that there are some people who are Muslims and are "seeking God."
Pastor Seth did not think that Christians and Muslims "worship the same God" because

My God is a God who has manifested in three persons—God the Father, God the Son, God the Holy Spirit. They only have Allah. They don't have God the Son or God the Holy Spirit... They reject our God because they don't see us as monotheistic.

When asked whether Christians and Muslims worship the same God, the respondents seemed, once again, to have been influenced by the violence associated with Islam. All but four said Christians and Muslims do not worship the same God. From a theological perspective, they cited Muslims' denial of the Trinity and the deity of Christ; the lack of a concept of grace in Islam and its orientation toward works; the angry and unforgiving character of Allah; and their perception of satanic characteristics in the religion. From a political perspective they argued that the God of the Christians is a God of peace, whereas the

Qur'an teaches violence, as seen in violent actions carried out by Muslims today. While the respondents made frequent references to violence in Islam, only one person attempted to compare and contrast it with violence explicitly commanded by God in the Old Testament. The four respondents who said that Christians and Muslims worship the same God typically cited the fact that there is only one God and God loves the Muslims just as he loves the Christians. A common omission from the responses of this group was any discussion of the biblical understanding of the exclusivity of Christ or the Trinitarian nature of God.

Q9: Some churches host social events like a dinner with their Muslim neighbors. Would you be comfortable participating in such a dinner? Why or why not?

John thought that "it would be great" because he sees a great "lack of knowledge" about Muslims among evangelicals and "lack of dialogue" between the two groups. "We need to talk," but

> I would be under no illusion to say that hosting that event would be incredibly controversial at my church. There would be a lot of people that would be tremendously upset. There might be a lot of people that might leave the church over that.

The reason for this is that "evangelical Christians suffer in many ways just as much of the legalism and lack of grace that you see on the other side." But then everything is "black and white. There is no gray." People do not have to agree, but they are not willing to talk or seek to understand.

Mike, emphatically stating, "oh, definitely," said Muslims need to be viewed "in terms of their relationship with Christ and with God." From this perspective, Christians need to recognize that God wants "everyone to have that view into who He is and if I can be part of helping someone see that, I'd love to be involved."

Other reasons for being comfortable about participating in this event that were given included: "They are my neighbors, they are God's creatures, they are God's children" (Debbie); "I would love to have dinner with him, get to know them" (Paul); "I would like to know more, ... right now maybe I've gotten a prejudicial attitude because of what I read and what I see on the news" (Sam): "These people are lost, they need to know who Jesus really is, not the Qur'an definition, but who Jesus really is. And if they did, ... they might be [willing to convert] to Christianity... I am commanded to do that, and I would like to do it too." (Paul); "I would be very happy to reach out to Islamic people, wherever they were, and welcome them, and encourage them, and show them the love of Jesus" (Stacy); "we need to reach out" (Matt); "build community bridges" (Joseph). Matt, a businessman in his 50s, also asserted that it is equally important that Muslims reach out. Muslims need to "understand that there is some distrust in them." The conservative Muslims, the "main body" of Islam "who don't profess to agree with jihad or any kind of holy wars, need to step up and let us know who they are, let us understand what kind of good people they are, let us understand what their religion is." Steve would love to have the opportunity to develop a relationship with Muslims so that he could get a "better understanding of them as people."

Lisa expressed some doubt: "I really don't know." She stated that as Christians "we want to be friends with other people, we want to invite people, we are a friendly, loving type of people, caring. We don't mean to do harm to anybody," but "we don't know what they are thinking. We don't know when they want to incorporate mixing with a Christian group what their agenda is." She admitted that she was a little suspicious about this. She also would love to believe that both groups can live peacefully with each other, but both groups have an agenda to convert the other group because "the other people are wrong, and we are not." Something like this would be "like mixing oil and water." Lisa went on to say that she would be uncomfortable with something like this because Muslims may "start working their way in."

Linda, in her late 50s and having served on the mission field, said it would be wonderful to do something like that in homes but not at a church. The reason she gave for this was that this was not the "goal of the church," whereas "evangelism" is. She envisions having such an event in a "neutral location like a park, and have a picnic together" where you could build a "personal relationship with a neighbor," and there would be the opportunity to "have an evangelistic impact" in a "large group" setting. If a church hosted and publicized such an event then people might think that it was "ecumenical," and evangelicals would "shy away" from something like this because "it gives the false impression of what we are all about as a church."

Susan, an accountant in her late 30s, had a similar perspective. If such an event meant "sort of the extreme pluralism that all religions are equal and we really are all on the same page about things, in a sense that really waters down the gospel in a very theologically liberal way that I feel like it would be a misinformation."

Hazel asserted that it would be "fascinating to meet some Muslims on a personal basis to get to know them, to understand what they believe and why they believe what they believe ... from a person that is truly a devout believer." Hazel would like to ask questions such as:

> What do you believe, and what are the basics of the religion, of Islam? Describe Allah to me. What do you, how do you worship him? What has he done for you? Why do you worship him? How did you come to faith in this? How did

you choose Islam over some of the other religions out there?
Or, do you know much about the other religions out there?
And, just try to understand ... how devout are you, what kinds
of things would you do on a daily basis to practice your faith?

Natalie asserted, "I think I probably would go out of my way to
attend such a dinner just to facilitate communication because I think
that would be a good thing. Yes, so I would definitely be comfortable
and I would encourage [it] actually. " She added that since 9/11 there
has been "such a tendency in this country to typecast Muslims." There
is a distance "between Christians and Muslims" that is greater than the
distance between "Christians and Hindus, for example." There is also
this "image of this radical person who is out to get us, and I just don't
believe that all Muslims are like that. So I think any time you can have
person-to-person interactions, it just helps to break down the
stereotypes, helps us understand each other better."

Rebecca admitted she would not be comfortable sitting down
for dinner with Muslims. Her concern was that "that information would
get to radical Muslims and they would kill me." While she admitted that
"that's probably wrong from a Christian perspective," she also said that
"I would like to be a little more judicious about my mission extensions,
not just showing up at a church."

The pastors' responses were similar in most respects to the
responses given by church members. Pastor Seth said that he would be
comfortable as long as both parties were respected, and it was "just an
opportunity to have a social [event] ... building relationships." If there
were religious connotations to this, then there would need to be some
"ground rules" so that it does not turn into a place where each side "is
trying to proselytize the other." He would not use such a gathering "for
the purpose of worship or for the purpose of preaching" but as a forum

for "presenting and helping to further understand the distinctions" between the two faiths.

Pastor Sawyer said that he would be comfortable with this and shared what he did in his church the Sunday after 9/11. He told the church that we could not one week say "'we want to share the love of Jesus with all the Muslims in the world' and this week '[we] want to nuke them all.'" He went on to urge his congregation to reach out to their Muslim neighbors, invite them to dinner, and "stand beside them because they need somebody to stand beside them."

Pastor Tim said that he would definitely be comfortable because "the way forward, our card is love, and it is to proclaim the good news and engage in good works and having relationships. Being good neighbors, serving, and caring for people is part of what we are called to." Pastor Tim had also done a teaching series at his church shortly after 9/11 titled "Middle East, Islam and War." They had invited a Muslim speaker from the Islamic Speakers Bureau in Chicago to "come in and represent Islam." They sent a female speaker who presented Islam as a "religion of peace." It was a "polite" and "cordial" gathering, but she was unable to answer "some of the more basic questions." For example, when she was asked, "You choose to live in a country that is predominantly influenced by a Judeo-Christian ethic. What country influenced by Islam would you choose to live in?" she could not name a single country. When Pastor Tim pointed out to her that they had invited her to speak but "we would not be invited there to speak," all she could say was, "What you are seeing is Islam is a religion of peace, it has been hijacked momentarily by these radicals, and that's not the true faith."

When asked whether they would be comfortable participating in social events such as a dinner with their Muslim neighbors that was hosted by their church, some respondents expressed reservations because they were suspicious of the Muslims' agenda to convert people or to do harm to Christians; one respondent said outright that she would not because radical Muslims might find out about it and kill her. However, in spite of their negative perceptions of Islam and Muslims and their cognizance of the theological differences between Islam and Christianity, most respondents said that they would be comfortable in participating in these kinds of social events out of interest in building bridges, getting to know their Muslim neighbors, sharing the gospel with them, breaking down stereotypes, etc.

It is not surprising that the respondents would be open to and would no doubt benefit from these kinds of social events with Muslims, in light of the fact that many of them had previously spoken in glowing terms about their interactions and relationships with specific Muslims. At the same time, many of the comments made by the respondents, such as not wanting mosques in their neighborhoods and fears about the real intentions of their new neighbors indicate a lack of hospitality toward Muslims. That is, what the respondents are actually articulating is that they have conflicted desires.

Q10: Do you ever talk about Islam or Muslims with other Christians?

Only four of the respondents said they do not have any discussions about Islam or Muslims. Amy said, "not very much." John had occasional discussions centered on "events and things like that, obviously that we see." The discussions are not focused on Islam because they "never really have taken time to understand Islam." Because they do not have "any deep understanding" of Islam, one of the biggest things that "evangelical Christians wonder a lot about is if it is true that Islam is being hijacked by a radical minority for political and economic ends" and why "mainstream Islam wasn't rising up and being more vocal than they are," a sentiment echoed by other respondents as well. John also wondered if Muslims are speaking out but that "the media has not given them attention." The Boston Marathon bombings was an example of events that they talked about, and their discussions included "the senselessness of the violence," what Muslims are thinking they can accomplish, why they would think that this was their "only course of action," and "what end are [they] trying to achieve." John summarizes: "I think it's mostly bewilderment."

Mike recalled one of the very few conversations he had had. In his perspective, "you have those certain limited people who have twisted the emotions of certain followers of Islam to do those kinds of things." Lisa recalled having a discussion about fearing Muslims, being wary of them, and watching them carefully. In her view they have an agenda to "come into the United States, set up sharia law here like they've done, and tried to do, and have actually done in other places." Paul has had discussions with his wife about "jihad, the terrorist aspect of it."

Stacy has lived in the UK for extended periods of time and has worked with Muslims. She has had only occasional conversations about Islam with American friends, but all the information that her friends have comes from the newspapers on the television, and she does not "want to appear too negative." Because the UK in comparison to the US is such a small country, people there have a lot of contact with Muslims, and so their information about Muslims comes through these contacts. In the US the view that people have is the view that the media wants to present, which is "a filtered view."

Eleven respondents said that they talk about news related events, with topics focused around the violence. One had talked about events happening in other Islamic countries such as Syria, Iran, Iraq, Egypt, Libya, etc. Another, Stuart, said that "terrorist attacks are 99% caused by Muslims," so why do all people, whether you are four years old or 80 years old or six years old or 50 years old, have to take their shoes off and get checked at airports? James said that when horrific events occur in America, it is not always the Muslims who are to blame; sometimes it is "whacked-out people like the kid in Connecticut, and he was as Caucasian as they come," other times it is Muslims like the Times Square bomber. He saw a "strong correlation still between terrorist activities and radically motivated jihadist types." Sam recalled a conversation he had the day of the interview where he was reminded "that there are good and bad in all groups," but most of his conversations regarding Muslims have to do with problems in Islam, such as "terrorism and uprisings in different countries." Hannah asserted that she finds herself "defending Islam ... when I hear things aren't right, or are not my experience with friends, or there is misinformation out there." On the other hand, Rebecca asserted that because of all the events that have happened, she has become "afraid of them." She has begun to "dislike them, to wonder what their secret beliefs are. I can't stand them, and I know that's wrong. I should love them, but mostly I have a repulsion."

Bill talked about Muslims in his Sunday school class. He recalled reading a story from Campus Crusade, which he shared in his Sunday school class, about how in an Islamic country Muslims had killed a Christian family. The respondent was quite moved emotionally and distressed that Muslims "kill their own people" and "rape the women." Bill was glad that he does not see these kinds of things frequently in the US except in occasional terrorist attacks. These kinds of situations are frightening to him because this is a "complete lack of respect for human life," something that he hates "the most about the Muslim faith." Natalie had discussions about Islam in her Bible study group regarding the fear "that more and more Muslims are coming to the US ... they're taking over ... the balance is shifting, ... instead of being predominantly a Christian country, now we are becoming more of a multi- religious country."

Debbie, an office worker in her 40s, said that her conversations about Muslims had to do with "introducing Jesus to them as a savior" and whether "the Jesus that the Muslims talk about" is the "same as the Jesus of the Bible." Joseph talked about wanting to learn more about Islam, reading the Qur'an, and having a meaningful discussion with Muslims and "sharing the faith with them."

Mary said that she talks with her husband about their views on Islam and about sharing the gospel with them. She thinks they should take an interest in their Muslim acquaintances, being "good neighbors" and "good colleagues at work" to them. She thinks they should take time to learn about Islam and "be able to understand their view towards Jesus Christ so that we can discuss that with them" and "about women in Islam and their situation in Islam." Mary and her husband also have had discussions about "end-time prophecy" and how Islam fits into the Book of Revelation.

Susan said that her discussions were centered around a concern for what Islam "actually teaches." Some people think that, based on the Qur'an, "this is not the peaceful religion we are being led to believe [it is]," while others claim that Muslims indeed are "really peaceful." She describes these conversations as "not really in-depth conversations."

Joshua has had discussions regarding Christians taking "too adversarial of a stance towards Islam" and that "we should have a dialogical stance." Even though Islam is not the "truth," Muslims are making an effort "to relate to God well," and Christians can use their "desire to do what is right" to "dialogue with them."

Of the four pastors interviewed, Pastor Justin said that this topic "doesn't come up much." Pastor Sawyer said that he has discussions only when somebody asks him something, which usually has to do with engaging Muslims in conversation. He simply responds by telling them, "just talk about Jesus and talk about blessing and praying them. Muslims love to be blessed. And they believe in Jesus, maybe more than you realize, so talk about Jesus." Pastor Seth said that his conversations are usually with other pastors, and they focus on whether they are doing any "outreach to the Muslim community" and what this outreach looks like "here or in other lands."

Pastor Tim has had conversations about Islam and Muslims in the context of the board that he serves on that funds PhD students from the majority world, a number of whom are African Christians "studying Islam." Some of the discussions have included topics such as "How do you prepare the church for the spread of sharia law?", and "What is the best posture against fundamentalist Islam on different issues?" This board hosts "ongoing conversations ... and dinners where people can ask ... questions."

The conversations Christians had with other Christians about Islam and Muslims can be grouped into two distinct themes. First, many respondents talked about the violence associated with Islam, for example: pointing out that terrorist activities are carried on by radically motivated Islamic jihadists; wondering about what was going on in the mind of Muslims who commit such violence; whether Islam has been hijacked by a radical minority for political and economic ends; why mainstream Islam was not more vocal in condemning terrorism; fear of Islam and Muslims; the agenda of Muslims who come into the US; terrorist attacks are for the most part caused by Muslims; etc. Second, Christians were concerned about evangelizing Muslims and wanted to understand Islam and learn to be better neighbors to Muslims. While the respondents' concerns about presenting the gospel to Muslims seem normal and expected, it is worth noting that the respondents are especially concerned about violent aspects of Islam and the perceived growing influence of Islam in American society, leading them to take an adversarial stance toward Islam.

It is quite noteworthy that every question asked caused respondents to bring up the issue of violence associated with Islam. Clearly the perspectives and attitudes of the respondents regarding Islam and Muslims are deeply shaped by the violence that they hear about and see in the media on a regular basis. These violent actions suggest to the respondents that there is a direct correlation between Islam and terrorism, arousing in some respondents a deep sense of fear and paranoia toward Islam and Muslims—so much so that that not only are they opposed to Muslims building mosques in the U.S. but they are even unwilling to engage Muslims in social contexts or to look at information on the Internet about Islam and Muslims for fear of some negative personal repercussions. Thus, the fearful perspectives and attitudes of the respondents have so shaped their practices toward Muslims that while most said that they want to show hospitality, in fact they practice the reverse.

Personal Reflection

Listening to the interviewees share their thoughts and experiences, I could identify with some of their perspectives, attitudes, and practices. My own thoughts and experiences spanned a spectrum from positive to negative and sometimes both at the same time. In some instances my position had shifted in one direction or the other. Perhaps you, the reader, can also identify with some of the thoughts of my interview subjects, and perhaps you can also identify with my own conflicted reactions. A key question emerging from this research was how these interviewees had arrived at their positions on Islam and how they maintained these positions even when they conflicted with their own most deeply held values. This is the topic of our next chapter, which considers my second research question: How have American evangelicals' perspectives, attitudes, and practices toward Muslims and Islam been formed and justified?

CHAPTER 6

SHAPING OF PERSPECTIVES, ATTITUDES, AND PRACTICES

I grew up in India as a Hindu in a culture where Hindu-Muslim differences were common. My parents lived through the time when the Indian subcontinent was partitioned into two countries, India and Pakistan in 1947. I have heard much anti-Muslim rhetoric over the years. I remember vividly one family member say that close family friends were "nice" Muslims —the implication being that other Muslims are not so nice. I have seen movies that have portrayed both Hindus and Muslims negatively, as well as clearly revealing the suspicions each community has for the other. Studying history as a high school student I learned about the Islamic Moguls coming to India and the Hindu-Muslim differences that have colored their encounter ever since. I was taught that Islam is a religion of the sword, that Muslims forcefully convert people. From an early age, my perceptions were shaped by predominantly negative perspectives and attitudes toward Muslims. Two instances, both related by my father, were particularly formative for me. My father's older brother was killed by Muslims when India was moving toward partition. My father's brother was living in Bombay (now Mumbai) at that time. Simply for wearing a Gandhi cap he was killed by a group of Muslims who were antagonistic towards Gandhi and his loyalists. Hearing this story I learned that Muslims were bad people who could not be trusted.

When I was 16 years old my father shared with me a story about the encounter his parents had had with Muslims. My grandparents had a successful business in Fort Sandeman but observed that Hindu-Muslim violence was on the rise and felt it would only be a matter of time before they were attacked or killed by Muslims. So they sold their business, sent all their children and household goods to Dehradun, and prepared to conclude their affairs and join them. On the morning my grandparents were due to leave by caravan, there was a knock on the front door. Their chief servant opened the door to find a group of Muslims armed with weapons who had come looking for the Hindus living in that house. The servant, a Muslim loyal to my family, told the Muslims at the door that they had already left and there were no more Hindus living in that house. After the Muslims left, the loyal servant quickly helped my grandparents escape out the back door. During their escape they stopped at a small oasis to replenish their food and water supplies. Sitting by the water to shave his face, the chief servant noticed in his hand-held mirror the reflection of the same Muslims who had come knocking on their door earlier in the day, approaching the oasis from a distance. Thinking fast and realizing that if they found my grandparents they would kill them just because they were Hindu, he hid each of my grandparents in big bags of clothes on the backs of two camels. When the Muslims arrived and asked where the Hindus were that they had seen traveling in the caravan, the chief servant replied that there were no Hindus, only a caravan of Muslims traveling to Dehradun. Not finding any Hindus, the attackers returned to Fort Sandeman. This was how my grandparents escaped certain death at the hands of Muslims in Pakistan. My grandmother was pregnant with my father at that time. It was because of the loyalty of this Muslim servant that my grandparents lived, my father was born, and then of course many years later I was born. This story vividly reinforced the negative perspectives I had of Muslims but also gave me conflicted emotions because of the obvious loyalty of this Muslim servant. In the end I came to view him as a fortunate exception to the general rule that Muslims were wicked and untrustworthy.

I would encourage you, the reader, to reflect on how your own perspectives, attitudes, and practices toward Muslims and Islam were formed and justified. I asked seven open-ended questions during the course of the one-on-one interviews to draw out answers to my second research question: How have American evangelicals' perspectives, attitudes, and practices toward Muslims and Islam been formed and justified?

Q1: Have you ever studied Islam or attended seminars or lectures about Islam?

From the lay evangelicals interviewed for this study, 15 interviewees responded affirmatively to this question, and one respondent thought that Islam might have been included when she studied other religions many years ago but was unsure. Two of the respondents had studied Islam in their class on world religions at a Christian college. Amy did not remember anything she had studied, while Mike clearly remembered a field trip where he sat down with the imam for 15 minutes prior to the service who talked to them about what they should expect to see. Mike remembered the imam's perspective: "Some Muslims' behaviors have been less than exemplary; we acknowledge that we have some challenges related to radical people."

Stacy had had the opportunity to attend seminars conducted by Sam Solomon, a Muslim convert to Christianity and an advisor to the British and U.S. governments on Islam. One of the things that Solomon discussed was that "first and foremost" a Muslim is Islamic "and everything else is secondary to that," whether that includes their nationality, or being parents, or their profession. Reflecting on this statement, she said she could not understand how someone could follow a person like "Muhammad, who clearly has so many flaws as a human being, but apparently the one thing that God will not tolerate from Islam is lack of belief. You can question anything but you cannot question God's existence." A person cannot pick apart the as they might the Bible. "It's not open to be picked." Solomon also said that Muslims might go to "state school during the day" and then go to Islamic schools in the evenings "where they are actually taught sharia law from a very early age." Stacy also said that "apparently they even have little plastic hatchets to role-play what happens when you steal. Your hands will be cut off."

Stuart had never done an in-depth study of Islam but had attended lectures by Joel Rosenberg, a Messianic Jew who "has very definite opinions about Iran, the leadership of Iran, the pending attacks on Israel, in his view, and whenever you have government stating that they will annihilate another nation, that's a big thing." He also listens to Ravi Zacharias, who in his opinion is "the premier apologist" and who foresees that within the next 20 or 30 years the population of the US is going to be 20% or 30% Islamic. Stuart asserted that Islam is "a cultural belief versus a religious belief" and that is going to be trouble in the future for the US on the religious front because "the whole Judeo-Christian system that we are built on is being dismantled."

Hilda, in addition to studying Islam in college, had also attended "three or four different seminars on Islam," all of which were given by her parents when they were back in the US during their tenure as missionaries in a Middle Eastern country. As far as learning about Islam was concerned, there was a difference between studying in the Middle East and education in the US. She asserted that from her perspective:

> there is such a lack of information here about what they
> actually believe, [whether] they [are] culturally and

religiously [Muslims], that for me personally starting into a discussion about Islam feels very complicated because you have to walk through so many underlying misconceptions.

She asserted that "so few Americans really have any experience with Islam. It's all new, and it's all sort of maybe a little bit, definitely foreign but kind of scary on some level." One of the misperceptions that Americans have of Islam is that it is violent. And it is a "critical" misperception: "It's not, 'Islam equals violent,' it's, 'Islam can be violent.'" She also had images in her mind from living in the Middle East "of people from magazines, from books, ... they're kind of how I process this group called Islam. And I am very aware that in conversation with other Christians, they don't have those images, they don't know the people, they don't know the spirit of the people." The images that she had in her mind included children who were "usually very poor, very downtrodden, hurt because the result of the misinformation, the result of the distance, the result of the lack of relationship is injustice." She asserted that when you get to know them as human beings, "something changes in the relationship, in the conversation: yes, they are Muslims, but they are first of all people." Joshua, in addition to looking at Islam in theology and apologetics courses, had also attended "lectures about Islamic thought." One of the lectures was at an Equip conference where he heard an apologist teach about different religions. He presented a "pretty adversarial position on Islam," saying things like "this is a satanic religion, ... Allah was based on the moon god and the moon god's name was Sin." Joshua was appalled and, slapping his forehead with his palm, asserted, "No, it's not the same word. It's not even the same concept." He recalled hearing the people react, and a woman in front of him gasped at this explanation. At this conference this apologist was the "dominant voice," arguing that "Christians are in this awful conflict and they want to kill us." On another occasion he was attending a Passover Seder put on by a messianic Jew who "made the same kind of statement: these Islamists are here to kill us." Joshua asserted that this comment did not really sit well with him but "made sense to a lot of the people in my congregation."

The experience of the pastors was different from the experience of their congregants—three out of four had attended lectures or seminars on Islam, whereas among the laity only fifteen out of the forty interviewed had done so. Pastor Justin mentioned that he had not engaged in any serious study of Islam. While he has picked up information about Islam "from conversations, maybe an article in a magazine, putting pieces together of people I've known who have worked with Muslims," but he has not had any "particular organized way" to get his "hands around that, either the theological framework or the social, cultural framework."

Pastor Tim had been part of a class titled "Middle East, Islam and War" that he had organized at this church. The class focused on "the history of the Middle East," followed by discussions, and he himself "gave a couple lectures on Muhammad and the history of Islam, Sunni, and Shia and what was going on." They had also invited a speaker to teach during this class. Pastor Sawyer said that he "might have gone to a seminar on Islam in the Urbana missionary conventions back in the early 70s."

Pastor Seth had not systematically studied Islam but had attended a four- or five-week-long Sunday school "series of lectures by a very well-versed missionary who was ministering to Muslims in France" and was teaching at his home church in Rockford, IL, while on furlough. The lectures he attended discussed topics such as "'What is Islam?,' 'The fundamental beliefs of Islam', some of the demographics of Islam in the world, and why some cultures were more amenable to the influx of Islam and the acceptance of Islam as opposed to other cultures." The last lecture in this teaching series "was a challenge of how do we as Christians minister or have a relationship with Muslims and people of the Islamic faith."

From the respondents interviewed, half of them had not attended any seminars or lectures about Islam or studied Islam. From the other half of the respondents, who had had some teaching on Islam, they received this teaching in a variety of ways: some had attended seminars or lectures, one person picked up information on YouTube and another via some teaching tapes, some had studied Islam in college and seminary, and some had done so in church settings. Respondents also received information from notable Christian leaders such as Sam Solomon, Joel Rosenberg, and Ravi Zacharias. Topics of study included the basics of Islam and Islamic cultural life, sharia law, violence in Islam, apologetics and evangelism among Muslims, the concept of jihad, etc., with all of the topics focusing on the issue of Christians being able to relate to Muslims from a variety of different vantage points. Two salient observations that can be made from this are, first, that a significant number of the respondents have not received any teaching about Islam, which means that the information that they have about Islam comes from other sources; and second, there is a need in evangelical churches for systematic and accurate teaching about Islam and Muslims so that the respondents are better informed.

Q2: Have you read websites about Islam?

From the lay evangelicals interviewed, 14 responded that they do not read websites about Islam, with Rebecca vehemently stating: "Never! I would never touch Islam on the web because I figured, you know, they will find me and kill me."

Lisa did not use the computer at all, but had access to numerous Christian TV stations such as Total Living Network, Trinity

Broadcasting Network, My Christian TV, and DayStar. Through these TV stations she had seen John Ankerberg's show on which he had interviewed two Muslim brothers who had become Christians. She felt that she got a good picture of things pertaining to Islam because she was getting to hear from someone who "knows both sides of the story; it isn't just somebody's opinion." Lisa also had the opportunity to see a program on the 700 Club where a man said, "this is what [it says in the Qur'an] about cutting somebody's head off and being willing to [commit] violence." She has also heard about the ways in which Muslim men "treat their wives." She recounted a story where a Muslim man in an Islamic country looked out of the window and saw his daughter-in-law brushing her hair. The man told his son about this and "so the agenda was to kill this woman for having exposed herself and [supposedly] trying to tempt this man who was nothing but a busybody peeking in the window." She thought that "there's no love between the man and the woman" because they blamed the woman and were ready to kill her "at the least thing." Lisa had also heard about Muslims in Islamic countries such as Afghanistan and Iraq strapping on bombs, blowing themselves up for Allah, and killing people quite senselessly: "Every time it's a group of people, it's a Muslim thing. That's who it's attributed to... It's really irrational-type thinking in most people's estimation."

Stuart had accessed websites such as The Wall Street Journal (http://www.wsj.com), Fox News (http://www.foxnews.com), and CNN (http://cnn.com). He recalled reading an article by Ayyan Hirsi Ali, a Dutch woman and a convert from Islam to Christianity, which appeared in the Wall Street Journal (Hirsi Ali, 2013). She wrote about the Muslim attack in London and the subsequent "lack of apologies or the lack of Muslim leaders standing up" and calling it what it was. The article was "not complimentary." Stuart also talked about Ali's prior experience of coming to the Netherlands as a student, becoming a Dutch parliamentarian, and the community "basically ostracized her because she told it as it was, what's happening in Africa, what's happening with Muslims."

Luke asserted that most of the things that he reads on the Internet are articles sent to him by other people. For example, he had recently read an article titled "Joys of Muslim Women," authored by Nonie Darwish, an Egyptian Muslim woman. From this article he learned that in Islam Muslim men can marry a female as young as one year old and consummate the marriage when she is nine; a Muslim woman cannot obtain a divorce; husbands are permitted to have up to four wives; Muslim men in America want sharia law to be implemented so that their wives cannot obtain a divorce; etc. Simon talked about picking up information such as the training of children in Islamic militant camps "to cut throats and to grow up detesting ... Jews and the West in general." Another website mentioned was Andrew Sullivan's The Dish, which provided information about the Boston Marathon bombers (http://dish.andrewsullivan.com).

Stacy had visited Islamic websites in order to "challenge them" and because she was interested in seeing how Muslims portrayed Islam and "what kind of people were manning the websites." She was interested because she thought "there must be a very good reason why so many people follow Islam, and I just wanted to hear their version of it." But her experience was that whenever she asked a challenging question, they would leave. "There was a lot of waffle about how gentle we are, and how loving we are, and how we want to reach out to Christians and look after our neighbors. But when you asked specific questions, there was never an answer."

Mary had visited websites "that were set up by former Muslims who have become Christians... They were addressing various spiritual issues that Muslims might ask questions about if there is some difference in Christianity and Islam." She also visited a website where a "Muslim was targeting Christianity [with] Islamic answers to Christian arguments."

None of the four pastors interviewed accessed any websites specifically about Islam. Pastor Seth had accessed secular news sources such as "CNN, Fox, News Max" and religious news sources such as the Gospel Coalition and First Things to read about "various events happening within the world of Islam." Pastor Sawyer mentioned that he gets news "once in a while [from] CNN or PBS but mostly BBC" He said Al Jazeera is another news source that is "pretty good" when you are traveling in some parts of the world. Most of what he reads is about "just straight current events, this is what's happening." He also added that "it is probably through some of those that I have become more aware of sort of the complexities of modern Islam, that there is so many different varieties and streams and so forth."

From the respondents interviewed approximately one third do not read any websites related to Islam. From those who do visit websites, most visited secular news websites across the political spectrum. These included: ABC, CBS, NBC, CNBC, MSNBC, Fox News, CNN, The Wall Street Journal, PBS, BBC, the Drudge Report and even Al Jazeera. The information they encounter on these websites focused on current radical events such as the Boston Marathon bombings; "misinformation," such as all Muslims believe in holy war and want to kill Americans; Islamic family life; etc. Some also accessed websites focused on Islam and contemporary politics—information that was for the most part negative about Islam and Muslims. Most of the respondents did not ask whether they should take this information at face value or whether this information is providing a balanced perspective on Islam and/or Muslims. They also drew information from

Christian websites and Christian radio regarding evangelistically engaging Muslims and answering questions related to faith. Others accessed Christian television, such as a 700 Club program in which a speaker pointed out passages in the Qur'an that advocate violence and killing, and other programs by TV host John Ankerberg who had interviewed two Muslim converts to Christianity. The respondent accepted the information from these sources as reliable without the sensing the need for any further scrutiny because it was coming from Christians who had been Muslim and hence were able to provide an insider's perspective. That Christian leaders who have converted out of Islam are trusted without question was also evident from the information obtained by one respondent from a website belonging to Walid Shoebat. Shoebat claimed that Huma Abedin, former Secretary of State Hillary Clinton's "number two person" had ties to the Muslim Sisterhood and the Muslim Brotherhood through her (Abedin's) parents. This led the respondent to jump to the conclusion that the information that Abedin had access to through Hillary Clinton was passed on to the Muslim Brotherhood. One respondent admitted that his information had come from a Christian source he characterized as "too right-wing"—to them anyone who looks like an Arab is a terrorist. He had begun to question claims from these Christians.

While respondents accessed a wide variety of media sources to obtain information about Islam, no clear pattern emerged as to which sources were accessed most frequently and/or which sources were most influential. The pattern that did emerge, however, was that information was obtained primarily from news outlets on the Internet and television. Only three respondents had obtained information from Christian sources on how to engage Muslims. Overall the majority of sources accessed by respondents focused on the violence associated with Islam, catalyzing and reinforcing their negative perceptions.

Q3: Have you read books or magazines dealing with Islam?

One third of the respondents said that they had not read books or magazines dealing with Islam, while the other respondents listed a wide variety of books or magazines that they had read regarding Islam, and some have also read portions of the Qur'an. Judy, a mental health professional in her 70s, recalled reading in a women's magazine an article about Muslim women who have gone back to an Islamic country with their husbands, were not allowed to leave, and had to "sneak out." She had learned that the culture supports the religion enough that these women are not able to go to the authorities and say, "I want to leave, and I came here with this understanding that I could go home with my children and my husband." In these kinds of situations there is no support for the women at all. Natalie had gathered from the Cairo Trilogy her impression "of the repression of women in the culture." She also recalled descriptions of the women that when they were away from the men, they were "just interested in hair, makeup, clothing," which is quite different from the "televised image" that she had of Muslim women covered in black clothes. But she also thought that her impressions might not be accurate because this book was set in Egypt in the 1920s.

Luke read Dr. Peter Hammond's Slavery, Terrorism and Islam: The Historical Roots and Contemporary Threat. He learned there that as long as the population of Muslims remains under 2%, "they will be, for the most part, regarded as peace-loving or a minority and not as a threat to their citizens." Luke stated that at the time that the book was written the Muslim population in the US was 0.6%. Hammond goes on to say that when the Muslim population is between 2% and 5%, "they begin to proselytize from other minorities and disaffected groups, often with major recruiting from jail and street gangs," and Luke asserted that there is recruiting going on in the jails in the US. Once the population exceeds 5%, Muslims exercise influence disproportionate to their size in terms of percentage of the population and "push for the introduction of halal [clean by Islamic standards] food, thereby securing food preparation jobs for Muslims." They also exert pressure on supermarket chains to sell halal food, "along with threats for failure to comply." And when the population of Muslims nears 10%, "they tend to increase lawlessness as a means of complaint about their conditions."

Luke went on to explain that Brigitte Gabriel, author of Because They Hate, grew up in Lebanon. When she was a young girl, Lebanon was a Christian nation, and the Christians treated the Muslims "much in the same way we do, with total acceptance for their religion and even brought them into the government, and they had equal rights in the government and through three waves of migration from Palestine and other nearby countries." But when the Muslims became the majority in Lebanon, they would stop the Christians on the streets and ask them to "prove who they were, and if they couldn't prove they were Muslims, they were shot."

Matt reads emails sent out by Joel Rosenberg, a Messianic Jew who writes about "praying for the world, praying for peace in Israel, praying for survival of Israel." Matt learned from his book that Muslims "are allowed to lie when they moved to a new country. As long as you are in a minority, you are allowed to lie because the end justifies the means. So, lying is perfectly acceptable as long as it is promoting the cause of Allah, their God." Karen learned from Walid Shoebat's The Case FOR Islamophobia that Christians "should ... be Islamophobic." The point of this provocatively titled book is that Christians "should definitely be far more aware of what is happening" than they are. Karen asserted that "it's like we are walking into the lion's den, you know, smiling and cheering and trying to make the lions our friends, and it could really, ultimately come back to bite us really badly."

Rebecca had read the Qur'an and Salman Rushdie's The Satanic Verses to look for "verses that are very violent," and she had "confirmed" that "they exist," and Nathan, a retired business executive in his 70s, had read the Qur'an to look for "jihadist passages" or "whether it really is indeed a book of peace."

Joshua learned about various aspects of Islam from a variety of different magazines. Newsweek covered "quite broadly" the war in Afghanistan and often published articles about how "Americans just don't understand Islam," which he thought was accurate "for the most part." National Review asserted that "we need to remember that the Taliban is our enemy and they're hurting Americans." Christianity Today talked about topics related to contextualization: "Should we call Jesus the Son of God when we're doing ministry to Muslims because God having the category of Son is just a nonstarter for them; when you meet God as a Son, that just doesn't compute." Joshua said that Christianity Today also reminded its readers that the Islamic world was huge, "some of which exists o.k. with Christianity, some of which doesn't. But we have to become more aware and intentional both globally and locally about how we're engaging that community." Of the four pastors interviewed, Pastor Justin had not read any books but thought he may have picked up articles from magazines such as Christianity Today and Leadership Journal. Pastor Tim had read books but drew a "blank about pulling up a book that has been particularly memorable or helpful" regarding the "Palestinian situation and the Muslims in Israel." The books that he had read "have been as much political when talking about Islam as they have been theological." One author he mentioned was Thomas Friedman, who writes about the Middle East and Islam. He had read a number of magazines such as First Things, Christianity Today, Time, Newsweek, The New York

Times, and others. He had also looked at blogs on First Things, which occasionally has "things that interact with Islam."

Pastor Sawyer had read books about the basics of Islam, the history of Islam, the life of Muhammad, and "stories of people who are Muslims who come to believe in Jesus and how that happened." Because his church is quite involved in "supporting churches in Muslim countries," he reads "anything that pops up in that arena of work." One book that was particularly memorable was Carl Medearis' Muslims, Christians, and Jesus. This book is about how to engage Muslims with the gospel and takes a very "blessing, positive orientation." Pastor Sawyer described Medearis in this way:

> The guy has got many friends in the Muslim world, he has preached in mosques in Lebanon in Hezbollah controlled territory. He has been in the house of the head sheikh of the Hezbollah, blessing him and his family... But he goes into all these places that people think Christians can't go and talk about Jesus, and he is loved by them because he talks about Jesus in a way that's nonhostile and that's not condemning.

To Sawyer, the effect of this book was "very powerful."

One third of the respondents said that they had not read books or magazines dealing with Islam, while the other respondents listed a wide variety of books or magazines that they had read about Islam: books by Mark Steyn, Sam Solomon's book Modern Day Trojan Horse, Kate McCord's In the Land of Blue Burqas, etc. Some respondents had also read portions of the Qur'an. The books and magazines they read, at least two of which were authored by Muslim converts to Christianity, covered topics such as: the oppression of the women in Islamic lands, the increase of Muslim population and influence, the killing of Christians by Muslims, lying to promote the cause of Allah, the need for Christian awareness and vigilance, violent and jihadist passages in the

Qur'an, etc. Other topics discussed included evangelizing and ministering to Muslims, Muslims coming to faith in Christ and the role of dreams in their conversion, and topics related to contextualizing different aspects of the identity of Jesus for Muslims.

While it is to be expected that the respondents would read about different aspects of ministry to Muslims, overwhelmingly the topics they read were negative in orientation, fostering and reinforcing the negative perceptions respondents had already had from the media. Evangelical leaders have influenced the development and reinforcement of these negative perceptions through the books they have written. The fact that some respondents approached the Qur'an and other books on Islam specifically to look for passages that talk about the violence connected with Islam underscores their preconceived negative bias. Most of the respondents had not read writings by Muslim authors. Thus, the only religious voice that they have access to, and hence are influenced by, is the voice of American Christian leaders.

Q4: Thinking about your own view of Islam, would you say that your view is positive, or negative, or cautious, or neutral, or several of these words, or some other word? Why is that?

To describe their view, respondents used one or more of these words, with 19 respondents using "negative," 16 "cautious," six "neutral," and four using "positive." John asserted that his view of Islam is cautious because he "always think[s] positively about people [and] likes[s] to give people the benefit of the doubt." He did not "believe that many of the people who are perpetrating [terrorism] are... even that religious." For example, the older brother in the Boston Marathon bombings "didn't necessarily live a very religious life really until recently." John asserted that he was "cautiously optimistic that at some point the truth would be told." He was not "anxious" or "concerned" but felt that we should go after the people who are doing these things, and "unfortunately it looks like there is no dialogue with them. That's an unfortunate situation. There is no other way to do it to keep you safe." John also felt that caution needs to be exercised because the Muslim community was not rising up "to the same level of public defiance or emotion or public rebuke of 9/11 and events like that." He also felt that Saddam Hussein and Osama bin Laden did not necessarily follow Islam but "invoked Islam for their own personal gain." Amy asserted that she would exercise caution toward the men because of the violence but not necessarily toward women who "don't seem to be the violent ones." She asserted, "I would make a friend with a Muslim woman. If she was my neighbor and she wanted to come for tea or something, I would be happy to sit down and have tea."

Mike commented that looking at a Muslim as a person, he would have "no trouble being a friend with them, sitting down with them, laughing with them. I would have no fear of harm or anything like that dealing with anyone." He added that on a "political, global level he "wouldn't use the word cautious" but rather "negative." He also asserted that he was not satisfied with his answer and "would have to think through and work on it a little bit more ... than it being just natural reaction to Muslims." Mary described her view of Islam as negative but, asserting that her "view of Muslim people is not necessarily negative," was not sure whether her view of Muslims was "positive or negative" because she saw them as people who need the gospel and who are "capable of believing in Jesus" and people who have gone through suffering and "who need help."

Lisa used three different words to characterize her views of Muslims: "scary," "very cautious," and "negative." It was naive "to embrace these people thinking you're going to turn them into friends.

[It is very scary] until they get rid of this jihad thing and sharia law idea and trying to push this on people." She felt extremely cautious because of "what's happened to European countries who have welcomed them" and because she did not think that it would be possible to "change these people." Stuart asserted that his view was "between negative and cautious, and more negative than cautious." It would be more positive if Muslims bought into the US lifestyles that adhered to "US laws, mores, and moral values while being a practicing Muslim."

Matt had strong feelings about Islam, using words like "fearful, anger, disgust" to describe his view of Islam. He was puzzled about "how and why would they be doing this;" he felt disgusted because of "how they treat their women," something that one respondent found "offensive" and another "sad;" he felt "terribly disgusted for the killings and the bombings that they do and [that] they kill innocent women and children" and felt "anger that they could kill Americans and get away with it." He had a "very negative perception of the people who have hijacked this religion," and it was very hard for him to imagine that Islam could ever stop perpetrating violence such as the Boston Marathon bombings. Matt was quite distressed because of the billions of dollars Western societies were having to spend "to protect their borders, for airport security," etc. He also felt that the Muslims "love" this and "it's very purposeful. They want to destroy us." Stacy added that Islam wants to "dominate the world." She asserted that whenever Islam is present, there is "conflict," "violence, aggression, everything that's evil; everything that Satan stands for somehow is represented in Islam." Peter viewed Islam negatively because it seeks to make converts "in a violent way," with "consequences for those that don't conform: ... chop the head off." James said that "Islam is the greatest tool of Satan in the persecution of the church."

Rebecca asserted that her view was "balanced" because her view was "based on study" and she was "informed." She said that she could not "stand them" and that "they are horrible ... and those people who think [there] are peaceful Islamists, they just don't know, they aren't. They're not Islamists. I don't know what they are, but they are not following the religion in a fundamental way."

Three respondents asserted that their view was positive. Debbie said that she did not have "anything against Islam, it's just a different religion"; Hazel said that her positive attitude came from personal experience with a Muslim who was "very eager to do well, ... very honest and conscientious." Hannah had a positive view because she sees "a lot of the good stuff in Islam." Steve characterized his view as "accepting" because, like people of any faith, Muslims should be allowed to practice their own religion if they are not hurting other people. He also said that his view was "positive, neutral" and that he was neither "in favor of Islam" nor "against Islam."

Two pastors (Justin and Tim) said that they felt "disappointed" or "sad" because Muslims do not have a relationship with Christ," and Pastor Sawyer said "incomplete" because of Islam's "view of who Jesus is." Pastor Tim also said that he was "at best cautious." He explained that Islam is a "broad tent," so it is inaccurate to say either that "Muslims are bad, Muslims are evil" or that "Islam is a religion of peace, everything is good ... It is not helpful for you to have a narrow snapshot of what Islam is like." Tim said, because Islam has more than 1 billion people, "everything you think about it is true somewhere in the world. There are wonderful, open-minded, highly educated, moderate Muslims. There are mean, trying-to-kill-you, fundamentalist, hate-women Muslims."

Pastor Seth used several of these words: "negative in the sense [that] it is not an alternative way to God"; "neutral in that I don't fear it,

I don't see it as a personal threat to my culture or to my conscience"; "cautious in how you would seek to minister or evangelize or proselytize people of the Islamic faith." He said people need to be "sensitive to who they are, to what they believe" and caring for them "as a person" and not "filtering them through the lens of 'you are a Muslim, but you are a human being, you are made in the image of God, you happen to have a different faith than I do, and how can we talk about that.'" He said that he would want to exercise caution so that he does not "come across as some overbearing WASP."

Looking at respondents' selection of words to describe their view of Islam and Muslims, the very fact that 35 of them chose either "negative" or "cautious" and 10 chose "neutral" or "positive" is a very clear indicator of the general outlook evangelicals have toward Islam. Respondents who used the word "positive" did so because they either saw Islam as just another religion, or because there are many good values stemming from Islam, or because of a positive experience relating to a Muslim, or because they thought that there probably are many Muslims seeking God and seeking to live a good life. Those respondents who used the word "negative" did so because, among other things, they thought that Islam is dangerous, it is a lie, it is a path to hell, large numbers of people are being misled by it, and it makes converts by force. Many respondents also expressed their views about Islam by using very strong negative words, such as "very scary," "dangerous," "fearful," "disgust," "deceptive," etc. One respondent was physically taken aback when I asserted that it seemed from her responses that her view about Islam was negative. While her views clearly were negative, she initially described her views as "cautious" and only later admitted that they were negative, because in her view, Islam itself is a negative religion. Clearly, the perception the respondents have of Islam is overwhelmingly negative in tenor. The respondents would do well to recognize that, in the words of Pastor Tim, Islam is a "broad tent."

Q5: Have the events of 9/11 or the recent Boston Marathon bombings affected your view of Islam and Muslims? Tell me about that.

John admitted, "Well, it can't help but influence you to some degree." There is evil in the world and "unfortunately individuals are co-opted by evil, sometimes in the name of a religion or a faith--we are sinful people." He also said that "we have to defend our nation," which "means that we have to do things that may be unpleasant." Natalie was influenced to the point of starting to think about Islam more because there was "so much in the news" and started to notice Muslims more, especially women because of their distinctive clothes. She started to wonder "what would cause someone to do this, ... this idea of getting into heaven by kind of suicidal means of getting to heaven, losing your life for the religion or some religious cause." She also began to question "whether the religion itself leads to that kind of action, or whether it's just kind of a radical group within them, just as there are radical Christians." Gabriel said, "I guess [these events] have shaped [my views] but not to the point that I'm more worried than I would have been before. I don't think they've changed my point of view that I'm worried about Muslims." He also said that he has become more aware of "some of the extremism" around the world. He recalled boarding a flight after 9/11 and having "crazy thoughts" when he saw "a guy with a long beard, dressed in robes."

As far as Lisa was concerned, "the 9/11 event really sealed it as far as [showing] what these people were capable of." She also went on to say that it was "terribly frightening" to her "to think that something like this can happen. You are not protected anymore in your own country, but still you live under a constant threat." The events of 9/11 made people "wake up and realize" that as a country we are "not immune to that sort of thing and that people hate [Americans]." People who are "steeped in Islam and who want to kill us are going to, and there is nothing that we will ever be able to say or do that will make them our friends. In fact, I think even if everybody in the country converted to Islam they would still want to kill us. " Darryl emphatically stated that, yes, 9/11 impacted him but the Boston Marathon bombings not so much. He said that for him there is no difference "between cancer and Muslim radicals that want to kill me" and that if "they want to kill me, I want them dead before they can kill me." Paul said "Oh, yes … it's clear we're not just talking about radical Islam--we know that there are certain groups like the Muslim Brotherhood that are dangerous." Matt said that Islam "brought the element of their religion [that] wants to destroy to the forefront." He asserted that since the 1980s he has followed "a guy named James Dines" who has talked about "the era of the coming holy wars, and he was right on." For Peter, these events have given him a "heightened sense of awareness and caution." Susan said, "I don't remember the last time I saw a Buddhist blowing up buildings that killed thousands of people and destroyed that much infrastructure and had the kind of societal ramifications, airport security, and the cost for security that that did."

Sam expressed confusion about what Muslims were fighting for and was of the opinion that they needed to accept that "we ain't going back to the 12th century." He said that he had "animosity towards most Muslims." He said that if he sees a Muslim woman who's covered up, "something snaps," and he has thoughts that run through his mind such as "if her husband thinks the way these guys did on 9/11, if her boyfriend or her brother, or whatever... What's going on in the mosque that they attend? Is there hatred being taught there?"

Carl felt that while these events have impacted his view, what was really bothersome to him was that he had "not heard the Muslim community that is more on the peace-loving side, etc., that is saying, 'oh, that's really bad, that was horrible.'" This lack of overt condemnation of these events by the Muslim community disturbed him and raised some questions for him, such as, "Does that mean that they're fearful of the people? Does that mean that maybe they secretly are approving all of that? I just don't know. I don't understand." He further asserted, "Just even apart from religion or Christianity, I don't understand that culturally. If you disagree with something, if you think something is horrible, why wouldn't you say that's horrible?" In this line of thought Hannah asserted it is easy for us as Christians to condemn actions of this nature committed by Christians because we are not born Christians but become Christians by making "the decision to follow Jesus." "For a Muslim, it's much harder for them because if you are born into a Muslim family, you are Muslim. It doesn't matter whether you [actually] follow Islam or not, you are a Muslim." For this reason, Muslims "can condemn it, but they can't say that that person is not a part of their community; they can't say that person is not a Muslim." Of the four pastors interviewed, three said that 9/11 and the Boston Marathon attack had not affected their views of Islam and Muslims. Pastor Seth explained that he was saddened because "a very small minority was able to do such terrible things and cast a really bad light on a large group of people." He also said that he was more influenced by the events of the last three or four years, such as the Arab Spring, the dissatisfaction within the Islamic countries in the Middle East, which made him wonder whether they want sharia law or more Western-style democratic freedom. But the influence that these events have had on him was to make him realize that he does not understand these things as well as he thought he might have.

Pastor Tim said "no" because he has not "learned much new on Islam in the last ten years." This pastor has traveled to numerous countries, done a lot of reading, has listened at great length to ten students studying Islam for their doctoral studies, and he has come to realize that "it's nuanced, it's complicated." He feels sad when he hears about "young kids blowing things up, it's sad for everybody. Their hearts are filled with hate; they are blinded. I am sad that the American church wasn't there in greater ways to love and to bring them in." He also feels frustration because of metal detectors at airports, having to take his shoes off because someone may use a shoe bomb, "the fences, the walls, the fear—that's very frustrating." He also shared an experience that he had sightseeing in Egypt where he heard some Korean Christians sing a Christian song in Korean and saw the backlash that they experienced at the hands of some Egyptians. He realized that this is a "pretty oppressive place." And then two days later, while shopping, he recalled coming around the corner and seeing a Muslim woman "in a complete burka," and he thought to himself, "'Wait a minute. I am in Lake Bluff, I'm not in Cairo, I'm in Lake Bluff.' So, occasionally you go, 'Oh my goodness, this is right here.'" He went on to say, "But, for the most part, tragically, I am more worried about strategic planning at the church, and budgets, and the person in the hospital, and, you know, that's sort of an all-consuming."

Pastor Justin said, while as Americans people are trying to say that "these people don't represent" all the Muslims necessarily, "it's really hard to get on an airplane and not just feel a little uneasy if you see someone who looks Middle Eastern." This pastor imagined that other Middle Eastern people probably feel a "little uneasy" as well. But you do not think this if you see "an Italian," for instance. This pastor saw these kinds of events "as the radical edge of something." He also thought that "we will have more of these. I do think that Islam will lay behind much, not all, but I don't know that it's fair to say, 'So, Islam is the reason why people are getting blown up.' I think that's a bit of an oversimplification."

Twenty-eight respondents said that events such as 9/11 or the Boston Marathon bombings have influenced their view of Islam and Muslims; eight said they have not, with several asserting that these events had only reinforced the view they already had. Representative of those individuals who said they were "influenced" is a respondent who asserted that she had started to think more about Islam because there is so much in the news; started to think more about Muslims, especially women because of their clothes; started to wonder what would lead someone to act out on the idea that killing yourself for your religion would automatically get you into heaven; and started to wonder if the religion of Islam itself leads a person to do this or if it is the actions of the radicals in Islam. One female respondent broke down in tears as she expressed disbelief, and shock, and bewilderment when recalling the events of 9/11. Other respondents already "knew" that this kind of violence was always part of Islam and that Muslims think this way, and hence they were not surprised when these events happened but were surprised that these events did not happen more often.

Q6: Does your pastor make references to Muslims and/or Islam in his preaching at your church? Have you had teaching at your church about how evangelicals should view Islam and Muslims?

Twenty-two of the lay evangelicals interviewed said "no" to the first question. Others had a variety of responses. John asserted that his pastor occasionally does that in the context of the "multicultural reality that we live in," and another said references were made in the context of evangelism. Three respondents, like Stuart, asserted that their pastor makes reference "in the context of Christianity being the right one versus the others"; Natalie said her pastor "preached a series called FencePosts" and sought "to clarify what we have in common with other faiths and where the differences are." Linda asserted that this only comes up "if they make reference to a news item," and she may have "heard a couple of sermons comparing beliefs, what the Bible says, with several different religions." Darryl said that this comes up "once in a while, in a good way, not in a negative way," and another said his pastor has talked about having a Muslim friend but never about Islam. Joshua recalled having an experience as a fourth or fifth grader where his pastor had invited a Muslim convert to speak about Islam. This "missionary to Muslims" talked about Islam and "framed it from a spiritual warfare perspective." He "fully believed" that Gabriel who gave the Qur'an to Muhammad "was a wicked spirit."

Mike said they had exposure to this when they had missionaries serving in Muslim countries speak at their church, and they have also known missionaries in their church who were "actually killed by Muslims." Because of this, "the tension has been always pretty much in front of you. It is not just the remote events in the news, it's people that you have sat with in the pew that have lost their lives due to Muslim violence in African tribal countries." Carl and Hannah said that their pastors do this often because they frequently go on mission trips and support churches in Islamic countries. Periodically they also have missionaries visit their church and speak about Islam and Muslims. For several weeks in the context of "culture in America there was a focus on Islam and how do you relate." This topic has also been brought up in the context of preaching about "differences between the faiths, people that he has talked to, [so] yes, it's pretty active."

From the lay evangelicals interviewed, 25 said "no" to the second question. Others had a variety of responses. Five respondents asserted that references were made "not directly but in the context of the gospel and that "Christ died for all," that we should love them, reach out to them, and accept them. Ryan, a retired medical professional in his 60s, said, "I think we had teaching about what Islam is, and a little bit about what their theology is... I think it's been covered to some extent." Linda said that references have also been made when they were "praying for the persecuted church," but she does not "recall it being prejudiced by a pastor to hate them or to fear them, only to be aware and to pray." Joshua remembered hearing about "what Islam believes and you should pray for Muslims to come to know Jesus."

Pastor Seth said that he does not discuss Islam any more than he discusses "other religious faiths." When he does, he "might acknowledge the influence that these faiths can have within our communities or within the world," but he does not "hold it up as a straw man." He will bring it up "if it's germane to truly understanding a doctrinal or theological issue for the purpose of theological comparison [but] not trying to compare people."

Pastor Justin would talk occasionally about his relationship with his friend, Muhammad, but has never discussed Islam in "theological terms or missiological terms." He does not "feel very confident about his knowledge." Furthermore, he has never had teaching about how evangelicals should view Islam and Muslims. Pastor Sawyer said that he had "told stories of Muslims who have personal encounters with Jesus usually in dreams or some kind of miracle in the process of telling something else" but had not "really given sermons on Islam, or about Islam, or about Muslims necessarily." Pastor Tim had done teaching in his congregation about Islam titled "Middle East, Islam and War."

From the lay evangelicals interviewed, 22 said that their pastor does not make reference to Islam and/or Muslims at their church, and 25 said that they have not had teaching about how evangelicals should view Islam and Muslims. Those who responded affirmatively to the two questions said that that there were no references that were negative in tone and that the references all had to do with the topic of evangelizing Muslims.

The information that the pastors communicated to the laity may be summed up very well by the comments of Pastor Tim: "I would say, treat Muslims and Islam ... treat people as people, listen, don't react out of fear or ignorance, love, serve, proclaim the good news, and engage in good works." Significantly then, negative perceptions that the respondents have are not being taught to them in churches they attend. At the same time, the fact that some respondents indicated that Muslims need to hear the gospel and that Christians need to minister to them is an indication that the respondents are also shaped, perhaps under the influence of their pastors and churches, by the biblical imperative for Christians to love all people.

Q7: Have you had discussions about Islam or about spiritual matters with a Muslim?

Fifteen of the laity interviewed responded "no." Rebecca's views were especially passionate. In response to the question she gestured strongly and emphatically stated, "Never. And I never would because I don't trust them, maybe they are secretly radical."

Lisa had had conversations with two Muslim men who had rented a room in her house. In the first conversation he talked about the return of Jesus, and she said that "the Bible doesn't give us the day or the hour, but we know by events that are taking place. It says when you see all these things happen, then you would know that your redemption draws nigh." By "things" she meant "weather patterns," "wars," and "the whole world being up in an uproar and people who are killing others believing they are doing God a favor." She told him that she believed that Jesus was going to come back in 2020. He responded, "Oh okay, if he doesn't return by 2020 I can come back and talk to you? And then are you going to listen [about Islam]?" In the conversation with the second Muslim man she said that he tried to get her to read the Qur'an.

Cathy had had numerous discussions with Muslims and shared one that was centered on matters of faith. Cathy asked a Muslim acquaintance whether she had read the Qur'an, to which she responded "no, not really"; she asked her if she had read the Injil," to which she responded "no, not really." At Cathy's invitation, the Muslim woman read both of them with her, and they had a discussion about them. Cathy noted, "She never made a profession of faith for Christ, but I don't see the only fruit is the profession. I think the seed itself is important." She also had discussions with her about Jesus, and the Muslim view of "Isa not really being crucified," and also about "historical records for it. What about Josephus?"

Stacy, who has had considerable experience working with Muslim women, had had numerous conversations, some of which led to "conversions to Christianity." Two of these women "had dreams the night they converted that Christ actually came up in their dreams, both of them." In another conversation that she had with a Muslim girl, she recalled that the girl said that "Islam is better than Christianity because God didn't come down to earth to have sex with Mary." After making the statement she shut the door to her shop and "wasn't open to any talking at all."

Mary had had numerous conversations with many interested Muslims when she was a college student, many of them focused on a "lot of misconceptions" that the Muslims had. She thought that for Muslims, evangelicals were "way off the radar" and they looked at them "as a little splinter group of Christians." She commented, "the only thing that they knew is that evangelicals were the ones supporting their enemy, Israel." Muslims did not understand the Reformation and had no idea "why there were different groups of Christians or what the differences between them were." They were interested in discussing "spiritual experiences" that they had in common with Christians, such as prayer. They were interested in "having a good prayer life," and one Muslim was interested in knowing how "as a Christian I didn't recite a prayer, but I actually prayed whatever I needed, whatever I wanted." Mary also learned that for Muslims "to come out of Islam is hard because of the family, and it's like if you are leaving their religion, you are leaving their family or you are leaving their society." The Muslims thought that Christianity was too "individualistic" "because it's not a social system, it's not a community that they can understand," and "they liked the idea that they were in an Islamic state, an Islamic nation, an Islamic society that was going to have certain moral standards for the whole society and that they were going to rule." Another respondent, Hilda, had also engaged Muslims, discussing topics such as "Who is God? What is God like? Is God an angry God? Is God a loving God? What do I have to do to get to heaven? Do I have to do anything to get to heaven?—those kinds of things. "

Natalie also had a very brief conversation with a Muslim neighbor after 9/11 who commented that "[Pakistan] is just ready to explode ... that part of the world is just in such turmoil and conflict." The Muslim woman was "horrified like everybody else, [and] sad about the whole thing," and concerned about how her family in Pakistan was "going to come through all of this."

After the interview was finished, Ryan, gesturing strongly, vehemently stated that Americans should "nuke" the Muslim nations, and "when we do that once, they will not mess with us again." In contrast, Darryl actually wept after the interview because he was extremely disturbed over his conflicted feelings: He knew that his Christian beliefs required him to love Muslims, yet he struggled with deep feelings of animosity toward them.

From the four pastors interviewed, Pastor Seth and Pastor Sawyer had never engaged Muslims in a conversation, and the Pastor Justin's discussions with a Muslim gas station attendant have already been discussed above. Pastor Tim had organized a Bible study at his home "on the life of Jesus" and invited his neighbors, one of whom was his Muslim friend. The Muslim man came every week and "was very appreciative," and at the end of the six- or eight-week Bible study said, "If you ever do anything like this again, I want to be in it." But at the end of the Bible study he also said, "I think Jesus is a prophet, so I am interested in Jesus. But I don't think we think that he rose from the dead."

Fifteen respondents had not had any discussions about Islam or spiritual matters with Muslims, with one respondent emphatic about not doing so. All those who did have conversations talked about the gospel, with the exception of three: One conversation was about Muslims evangelizing the Christian, the second conversation was about misconceptions that Muslims have about Christians and Christianity, and the third conversation was about the events related to 9/11. In general, there is a willingness among both religious groups to engage in in-depth dialogue, discussing matters of serious substance. Most of the respondents had not looked to Muslims they associated with to get their perspective about Islam or about events related to Islam and violence. That is, the perspective that the respondents espouse is for the most part not shaped through dialogue with Muslims and a thoughtful engagement of their views.

The negative perspectives that the respondents have toward Muslims and Islam are shaped for the most part by the information presented on the media, most of which puts the spotlight on current events that focus on the violence associated with Islam. These negative perceptions are also shaped by American Christian leaders through what they say and write. The view that the respondents seem to have of Islam is that in general it is an evil religion, no different from the evil and violent characteristic that it espoused when it began in the 7th century CE, and that it will continue to be this way in the future, perhaps even become more evil and violent toward Christians and Americans. At the same time, individual Muslims the respondents had come to know in a variety of settings and on numerous levels seemed to be respectable human beings. That is, there is dissonance in the minds of the American evangelical respondents in terms of their extremely negative views of Islam on the one hand and positive views of Muslims on the other. There is also dissonance in their minds in that while they view Muslims as decent people, they are also suspicious of the motives and actions of Muslims. In some cases these conflicted perspectives were expressed by the same respondent.

Personal Reflection

It would be helpful at this juncture for you, the reader, to reflect on what your own perspectives, attitudes, and practices are toward Muslims and Islam as well as how they were formed and justified. To shed further light on this subject, I did a focus group study of American evangelical ministry leaders who engage Muslims in the US on a daily basis through their helps-based ministry. This study not only provided information about how individual evangelicals approach Islam but also how the ministry itself serves as a positive example for evangelical ministries and individual evangelicals in outreach to Muslims.

CHAPTER 7

ENGAGING MUSLIMS: A FOCUS GROUP STUDY OF COMM

The mission statement of Christian Outreach Ministry to Muslims (COMM) explains the purpose of the ministry as providing "a positive and active presence in the heart of their city's Little India neighborhood, proclaiming the uniqueness of Jesus Christ in word and deed."[4] As a friendship center and helps-based ministry, COMM is a church-supported organization that strives to create an inviting community-oriented atmosphere toward those who visit. This is reflected in the manner in which the leaders engage and talk to the visitors to their bookstore; the easy access to a wide variety of Christian books and pamphlets, Bibles, DVDs, Internet and faxing services; and the positive response from the community in availing themselves of the resources that COMM offers, especially weekly tutoring classes for students. COMM was established with the goal of providing a "platform" in the marketplace to reach recently arrived Hindu and Muslim immigrants from South Asia and seeking to meet their needs and help them get adjusted. It is an incarnational ministry whose raison d'être is to be a witness for Christ and share His love. I spent over two hours interviewing the nine ministry leaders in a group setting, asking questions to draw out their experience ministering to Muslims. Their responses to six questions I asked during the course of the interview are discussed in the first part of this chapter.

---

[4] The name and location of the ministry have been changed to protect respondents' anonymity.

COMM also has a ministry of apologetics in which a staff apologist defends the Christian faith regarding Islam. In order to protect the identity of the apologist, this ministry is not advertised. The COMM staff apologist and I spent almost 40 minutes talking about his experience with Muslims; his responses to the nine questions I asked him during the course of the interview are discussed in the second part of this chapter.

The COMM staff has between them a cumulative total of more than one hundred years of experience ministering to Muslims, overseas as well as in the US. They have much wisdom to offer about the practicalities of ministry to Muslims. In Chapter 10 I will offer some missiological recommendations for evangelicals, but as you read through this chapter, I would encourage you, the reader, to keep your eyes open for important lessons from the comments of the COMM leaders.

Interview Of COMM Staff Engaging In Helps-Based Ministry

Q1: If someone who is not familiar with COMM were to ask you why you are doing the things you do with Muslims here, what would you say?

Frank said that his answer is different when he is responding to someone from the Christian community as opposed to someone from the Muslim community. However, Luke said that his response is the same for both groups: "The whole purpose that we are here is to share the love of Christ, as we are called by God to do so. That's it." COMM, which came about because Christians were concerned for the newly arriving immigrants in the US and wanted to help them get adjusted, exists to meet the needs of the South Asian community, including Hindus and Muslims.

When COMM, "a church-supported facility," began this ministry, the leaders believed that historically the evangelical church had been slow in responding to the challenge of Islam and Muslims all over the globe. So, when COMM leaders started praying about this ministry 20 years ago, they wanted to have a "platform" in the marketplace, a presence, so that they could reach the Muslim population in this area. They began with the goal of establishing an incarnational ministry in which they would be completely open in their witness of Christ, in contrast to a similar ministry in another large metropolitan area that engaged Muslims with the gospel covertly. COMM wanted to make sure that when a Muslim walked into their bookstore, the gospel and other Christian resources would be easily accessible to them.

The founding director of COMM, a Christian man named Hassan, is originally from Pakistan. Despite the fact that his brother was killed by Muslims, Hassan felt sympathy for the plight of Muslim immigrants: "We feel that a lot of people who come here from our part of the world are out of their comfort zone; they are out of their countries; they are lonely; they are struggling; they sometimes have a hard time getting connected with the local Muslims, initially at least." COMM is able to offer them the "love and care" they do not always receive from mosques and other Islamic institutions. While they do receive "Qur'anic teaching" in these places, "the love of Christ is not there. So those were the reasons" for establishing COMM with the focus that it has.

One of the female leaders, Ruth, has been with the ministry since its inception. She noted that they begin with the premise that this is a Christian bookstore. They explain their purpose to Christians as serving the Lord by serving the community. To non-Christians, they explain that they offer "community-oriented services." COMM serves as a bookstore and provides Bibles and various pieces of literature in different languages, provides faxing and photocopy services to the community, offers English classes, and provides tutoring services for children. Ruth characterizes COMM as a "helps-based" ministry: "Depending on what the need of the community is, we will tailor it accordingly. But the bottom line is we are here to share Jesus Christ with people."

Q2: Are there biblical teachings and themes that are especially significant to the mission of COMM?

One theme that is core to this ministry is the conviction that there is no salvation in Islam and that Muslims are lost. From the start of their ministry the leadership team was convinced that Christ is "not part of Qur'an or Hadith," that Muslims need to come to faith in Christ the Savior in order to receive salvation, and that by bringing the gospel to Muslims they were fulfilling the mandate of the Great Commission given to them as a ministry by God.

Jake found Acts 17:26 to be "key." He explained that God has brought Hindus and Muslims to this country so that they may have the opportunity to find Christ and that God has placed their ministry in that area so that they can "share the gospel with Muslims and Hindus and whoever comes in the door." This is the ministry's "heartbeat." Another passage he considered key to their ministry is Acts 2. Just as God had brought people from every nation to Jerusalem during the feast of Pentecost so that they could hear "the gospel in their own language" and take the gospel back to their homeland, so also their hope is that some of these immigrants will "go back to their own lands and carry Christ and the gospel to their own people." "These are our strategies," asserted Jake.

Another biblical theme that is key to their ministry is prayer, which they call a "strategy." Susie remarked that the fact that they have "direct access to God through prayer" is especially welcomed by many women in the community who intentionally come in order to share their prayer requests. Having worked in Islamic communities for years, Jake asserts that Muslims "carry a lot of burdens" and have "longings and feelings that they can't share with others of their community because others will use it against them." The ministry leaders are in the habit of praying in the name of Jesus and doing so immediately when needs are presented. When God answers prayers such as obtaining US citizenship and passing tests, they are perceived as godly and spiritual people, and this makes them "acceptable" and "attractive" in the eyes of these Muslims.

Prayer has been an important value since the founding of the organization. Hassan noted that COMM began in the fall of 1997 in answer to "3 and a half years of concerted prayer" by numerous churches in this city. While many denominations have tried to establish ministry among Muslims and spent hundreds of thousands of dollars in their efforts to do so, they all failed. The leader concludes that "dollars do not reach Muslims. I think it's the servants who are passionate, who are burdened, who depend on the Lord."

At the start of this discussion, Hassan brought up various models of doing ministry among Muslims. While there were many efforts to reach Muslims by numerous denominations, the only ministry that had been established was located in another major metropolitan area in the United States. They desired to establish a "friendship center," but the only model that was available was the Arab-American Friendship Center in that town. After a few days of observing this ministry it quickly became apparent that although Muslims from a variety of ethnic and national backgrounds walked in, the Word of God was inaccessible to them. This observation convicted them to start a friendship center that would provide easy access to a bookstore with Bibles and other Christian literature in immigrants' mother tongues. In time this ministry has become a model for the Asian Friendship Center in East London and a similar ministry developing in New York City.

Roger explained a church-planting model including five steps: "survey, contact, evangelism, conversion, and discipleship." Surveying the community involves informally finding out through prayer and living in the community the kind of people who live in the neighborhood and the needs they have. They make contact with the people through various services— photocopying, English classes, tutoring, etc.—offered at COMM. This kind of contact creates opportunities to share the gospel "in a real and living way. And from that you would hope to have converts and eventually establish churches." This cycle keeps going as contact is made with new people and as the ministry leaders continually discover new things through their informal survey work.

Another way COMM serves the community is through an afterschool program offering children help with their homework on weekday evenings. The program begins with a brief discussion and explanation of a Bible verse and prayer. Children are encouraged to talk about the verse as they are doing their homework. On Fridays COMM runs an extended Bible club that involves learning a verse followed by an "object lesson, or a story, or a discussion" in order to "reinforce the verse and the biblical concept." Friday evening sessions end with singing. About this experience, Abby commented:

> So just for me, I've seen a lot of amazing things happen over the life of these kids. The majority of them are Muslims. Some of them are followers of Jesus and most of them are beginning to be very bold about it. In the beginning it was

kind of like hush-hush, but now they're beginning to be very bold about it. So my experience with Muslim kids is that we keep on lifting Jesus high, we keep opening God's Word. And God's Word is a lion, and so you just let it loose. And you see what it does. And it's been doing amazing things in their lives.

The afterschool program averages about 25 students on a daily basis, something that missionaries who have served in Pakistan for many years had not been able to accomplish. Hassan asserted: "We are not talking about one picnic here and one picnic, or a Christmas show, or an Easter play, or eid show, or whatever" but seeing consistent high numbers in attendance. Their work has been so well received that Susie asserted: "We have kids that have grown up from across the street bringing their nieces, or nephews, or their cousins, their little cousins here." With great excitement, Hassan pointed out that there is "longevity" to their ministry and they are planting seeds, all of which is evidence of "God's grace, and sovereignty, and his mercy," but that also speaks to the ministry's accessibility: "For people also to have accessibility to the place is very important."

During the summer COMM does not run the homework center but a three-day program that includes taking the kids to a park on Mondays, a field trip on Tuesdays, and activities involving arts and crafts on Wednesdays. The summer activities keep the kids who have worked on the homework as a group throughout the school year in contact with one another and interested, "and the conversation about Jesus keeps going."

COMM has also done outreach ministry among women, such as taking them on shopping trips. Because some of these women rarely are able to leave their homes, shopping becomes a significant activity and is a great opportunity to develop relationships. Other community outreach activities include picnics and an annual block party.

I followed up by stating that Islamic, Indian, and Pakistani cultures all tend to be conservative. I asked about their experience reaching out to women and how it compared with their outreaches to men. Agreeing that it is a lot easier to work with women, the leaders mentioned numerous ways in which they reach out to them. First, they simply pray for them because, as Susie pointed out, "There are always needs and there are always things to pray about. So, that opens up the conversation very, very easily." They also connect with women through ESL classes and monthly luncheons, which create opportunities to get to know the women and their problems, pray for them, and find other ways to help them. They help network the women with other organizations, such as Battered Women, that are able to "bring the help that's needed." For example, Ruth recounted a story of a young Pakistani woman attending their ESL class who came to them for their help because her husband was living with "another white woman." Her husband decided to take her back to Pakistan on a vacation. When her ESL teacher heard her story, she realized that something was not right, so before she left, the leaders at COMM "took pictures of her green card, her passport, her ticket, everything." Ten days later, recounted Ruth, she got a call from the young woman saying that her husband had divorced her and had stolen all her documentation, and there was no way for her to get back. The girl had been married at 15, had come to the US at 17, and had been divorced not long after that but did not want to stay in Pakistan. Having photographed her documentation, the leaders at COMM were able to help her get back into the US. After she returned to the US, she did not want to go back to her husband, so COMM helped her get a court order of protection. In fact, Ruth remarked that she has had to help several battered women by taking them to organizations that provide legal help for them. On the basis of their abuse, some of them have been able to obtain green cards.

Before 9/11 they assisted women, many of whom were undocumented, in many other ways, such as helping them find doctors, pro bono lawyers, free clinics, etc. Ruth remarked: "So, [we] actually used to make home visitations with a doctor, a nurse, and a physical therapist, and I was the translator." After 9/11 things have changed a lot because many of these people with whom leaders at COMM developed strong relationships have been deported. But their hope is that because the gospel has been demonstrated in their lives very clearly, "the Spirit of God that makes it real to them and ... God who makes it fruitful in their lives ... will send somebody else alongside to finish the work that we began." The women leaders strive to share the gospel in every relationship that they develop, and one very powerful way of doing this is by sharing their testimonies and what God means to them. Ruth remarked, "I do not believe in belittling Islam or belittling anybody's religion to raise Jesus. He's already up here. But we can always talk about what God means to us, what He's done in our lives. And that is amazing. And as you share the gospel and you also live the gospel, people are impacted."

At other times Ruth has "gone to the police station with some of the women whose children have been caught stealing and who are afraid to go." And she has also supported them by going to court with them. Sometimes she has met with the school board of education to intervene on their behalf when there has been a problem. Being there to help them when these needs arise helps develop friendships and strengthen relationships, all of which helps develop a level of trust among them. Ruth remarked, "So that makes a huge, huge, huge difference. We become friends."

In addition to the several ways in which they meet the physical needs of people who come into COMM for help and through that share the gospel with them, they also engage in street evangelism. Frank described how they have several teams comprised of students from a local Christian college who "work from 1 to 3 every week to interact with people on the street and proclaim Christ in more traditional and assertive ways." Some people on these teams are also able to go into people's homes and develop relationship with them, "looking for opportunities to gracefully share the gospel." Some Christians have even moved into the neighborhood in order to be "the yeast of the kingdom of heaven here within this dominion of darkness."

Another aspect of this ministry that is very attractive to the visitors is that many of the COMM leaders have been to India and Pakistan and are able to connect with the visitors by talking about the cities they have visited. Because of their sojourn, they are familiar with the culture as well as the language. So, when somebody walks in, Luke greets them with "Kya haal hain aapka?" ["How are you?]" and "Kya aap chai piyenge?" ["Will you drink tea?"]. Speaking Urdu, Hassan remarked, establishes a connection that diminishes "intensity" or "hesitation" on the part of the visitors, engenders trust, and enables them all to "open up" much more quickly.

Luke reflected that Jesus was a person who was "acquainted with grief and sorrow." "Sadness, loneliness, loss of love, grief, sorrow"—these are universal experiences. People who come to COMM understand the language of suffering. Because the ministry staff can relate to these experiences, the people who come to COMM know "they are safe from someone seeing them talking to a Christian ... who is trying to convert them..." Relating to the people in this way allows these leaders "to share the real and meek Jesus Christ."

Q3: From the various activities you do to engage Muslims, which are the ones you enjoy the most? Why? Which activities are the most challenging or difficult? Why?

Abby began by explaining that all areas of ministry that she is involved in, including working with children and "ladies stuff" in evangelism, are enjoyable but also have their challenges, which is "normal" and to be "expected." It is a joy to engage in this work because they are doing it for Jesus, and God gives them the grace to come out of the challenges in a "triumphant" manner.

When I mentioned that Islam poses some theological challenges, e.g., its contention that God cannot become a human being, and asked whether they face opposition from this perspective, Ruth responded by sharing an encounter. A woman in the community, desiring to bring her children to COMM's homework center, befriended the leaders. When some of the people in her community told her not to do this because this was a Christian place, she stood up for COMM and responded, "No, they're good people. I will not send my children anywhere but there." The leaders at COMM have come to realize that women in the Muslim community "don't care what the mosque or their husbands" are saying. When they are at COMM, they are unconcerned about the teaching because they know that the leaders at COMM care for their children, pray for them and have their prayers answered, understand their culture, and are not "pushy" but also "not afraid to talk about reading the Bible." Even when COMM staff members have encountered women that they don't know very well and who try to tell them "how wonderful Islam is," when these women get close to the leaders, these types of comments diminish and their relationships with these women become "more real." "We have favor with the vast majority of the Muslim women," remarked Sarah.

But they have also had occasional "run-ins." On one occasion Sarah was taking 25 children on a field trip. While she was waiting with the children in front of COMM, a mullah walked up to her and said, "I know what you're doing. You're converting these children." The children did not know him, even though they were Muslim. He proceeded to grab the children, two boys in particular, and started dragging them down the street, saying, "I'm taking you. You cannot be here. They're trying to convert you." Sarah started yelling at him, and several cab drivers stopped and started yelling. She went into the COMM office and Frank came out and calmed the situation down, and then some of the male leaders went to the mosque and informed them that "this is not acceptable."

On another occasion two "totally veiled women," one of whom was accompanied by a 10-year-old boy, approached Ruth and said they had a problem. Unable to find a room inside COMM to have a conversation because all the rooms were occupied by male missionaries, they decided to sit on a bench outside to talk. A Muslim man driving by in a car recognized the boy and told the women, "Don't you know that these people here first give you the Book, and then they convert you?" Then he ordered them to take the boy away. The women ran away in great fear. When Ruth said to him, "Excuse me!," he responded, "You shut up, woman, and you don't interfere! This is none of your business!"

Frank indicated these were earlier experiences but not common anymore because COMM has become established and belongs there. People in the community have come to realize that they're there for the long-term, that they "love them and care for their children." Even though there are people at the mosque who do not like them, COMM has come to be accepted as part of the community.

Hassan explained that it took about "ten years or so" to come to this point. There were a number of factors that contributed to this. The ministry leaders were intentional about speaking on behalf of COMM and promoting its ministry. They also attended many of the Muslims' own programs such as Mushaira, a poetry recitation at the Holiday Inn, or the program organized by and for the Pakistani community leaders honoring a Muslim journalist, which calmed their fears and made them realize, especially after 9/11, that COMM leaders are not "bad people" but genuinely caring and helpful. Many of the Muslim women who have been served by COMM and have had their kids taken care of have been able to "calm their husbands down."

The ministry leaders realize that even though "there is a segment of Muslims [who] will never accept" them, they are unwilling to "water down the gospel or tone it down" in order to be accepted. There are major theological differences, but compromise on ontological and missiological issues is not an option. They have consistently and boldly shared Christ, prayed for "active conversion," and have seen Muslims "come to Christ." Some of these Muslim converts have been baptized, while others have gone back to Islam. From their perspective, "if there is no opposition, there is no ministry." Hassan explained that for them there is no new methodology for doing mission among Muslims in the 21st century that is devoid of "pain and persecution." He asserts, "So, in Muslim evangelism you confront them with the love of Christ, but you also have to be bold. And I think by God's grace we have stood firm. And we have received respect." In fact, two of their leaders were also recommended by the Muslims in the community "to receive mayor of Chicago's honor award." COMM has made sure that whenever they had a community function, Christ was presented boldly and openly. For example, said Hassan, at the New Year's Milan Party (milan is the coming together or gathering of people) where there were approximately 500 Hindus, Muslims, and Sikhs present, COMM leaders had set up a book table and presented the gospel through various forms of literature, including Jesus DVDs. In fact, COMM had passed out so many Jesus DVDs that for some time to come over the next few years many Muslims would remark that whichever Muslim home they went to, there were Jesus DVDs to be found. There have been other groups as well who have come and passed out these DVDs and evangelized on special occasions, such as on Pakistani Independence Day.

Another incident happened when a "small but very strong minority of Muslims" refused to rent out building space for COMM's ministry. Their previous landlord refused to renew the lease, saying, "No, I am having dreams and visions, and one day I have to stand before Allah, and what will I say?" Being refused by several landlords was a "wake-up call" for COMM: "They own almost all the buildings on this street," which is a "tension" that "kept us on our knees, and that's why we ask people to continue to bathe this ministry in prayer." Roger remarked: "Thank God for the Hindu landlords" who are willing to rent them building space.

After this I asked a couple of sensitive questions in relation to recent events such as 9/11 and the Boston Marathon bombings that had taken place just a few days before this interview. I remarked that, as a person of Indian heritage myself, when I heard the bomb was made out of a pressure cooker, I thought, "Oh, gosh, Indians, Pakistanis, we use pressure cookers. One of us." To this remark Hassan quickly responded by saying, "Well, to be a little bit more fair, I thought it's not one of us. Maybe Kashmiris." I mentioned that the news media thought that they might be "Chechens, and they connected that with Islam very quickly." Frank added, "Or, Muslims." In light of these events, I asked what their opinions were about Muslims and Islam. Their opinions differed considerably.

Luke openly shared that there was a time when he hated Muslims with great passion. Now he does not hate Muslims but still hates Islam. He saw Muslims as "victims of a lie" and not as "internship projects or short-term projects" but as people who are lost and who deserve to know the gospel just like us.

Roger's opinions were influenced by his experience serving as a missionary in Pakistan and working among Muslims in America. He asserted that most Muslims in Pakistan "are pretty good people," but a few were radicalized enough that "you had something to fear from them as a Christian or even just as a foreigner." Muslims living in America, asserted Roger, are just normal people trying to get a job or trying to make a living, but they are part of the system of Islam, which in its very nature tries to change "other cultures so that they all become Islamic and everyone is forced into Islam." For this reason the average American is confused because they think that all Muslims are attempting to "turn America" and make it part of the Islamic world. Yet the Muslims that he knows are simply trying to go to school, drive a taxi, visit the hospital, etc., and are not "affecting America in a bad way." On the other hand, Islam as a system has been established, and it has its effect, eventually forcing people to give in to Islam. This is very severe in Pakistan where "Christians have fewer and fewer rights." While Christians in Pakistan are under a lot of pressure and have a lot to fear from Muslims, "the average Muslim you meet in America is just a good guy trying to make a living."

Another leader, Jake, who has also served as a missionary in Pakistan, asserted that Muslims in America have a long-term agenda. One Muslim in America said to him, "You're a Christian, but your grandkids will be Muslims. Your grandchildren, your posterity will be

Muslim. We have a long-range perspective here in America." Jake asserted that the Muslims living here—"those who are involved, actually involved in jihad, which here is a passive jihad, for the most part"—are quite happy with the way things are progressing in America. These Muslims are trying to present Islam in a positive way and do not want incidents such as the ones I mentioned above because that disrupts their agenda of becoming increasingly acceptable and coming to a place where they can influence the society. They have already made "a lot of inroads, politically and otherwise, as we all know. Five of the cabinet members of [Obama's] administration are Muslim ... [and have] ties to the Islamic Brotherhood." Jake observed, even though we do not see "active opposition," there are those who are engaged in "passive opposition." Some Muslims "hate us," and some "walk by our window and curse us." Regarding this hate, Hassan added, "We can see it in their eyes." Jake also expressed the same perception of seeing the hate in their eyes. He also said some of them would hold up an "open hand" toward another person as a symbolic gesture of a curse. He also agreed that the Muslims are victims of the satanic system of Islam. The COMM leaders "pray against and seek to deliver souls" from the system. They too have a long-term vision. They are sowing the seeds of the gospel. Jake remarked that although they have not seen much of a harvest yet, they are convinced that "God will bring about a harvest" if they continue to sow patiently, "watering and cultivating by our attitudes, by our willingness to be available to help, to give of our time and our leisure to go and help someone with their problems."

Abby added that Saudi Arabia is a rich country that provides a lot of funding. They are "very united, and they have this brotherhood" that has the goal of taking over America. "And they're doing it. They move into a neighborhood and they take over the neighborhood. It's happened in Minnesota and in Dearborn, Michigan." She recounted the story of her friend who had converted out of Islam and had become a Christian. This convert's brothers call her on a weekly basis to intimidate her and tell her that "Islam is going to take over America before your eyes." When she responds by saying, "Well, let's see what happens according to Scripture... I know that Jesus is the King of Kings," they assert that "Minnesota is already a Muslim state." Abby warned that Muslims have an agenda, they have finances, and they are ready, and this is a "wake-up time for us. We cannot shrink back." Susie was of the opinion that Muslims are "always permeating everything." When they "buy something," such as property for a mosque, they would never sell it to anyone else, and it will "always stay in Muslim hands." This concept is foreign to Westerners, Susie added. While we as Americans sell to each other, Muslims do not. This is just one of the ways in which they are taking over, "they're claiming land." Jake agreed, asserting, "they love to buy churches." Adds Susie: "Once they claim it, they're not going to give it up. It is now in Muslim hands"—a concept that needs to be communicated to "Western churches" because they do not "really get that."

In response to the question, "If you had the chance to tell the American church something about Islam or Muslims, what would you say?" Hassan had a two-part response. First, he commented that many evangelicals are scared and have allowed "Islamophobia to take them down, to depress them, to scare them." This fear "is a wonderful weapon of the enemy" because it makes us complacent. Because evangelicals are resigning in defeat, "our own people are now becoming a danger. We are pretending that somehow this is going to go away. [But] they're not going to go away. The majority of the refugees who come to this country are Muslims." Part of the problem, according to Hassan, is that while initially the American church is very interested in learning about Islam and Muslims, their fear paralyzes them. He added: "Our reaction is that disengagement from Muslims and Islam is not an option. If we want to live in this country and if we want to practice our faith, we have to engage with these people from a sociological perspective."

He highlighted some concrete steps that American evangelicals must take through the following questions: "Will you start praying for us [COMM]? Will you come alongside us? Will you help us to do more outreaches?" Second, and more importantly, is the "biblical perspective." Muslims are "lost people who desperately need God. And once they find Christ, things can change [and] will change."

I pressed for more information about the leaders' thoughts and perspectives regarding Islam or Muslims. Jake asserted that while people claim "that Islam is a religion of peace, it's not." The other interviewees vocalized their agreement. Jake continued, "We all understand that and we need to continue to communicate that," but "we never want to communicate a feeling of fear from Muslims, or resentment, or hatred of them. We want people to understand and have a compassion for Muslims. That's very important."

Roger echoed this sentiment by saying that they wanted people who were supporting and praying for them to develop relationships with Muslims where they could say to them "face to face, 'let's talk together, how are your kids, come to my house, let's eat vegetables and anything halal, and, yeah, let's talk.'" Fear will only make you "cut yourself off" from Muslims. What American evangelicals need is a willingness to reach out to them, to realize that it's possible to learn to become "able to meet a guy at a gas station, and give him a Jesus video, and have a conversation." Jake said that it was very important that they were a resource center and were able and willing to provide DVDs and literature, teaching about Islam, and encouragement to overcome their "fear of offending" and take the initiative to reach out to Muslims. He said that "you will not offend, the gospel may offend them," and that they should let the Holy Spirit use them to "put the Word of God, the seed of God's Word into Muslim hands that will reach their heart." After this I brought the dialogue back to the claim of Muslims that Islam was a religion of peace and asked them to talk more about this theme. Hassan responded by saying that this claim is "packaged and presented in the West." He asserted that there is not a single Muslim country where there is this "so-called" peace. "From Egypt to Indonesia, where is peace?" Islam talks about human rights and championing women's rights, but they do not exist, and women are not treated equally. "In the heart of Islam, Saudi Arabia, the bastion of Islam, there is not a single open church or house of worship. People are kicked out, deported, abused, punished." This discussion about peace happens "among the American audience." In Pakistan the subject is not even brought up because "they are ashamed of their religion, all of their country, because they know ... it's a blatant lie." And "we can show them it's a lie," added Jake. Hassan agreed: "This whole notion of peace and all those things, it is basically baloney."

Hassan continued, "From the very beginning, the foundation is a headache." In his view, violence is a part of Islam, and if you read the Qur'an through, which they claim to be "Allah's revelation" or "divine revelation, you will find verses that teach this." He also asked a series of questions: "In what country? Where is this so-called democracy? Where are human rights? Where is the protection of minorities?" Christians are "second-class citizens ... in many Muslim countries." They "do not have equal rights, are discriminated [against], don't have jobs." Having said this, he asserted that we need to love the Muslims, who are in bondage to the teaching of the Qur'an, and we need to love them without being naïve about Islam. The lesson for American churches is that while God can appear to Muslims in dreams and visions—which He is doing in many parts of the world—we need to love them and care for them unconditionally if we expect them to respond.

Jake added that the peace Muslims are talking about is the "peace when the whole world is submitted to Allah, and there is no religion but the religion of Allah." Others quickly echoed the significance of "submission." Jake continued: When Muslims claim, "'oh, salaam [Islam] means peace,' it doesn't. It means submission." He shared that in his experience, many come to COMM and gladly receive their practical services, yet at the same time some Muslims despise them. Part of Islamic teaching is to take and use the resources of the kafir [unbeliever]. Hassan had overheard Muslims saying, "Looto unko. Looto. Looto. Kafir hain." ["Rob them. Rob. Rob. They are unbelievers."] Hassan remarked wryly, "I was being blessed with curses." While all of this is "very much part of our community" "under the radar," they love them in spite of it and are willing to share what they have. This led Jake to say that "they're totally disgusted with the fact that we don't fit that stereotype of" hating the Muslims for their behavior. "They want to hate us, but they can't."

Frank pointed out the "false dichotomy" that exists among American evangelicalism": "Either Islam is evil, Muslims are scary, I have to keep them at arm's length because they're out to destroy us. Or, Islam is a religion of peace. Isn't that nice and wonderful?" To this a number of the leaders said, "[Muslims] are just like us." Referring to Matthew 9:36, Frank asserted that just as in his context Jesus was moved with compassion for the people and healed them of their diseases, interacted with those leaders who exhibited "false legalisms," sent the disciples to cast out demons, so also "we have that same thing with Muslims. They're sick and in need of healing and spiritual healing as well. They are under oppression of religious legalisms, of law that's not from God." And we who have the "Spirit of God" in us "should be beating in our chests for Muslims today in our neighborhoods and our workplaces."

After this I asked them how their perspectives on Islam and Muslims had changed after 9/11 and the Boston Marathon bombings. Sarah shared her experience before and after 9/11. She and two other women leaders had many Muslim friends before 9/11, women who were totally veiled in burkas. After 9/11 she was walking on the street and really feeling the shock of the event as a "red-white-and-blue blood" American. She visited a Muslim woman and remembers thinking that they did not "want people to unfairly harass them." But, at the same time, she came to realize that the Muslim woman was part of a larger community and the larger system of Islam. If they were living in a different country and were in a different setting, she would throw her under the bus, in spite of the fact that they were good friends. These leaders have come to realize that "the vast majority of Muslims would choose Islam" over them. And they may do it "apologizing, 'I'm sorry, please forgive me,' but they would still do it." They are more faithful and loyal to Islam, and it is Islam that people need to be afraid of, not terrorism.

Frank recounted a similar story. About a couple of years ago he ran into a Muslim man that he knew from the Islamic Community Center (ICC). As they sat down and talked, they were both "very nice, and cordial, and friendly toward each other," but at one point in the midst of this nice conversation he said, "Make no mistake, Frank. When the real jihad thing comes down, I'm coming after you first." And this comment was made "after years of relationship" and after hosting Frank's groups at the ICC for years. Frank commented: "It's not all [about] wonderful, good relationships."

Susie warned that we need to be concerned about Islam, "even if they're peaceful." In her opinion the problem is not just with a particular subset of extremists, but "it's Islam. It's their system. It's that group that people need to worry about." Along these lines Ruth shared a remark made by a Muslim: "One of our friends told us while she was in Pakistan after 9/11: 'Oh, we will take your Sears Tower too.'"

Luke described some significant lessons he learned while living with a Palestinian Muslim family for three months. The Palestinian man described himself as a radical, "a fundamentalist." Luke responded by saying, "I'm a crusader." He said among the different types of Muslims he has met, none of them "have ... respect for sheepish, wimpy Christians who hide their Bible or cover it up: 'Oh, well, let me hide my Bible. I don't want to offend anyone. I don't want to show anyone that I read the Scriptures' ... and all of this." This kind of behavior turns them off, and it indicates to them that you are "not sincere about your faith," and at the same time "you're trying to sell them something that you're not sincere about." What is needed are Christians who will be direct in their proclamation. In our engagement with Muslims, Christians are "going to be attacked," which may lead some to become "too protective" of themselves: "I don't want to put myself out there and, you know, they'll hate me, and this and that." Yes, we will be hated because Jesus said that we would be hated for his namesake, asserted Luke. But if Christians do not share the gospel with Muslims "for the sake of getting along," what kind of friends are we being to Muslims and how much do we "really love them?" asked Luke. Jake added that even though many Muslims reject the message, there are many who come in, and the COMM leaders pray and take small steps toward sharing the gospel with them openly: "A little bit more, open the Word, give them a verse, or whatever, and share the gospel." There is a tension in all of this and "they bristle." The Christian leaders know them as individuals and respect the fact that they do not want to hear, but they also urge them by telling them that this is for them and that they should consider it and then "come back and talk." The Christians do whatever they can to encourage them to take the Gospel. For example, if someone's car breaks down in the middle of winter and they cannot get it started, or they have a flat tire, the Christian leaders are "right there" to help them. In fact, on one occasion a Muslim had his car tires slashed at the hands of an enemy, and Jake called up his own tow truck service to help. Jake noted these small gestures are meaningful: "We're sowing seed for future reference in these people when we do things they would never do."

Sometimes Muslims accused these Christian leaders of trying to convert Muslims. On one occasion a hostile Muslim came and started inquiring what COMM was. After a brief exchange Luke asserted that this is not a Christian place but that they are Christians who are there to "share the love of Christ with the community." When the Muslim man asked if they convert Muslims, Luke responded by asking two questions: "Who moves your heart, God or man?" and he responded by saying, "Allah"; and "Who sees your heart, God or man?" and again he responded by saying, "Allah." Luke then asked why the Muslim man was afraid, if he knew that only Allah has power to "move" and "see" a human being's heart. After responding that there are too many people there and that he was confused, the Muslim man left. Luke summarized this exchange by asserting that they are not able to convert anyone, only God can.

Q4: From your perspective, what are some indications that the ministry of COMM has been successful?

Susie observed that Muslims keep coming back to COMM in spite of the attitudes of the people and other places where they could go to learn English. They tell them that they come there because the leaders at COMM are "better" and "love them better": "You love us here, we're safer here." Another reason Muslims keep coming back is to ask for prayer. For example, women in their ESL classes have asked for prayer for healing for themselves and their family members, or because their kids are having problems, or to receive prayers for US citizenship interviews. On one occasion, when some leaders were visiting a Muslim family at home, they prayed for blessing for their house and household, and the next day the Muslim family said their prayers were answered because they were able to get a bed for their home. "They think that prayers in the name of Jesus are effective," remarked Susie.

Luke believed COMM has planted lots of seeds, some of which "have grown," and others are "in the process of growing." At the same time he asserted that Muslims "are also a gift and a blessing" to them. He considers his ministry a privilege because Christians "serve a unique God and this is a unique place with a unique purpose." COMM leaders also see signs that they interpret as God working in Muslims' hearts. For example, "another Muslim boy had a dream last night about Jesus," according to Abby. Another leader sees progress in the fact that "people are responding." Frank said that what keeps him working is "to see a Muslim get it," to see their prayers answered and that the Muslims know that "it was prayer in Jesus' name." This "is success enough to keep us going."

Hassan vehemently protested that the question was a "classic example of a Western way of measuring success." He asserted that he did not look at success "from a secular perspective of numbers." They had been faithful to their "calling and commitment from the very beginning," and the success of the ministry was that their small group of people had been allowed by the Lord to minister and reside in the community for approximately fifteen years. From Hassan's perspective, success was "God in his own sovereignty" bringing children to COMM so that they could serve them on a daily basis: "I ask this question to my

American friends, 'Will you send your daughter or son to a Muslim friendship center for tutoring?' 'No, we cannot do that.' 'Well, then why do we expect them to send their kids to a Christian friendship center?'" But there is a waiting list for children to get into COMM. Again Hassan repeated, "all the glory goes to God" because God in his sovereignty "has had mercy upon us in our small efforts that these kids come, these women come, these men come, our prayers are answered."

Even though to Hassan "'success' from a human worldly perspective is a foolish term to use for Christian ministry," they do evaluate their ministry, write reports, and do a self- evaluation during the monthly meetings to see if there is anything that they need to "tweak" because of increased opposition. COMM has gone through different seasons and has had to make changes in their women's ministry, which Frank expanded upon later. COMM leaders started taking women on shopping trips to the mall after learning that Muslim husbands kept them "imprisoned" at home to protect them from the "wicked society" around them. Once the COMM leaders helped these Muslim women "establish a modicum of freedom" and develop friendships with other Muslim women, the need to take these mall trips no longer existed. Presently COMM hosts monthly potluck lunches for the Muslim women. Their children's ministry has also evolved, moving from weekly "kids club" to a daily tutoring center; the Sunday afternoon church service that was contextualized for both Hindus and Muslims has evolved into a daily morning prayer service, and Sunday morning church service contextualized just for Hindu seekers, and a Friday evening service contextualized for Muslim seekers. However, the latter has since ceased completely because they were unable to draw Muslims to these meetings.

COMM also has a strong Internet presence. The website Answering Islam (http://answering-islam.org) is an apologetics website with a global reach. Mansur Murad, the website administrator, was trained by Vern Rock, a former missionary to Pakistan who is now deceased. This apologist uses the Internet to train people "from here to India," affecting many people who they are not even aware of. Hassan recounted an incident that occurred several years ago, in which an American woman married to a Saudi and living in Saudi Arabia was searching the Internet to "find dirt on Christianity" and found her way to Answering Islam. Upon reading the articles posted on the website, she came to believe in Christ. She began communicating with the leaders at COMM and said, "Oh, I'm convinced, I want to follow Christ. But my problem is this: I'm married to a Saudi, I'm in Saudi Arabia. If I tell him now, that's the end." She moved from Saudi Arabia to Ohio and "gently" told her husband that she had become a follower of Christ. Upon hearing this, her husband divorced her, but the Internet-based apologist at COMM was able to continue discipling her in the Christian faith. After telling this story, Hassan said that success is that those who have come to know the Lord continue to serve him. He noted that COMM personnel have invested "hundreds of hours in the lives of our young people from three Christian colleges," many of whom are now serving in Central and South Asia and around the world. Hassan referred to these young Christian leaders as "fruits of our labor." Luke approached the question of success by describing what failure would look like: "Failure would be if we are seen in Christ's place, if all the glory would not go to Christ. That would be failure. We should be invisible." COMM leaders are convinced that only God can change lives and bring salvation, that by themselves they are not able to convert a Muslim or Hindu: "That's the work of the Holy Spirit," said Jake. God has called them to sow the seeds by getting out his word so that the Holy Spirit can use that in that person's life. They see themselves as farmers and realize that the crops do not grow in one day. Similarly, faith is a long process, and they are there to be involved in the process, trusting that the Lord will bring salvation in the lives of whomever he chooses. Jake noted this is God's work and in his grace he uses them: "All He asks us is to be faithful in sharing with those He brings to us and those He sends us out to."

Hassan explained that in many "creative access countries" such as Pakistan, missionaries are starting to pull out because the situation is getting hard. Some missionaries are "house-arrested"—not allowed to move about freely without a police permit. Even though Muslims will not kill them, they are targeted and reported to the police. But God is bringing some of those people here to the US, and in his grace he has allowed COMM "to remain in this neighborhood despite of the opposition and their bitterness." Some Muslims in their community hate COMM, but there are also many who love it. Even though there are other places, such as the Indian-American Foundation (a pseudonym) or Mercy Center (a pseudonym) less than two miles from COMM, Muslims bring the children to this group knowing that they are Christian. "That means what they're getting here they cannot get from the state-funded Muslim centers," asserted Hassan. In fact, some organizations such as the Muslim Community Resource Center (a pseudonym) have closed down "because they cannot offer anything that we offer, even though they get funded by the state. Money is not an issue for them, but no one volunteers. Who is going to work there?" In the leaders' view, God has always provided the resources for COMM to operate.

Q5: As you have engaged Muslims over the years, have you found that your perceptions of Islam or of Muslims have changed? In what ways? Why?

Jake had lived among Muslims in Pakistan and faced persecution nearly to the point of death at times. He indicated that seeing the things that have happened in America deeply hurt him. Having served in Vietnam, he said that he would give his life for this country and that his attitudes toward Muslims were a "continuous struggle" for him. When he sees a male Muslim with a beard and traditional clothing or a veiled Muslim woman, he has to stop himself and "willfully stop and pray for them" in order to keep himself from becoming bitter. He has come to realize that it is easy for him to become bitter. Jake asserted:

> We all have the tendency: the more you know, the more you understand, the more you see the deception, the more you know Muslims who are suffering under Islam, and the more you understand what they would love to do to us as an enemy, the tendency is to become more bitter. It doesn't go the other way. The more you know, the tendency is to become more resentful.

"You've got to guard your heart" constantly, asserted Susie, to the agreement of Jake. Pointing to Hassan, Jake reminded me that his brother was murdered by Muslims, which naturally has created a struggle with bitterness. Yet this struggle is not limited to such an extreme circumstance. Instead, "We all do. We struggle."

Hassan explained that the only way to overcome this tendency is by daily surrendering to the Lord at his throne of grace and pleading with him on a daily basis for "grace for each day." Otherwise a person can harbor such a deep, strong, and bitter hostility that it is impossible to love from a human perspective. They are able to love because the grace of God enables them, and you have to go back to Him constantly for that grace, especially when you have to "pray for your enemy," which is not easy to do. He added that in the churches in the West persecution has been romanticized and "we have a tendency to glamorize martyrdom." But Hassan commented that if you were to ask a person "who has lost his or her loved ones," they will tell you that it is like getting your arm amputated, which heals, "but it's a constant, daily reminder till you die that you've lost someone. And that gap never fills." It is only by the grace of God that a person can go on daily. The death of his brother changed his perception in that it made him more zealous about preaching the gospel, globally as well as in this country. It also reminded him of the brevity of life. Hassan's brother was standing near him when he was shot and killed, and this reminds him of the "urgency" to sow the seed of the gospel. His prayer is that no one "goes through this gift of martyrdom" because it is difficult and "very painful," but as a result of it they are all "dedicated."

Hassan continued that when they wake up in the morning, they have to ask the Lord to help them because "it is not easy to love a person who hates you. The hate is in their eyes. We pray, 'Lord, open their blind eyes,'" knowing that the gospel will set them free from the "bondage and the oppression." Hassan added that these people are in a dark place and extremely desperate, otherwise how does a person "kill like this?" Ruth asserted that no matter how difficult, it is important to remember that Jesus died for each one of us, that we are undeserving, and that he extends the same grace to every person. There is no choice but to love Muslims. When problems arise, "you draw on the Lord" and say to him, 'Give me your heart.'" Ruth says that regardless of their perceptions, they try to continue being "intentional in reaching out."

Q6: Based on your experience of engaging Muslims through COMM, if you had the opportunity to share with American evangelicals about Islam and Muslims, what would you say? What do you wish they knew about Muslims and/or Islam?

Hassan responded that there were two lessons American evangelicals need to keep in mind. First, having a "biblical foundation is crucial in loving Muslims." This foundation includes recognizing that "they are lost" and need Christ and that "the Word of God calls us, enables us, equips us, trains us, and keeps us going in Muslim ministry." There is no "sleek methodology" that has been developed by American missiologists that can take the place of this. Second, American evangelicals should not accept defeat in the face of Islam. History has shown that "whenever and wherever the church has taken the second place, evil has grown." For example, Dr. Erwin Lutzer, in his 2013 book The Cross in the Shadow of the Crescent, reflects upon the pre-war churches in Germany and America. When the church in Germany remained silent, Hitler came to power. The American church needs to wake up from its sleep, otherwise there will be "drastic consequences." Lutzer is not "promoting Islamophobia" but calling upon American evangelicals to love Muslims with the "love of Christ." The church in America needs to wake up and "march on in grace, and mercy, and forgiveness." The answer does not lie in an attitude described by Frank as "cuddly, cuddly, well, let's co-exist together" but in presenting Christ and the "message of cross." "We present it, and people still come, by God's grace," asserts Hassan.

According to Frank, a good portion of the evangelical church has bought into the whole idea that Islam and Muslims are evil, that they are our enemies, and that they are out to get us. While it is true that "Islam is evil," American evangelicals need to keep in mind that Muslims are "just people," who are "in bondage to sin and to Islam."

American evangelicals should not be afraid of Muslims or "hold them at arm's length" but should boldly engage them in dialogue without, in Sarah's words, the "fear of offending" them.

Jake noted that some American evangelicals labor under a "fear of being labeled intolerant." But what is intolerant, asserted Jake, "is to sit back and do nothing, keep your mouth shut while these people are in bondage and going to hell right before our eyes." Many Muslims have the stereotype that Christians are weak; there is "nothing there," they are "secular, hollow, empty, no prayer, no relationship to their Creator." American evangelicals need to break that stereotype and show Muslims that they "really love God ... and are willing, in kindness and love, [to] present that to Muslims."

Hassan gave the example of a student in a Christian college who, after returning from Jordan, felt that she needed to hang out with students at the Muslim Student Association's chai room at a university in the area. She befriended many women from Saudi Arabia and developed relationships with them over the course of a year. Now they have requested to study the Bible, with no precondition that "you study the Qur'an and we will study the Bible." Hassan firmly believes that these women will not remain Muslim but will come to faith in Christ. He also encouraged another Christian student to go to the Somali restaurant across the street from the gym where he works out and talk to the Muslims there. According to him, these Christian college students are a "microcosm" of the American church. It does not even occur to them that they could go to restaurants like these "to just grab a cup of tea"—they would rather spend money in Christian coffee shops than go there. The student responded, "I never even thought about it." Another student said, "Oh, I don't want to offend them," to which Hassan said, "You're not going to offend them. Go and talk to them." After trying this, the student went back to do it again. "Once you start talking, things change. When you don't talk, walls are created." Susie added, "It's OK to make mistakes in front of them as long as you are sensitive, and open, and sharing yourself. Just do it! Just go! Say hi. Don't ignore them. Don't be afraid."

Abby remarked, the idea here is to work on building the relationship and trust, and "then they're going to start asking you questions." Muslims are searching for the truth, and we should not be afraid of presenting the truth to them but be willing to open God's word, which is "alive, and it goes deep." Muslims have questions they want to ask about Christianity but have no one who they can trust and talk to. If we establish trust and answer their questions, "we clear those misconceptions. And then the veil is removed, and then before we know it, they are a follower of Jesus. And after a few months they're being bold about it."

Jake explained that Muslims who have been educated in mosques think they know Christianity and that they know "about the Bible." They have "been told a lot of things," but much of what they have been told is lies, and Christians need to show them that the things they have been taught are in error. Jake's approach starts with the Old Testament. He tells them to read Isaiah 53 and asks them to tell him who it is about. "Every Muslim I've ever asked, with very few exceptions, will say that's Jesus." He then tells them that this was written "700 years before Christ died." He asks them a series of questions, such as "Here, what does it say about the one you say is Messiah? What does it say that He will do?" They go through the text "step by step, verse by verse." This draws the Muslims in, and they are fascinated because they have never heard this before, and they have never seen that "what God foretells has come about, what was foretold by the prophets has come about in and through Christ." This is contradictory to what they have been taught, for example "that He actually did die." Sometimes he goes to other passages, such as Psalm 2 or Isa 9:6, to show Muslims that Jesus is the Son of God. Any Christian who is familiar with the Scriptures "should be able to do that," asserts the leader. "Show them Jesus from the Old Testament." This breaks stereotypes, confuses them, and gets past the armor that they have developed through what they have been told what Christians believe. Doing this, Jake asserted, "hits at their heart because it's what they need." Tell Christians, added the leader, "go to Isaiah!"

Roger advised that while it is "good to know a little bit about Islam," Christians should "spend a lot of time studying about Jesus." It is not helpful to "present Christianity for Muslims." It is "much better to just know what Muslim hang-ups are and then present Jesus. Let Jesus deal with the Muslim's hang-ups." Luke asserted, "The thing is obedience. Even if you're afraid, go anyway." Christians need to be prepared, and part of that preparation includes "knowing Scripture [and] contending for the faith." At this Sarah chimed in that sometimes Christians think that they have to go through seminars and learn "how to refute Islam." Her advice was, "just go. Don't even worry, just go and start loving on them." In Frank's opinion, many Christians are "a little too hung up on education." All leaders echoed the sentiment that "you don't need this class or this seminar, just do it."

It is also "really important," asserted Abby, "to create an environment that is conducive for Muslims to feel comfortable." She stated that COMM is a friendship center, not a church, and it does not meet in a church building, which "would be a complete turnoff, in my opinion." It is important, said Ruth, "to build bridges to Muslims rather than to look for ways of fighting with them"—the way to do that is to begin by developing a friendship. Friendship-building is "relatively easy," and in that context "you are not critical; you accept the person the way he is. And that's what the Lord did too. So, I think if you love with the love of Christ, things will change." In the context of developing these relationships, Susie asserted that people need to remember to not get "discouraged." Developing relationships and establishing trust takes time, and a person may never see for themselves the breaking down of barriers that have been set up by Islam. "But you can't worry about that. Do it anyway."

Jake agreed that while Christians need to "look for the long-term relationships," they should not "forget the chance encounter, the individual brief encounter." With this in mind he suggested: Instead of paying at the pump, go inside, meet that person behind the counter, ask him, "Where are you from? How long have you been here? How is your family? Are they safe? Are they here in America, are they back in Pakistan?" And then have something to give them, "Here's my number. If you need anything ... I pray, and God hears my prayers. And here's some verses from the Holy Scripture. Take this and read it, it will be a blessing to you. You'll see. It'll be something that will bless you." Give them the DVD. Just, little, a brief encounter, sowing seed. Remember, the sower went forth to sow and he just scattered seed wherever. He just sowed. Some will fall on good ground. You don't know who is going to be the good ground.

As we are developing relationships, it is also important "to be faithful doing what we do" and also "to pray that God moves Muslims towards God," asserted Frank, because it is "the Holy Spirit that does the converting." Jake added, American evangelicals need to "have a vision of hope for Muslims. Just as Christians were praying in the 60s and the 70s and 80s for Russia and for the Communist bloc and God eventually brought down those barriers and the gospel was able to go in and "thousands and thousands within those closed areas heard the gospel and came to Christ," the same thing can happen with Islam. Islam is "a barrier, it's a block, it's a stronghold of Satan," which God can break down and "release the captives. Let's just have hope that God will bring Muslims to faith eventually." Hassan interjected, "Sometimes when we think there is a barrier, there's really not. They push the barrier, and you find there's nothing really there."

Interview Of COMM Staff Apologist

Mansur Murad is a Christian apologist who engages Muslims on the Internet via chat forums. He does not deal with all kinds of Muslims but only with those who are actively engaged in da'wah, an activity that involves evangelism by Muslims. For the most part he engages people who are "aggressive, in–your-face, and unfortunately many of them are also very disrespectful and blasphemous." For this reason he believes he has to be "very confrontational, very in-your-face." The format of his ministry does not allow him to sit down, and have a cup of tea, and develop a friendship. He described his ministry by saying: "You're in there, and you are doing battle."

Q1: If someone who is not familiar with COMM were to ask you why you are doing the things you do with Muslims here, what would you say?

Mansur asserted first that he bases his ministry on 1 Pet 3:15 where Christians are exhorted to preach the gospel and to "give an answer or defense for the hope that is within us to whoever asks," which includes Muslims. In preaching the gospel to Muslims he has come to realize that when they ask questions, some questions are sincere efforts to understand what Christians believe, while others are intended "to get you to lose faith in your own religion. They will ask tough questions to get you to doubt Christianity." Hence, he studies the pertinent issues and seeks to answer the "unique questions" that Muslims have. "That's why I do it."

Q2: Are there biblical teachings and themes that are especially significant to your mission?

Besides 1 Pet 3:15 Mansur presented numerous other passages that are significant to his mission. Drawing from Jude 1:3, where God appoints Paul not only to be an apostle "but also an apologist," and from Phil 1:16, where we find the word apologia from which "we get the word 'apologetics,'" Mansur asserted that "the biblical theme is that the apostles commanded, and by their example demonstrated," the ministry of apologetics. Furthermore, they also functioned as "polemicists." Whereas an apologist is a person who "defends and explains his worldview, a polemicist critiques another position. And you will find in the New Testament where the apostles do critique other worldviews that are in conflict with the truth of the gospel. So, I do both."

Q3: As you engage Muslims through your apologetics ministry, what are you hoping for as far as outcomes or results are concerned?

Mansur asserted that the reason he did this was so that Jesus Christ may be glorified, and to that end he prayed that God would give him the grace "to do it in a manner pleasing to him." First of all, Mansur's hope was that the Lord would use his "meager efforts to strengthen Christians who have encountered Muslims in evangelism but because of the nature of the questions and the objections have been shaken." Mansur asserted that he began his ministry of apologetics after an encounter with a Muslim polemicist at a local church. This Muslim came with a group of friends prepared with a binder full of "verses and questions he used to attack and insult Christians," pointing out contradictions in the Bible and calling it a "porn-filled Bible." During this encounter the Muslim "humiliated" and "embarrassed"

Mansur, asking questions that troubled him and caused him to "go back and just cry out to God in tears, saying 'God, how do I answer these questions? What am I supposed to believe?'" The Muslim was very specific in his attack: trying to show that the concept of the Trinity is "not biblical or rational," attacking the deity and humanity of Christ, criticizing the Bible and its "apparent contradictions," etc. Through this encounter, Mansur made a commitment to be used by God "to strengthen my brothers and sisters and protect them from going through what I went through because it was emotionally traumatic for me." Second, Mansur hopes that Muslims get saved, "escape Islam, and give their lives to Jesus Christ as their Lord and Savior." Those are Mansur's "two main objectives."

When asked what the different components of his ministry were and whether evangelism was a part of it, Mansur replied that when he reaches out and answers the objections raised by Muslims, he is being evangelistic. In fact, each time an objection is raised, it is an opportunity for him to respond and "then to clarify the gospel in order to remove hindrances and obstacles." He does this in four ways. First, by writing articles for Answering Islam (answering-islam.org), one of the best-known websites, "defending Christianity" and "offering a criticism of Islam." Second, he develops a show for the Aramaic Broadcasting Network, a satellite network station in the Midwest. He creates shows once a month and airs them once a week, with one show broadcast live and three as prerecorded shows. Mansur deals with various challenges brought up by Muslims and raises "objections against Islam." Some of these shows are available on YouTube. Third, Mansur operates an Internet chat room on which he responds once a week to objections against Christianity. These are recorded and reposted to YouTube for general public viewing. Fourth, Mansur also debates with Muslims, although he would prefer to not debate but "sit, and dialogue, and have him hear me out, then me hear him out, then bring up questions that we can answer without getting angry at one another." He would much rather have a friendly and respectful conversation, "but that hasn't happened for me."

Q4: From the various activities you do to engage Muslims, which are the ones you enjoy the most? Why? Which activities are the most challenging or difficult? Why?

Mansur asserted that the activities he enjoys most are the ones where he has the opportunity to take an objection and answer it, as opposed to engaging in debates with "limited time" to respond. For example, in the context of a debate, if his opponent brings up "10 passages from the New Testament, all out of context, to demonstrate, let's say, 'Jesus isn't God' —how much response can I do in 5 minutes? Not much." Instead, Mansur would like to get onto Paltalk (an online video chat platform), take an objection, such as "If Jesus is God, why does he say no one knows the hour, not the angels of heaven, nor the son but only my father?" (Matt 24:36), and have "unlimited time" to address it. This may take 40 minutes or an hour, but people listen intently because they want to learn and understand.

He also does not enjoy settings where he has to engage Muslims whom he characterizes as "very blasphemous." Mansur reluctantly shared some of the things that he has heard:

> I am even a little ashamed to mention some of the things because ... the Lord forgive me for repeating it, but, for example, "your God came out of the woman's [genitalia]." See, saying that bothered me. It's bothersome, right? "Your God went to the bathroom, peed on himself, pooped on himself." "Your God ran away like a rat." Stuff like this. See, I told you, it's troublesome. And then the so-called porn aspect

of the Bible. You know, ... Song of Solomon--Muslims say it's a book of porn, or Ezekiel 23 where God [refers to] the genitalia of the lovers of Israel and Judah... Stuff like this that I hear. And then personal attacks, "you pagan, you cross worshiper, you child of Satan, you slob..." That's what I'm dealing with. The ones that are the most anger-inducing for me are the ones that are attacking the Scripture or God, like what I just told you. And then sometimes they even use F-bombs: "F-you," "F-this." You think they respect Jesus, but I've also had some of them throw F-bombs in His direction.

Mansur attributed this "blasphemous" reaction to the fact that Muslims think that Christians worship not the Jesus of the Qur'an, which they view as the real Jesus, but a "counterfeit Jesus" that Christians "have created and made him something he isn't." For this reason, from the perspective of Muslims Christians are "the worst of creatures," like "dogs that love their own penis," asserted Mansur. He added that Muslims think Jews are worse than pigs, an unclean animal in both Islam and Judaism. There are several chapters in the Qur'an— Chapter 2, Chapter 5, Chapter 7—where it says that Allah "punished a group of Jews by transforming them into pigs and monkeys, swine and monkeys." Qur'an 98:6 says that both Christians and Jews along with "disbelieving idolaters" are the worst of all creatures. When Mansur hears these things, they weigh him down, bother him, and make him "really angry and irritated." He has to pray and ask God to give him "the peace to not react in the flesh." Bad as it is when "someone is insulting your wife [and] there is only so much you can handle before you snap because you love her so dearly," it is much worse when someone is blaspheming "the God that we love." These are the aspects of his ministry that he wishes he could "avoid."

Q5: From your perspective, what are some indications that your
ministry has been successful?

To Mansur, achieving his "two main objectives" indicates to
him that his ministry has been successful. He receives emails from
people all over the world, especially from South Asia, India and
Pakistan, as well as England, "praising God." Some of these people
glorify God because they were about to convert to Islam or their "faith
was shattered," and they happened to find his website and his lectures,
and "God used that to strengthen them." He also receives emails from
people reporting that Mansur's teaching "forced" them "to go back, and
study, and [see] the truth." Because of this, some people have reported
leaving Islam. These emails are the only way he knows that he is
achieving his objectives because the nature of his apologetics ministry
precludes him from developing face-to-face friendships with people.
Whereas COMM's approach is "to earn their trust, build their
friendship, and then share Jesus," in apologetics and polemics, "this is
hard to do without getting into an argument."

Q6: What do you think of Islam as a religion?

In Mansur's opinion, "Islam is one of the most vile, wicked, evil
anti-Christ systems in the world today." He notes 1 John 2:18-23
teaches that there are "many antichrists" and gives us the profile of an
antichrist: "Who is the liar? It is whoever denies that Jesus is the
Christ. Such a person is the antichrist—denying the Father and the
Son." He pointed out that Muslims do not deny Jesus Christ, but in the
Qur'an Muhammad asserted that "Allah is the father to no one and
Jesus is definitely not his son." In the Qur'an, Chapter 9 Verse 30 says
that "Allah will fight anyone who says that the Messiah, son of Mary, is
the son of Allah or that Ezra ... is the son of Allah. Allah will fight you
for that." The context of Chapter 9 is jihad; Muhammad is about to die,

and he is giving Muslims his final instructions, his "final marching orders." Mansur explained that Muslims believe Allah fights through "the medium of Muslims." They are his agents. "So, this is enticing, inciting Muslims to subjugate Christians because Christians believe that Messiah is the Son of God."

Because the Qur'an "comes after Judeo-Christian revelation and it was developed in an area saturated with Jews and Christians," it is not unreasonable that "part and parcel" of Muhammad's message was attacking "core and essential Christian doctrine," which is also central to "Islamic theology." In fact, "you cannot be a Muslim without attacking essential, core Christian doctrines. It's the antichrist." In Mansur's opinion,

> Muhammad is the most wicked antichrist that has shown up thus far in history. The damage he has done is not just spiritually used of Satan to deceive billions to hell but economically, socially, politically—the damage, the hell he has created for mankind.

Mansur asserted that Muslims all over the world were persecuting Christians and other non-Muslims and beheading them. In fact, recently he had seen a video filmed in Syria where a Catholic priest along with two others was brought into an open area "filled with Muslims, even young boys," and beheaded like animals "to the chant of, 'Allahu Akbar.'" And their only crime was that they believed in the "triune God." Christians for the last 1400 years have faced persecution, lived as second-class citizens and third-grade minorities, have not been allowed to "evangelize and practice their religion freely," and have had "restrictions imposed on them. Otherwise they would be killed." Islam is an evil religion to its core. "Anything good in it is taken from the Judeo-Christian revelation," and "that good is buried with all this evil, with all this filth, with all these lies and deceptions."

At the same time Mansur emphasized that even though Islam is an evil religion, it does not follow that Muslims themselves are evil. In his view, "Muslims are victims because they are convinced that this is the religion of God, that this is the way that God has prescribed for them to attain salvation, and they don't want to go to hell." If the Qur'an says that Muslims should hate infidels, they will hate infidels. Furthermore, if a Muslim does not hate the infidel, "then Allah is going to hate them." The Qur'an is very clear that Allah only loves "believers" and the "righteous," i.e., Muslims. "Unlike the God of the Bible who loves his entire creation and he wants to redeem them and transform their character," Allah "does not love the prodigal." Muslims do not know that "they are victims," "that they have been taken captive by the spirit of antichrist," and that they are being used as the agents of Satan "to bring destruction and chaos" into the lives of non-Muslims. Muslims also kill each other:

In Syria you have the Salafi sect that has entered Syria and wants to dethrone Assad because he is an Alawi. And then you have the Shiite Muslims coming from Lebanon to fight the Salafi Muslims who are from Sunni Islam. So you have Sunnis and Shiites killing each other, beheading each other, making life hell for one another.

To summarize his thoughts, Mansur stated: "Muslims are victims taken captive by Satan."

Q7: What is your view of Muslims in general and/or Muslims you have been in contact with?

Mansur made a distinction between the two types of Muslims he encounters. First, the "Internet apologists or polemicists" are "very vile people," who get on the Internet in order to target Christians and mock the Christian faith. Second, those he meets at COMM are "average Joes like you and me" and are "human beings" who have the same problems, same issues, same concerns, ... who wear a hijab or have long beards but are struggling to make ends meet, to manage kids who are a little rebellious, and not completely happy because daddy is busy working all day and they don't get to see dad, and mom is too busy cleaning the house to give them attention, or young kids whose parents don't get along, and who need the same grace, mercy, and love that Christ offers us. They are "human beings" whose "religion happens to be Islam."

Q8: As you have engaged Muslims over the years, have you found that your perceptions of Islam or of Muslims have changed? In what ways? Why?

Mansur responded that as he has engaged Muslims over the Internet, all of the "vitriol and the hatred" has caused him to view Islam as more evil than when he first began his ministry. The Muslims he encounters on the Internet are zealously trying to be faithful to Islam, and the more he encounters them the more "hate," "filth," and "blasphemy" he sees, so much so that as he has encountered what he calls "real Islam," the more evil Islam has seemed in his eyes. This change in perception has in no way been tempered by the average Muslim, "who is a Muslim culturally but not by practice."

Mansur admitted that indeed there are moderate Muslims, but "as Robert Spencer says," while we can have moderate Muslims, "there is no moderate Islam." The first Muslims, including Muhammad, believed that the Islam that was practiced by the first three generations of Muslims was the "most complete, perfect Islam." In fact, there are statements that are attributed to Muhammad asserting that his generation was the best generation and that "if you want to know Islam, true Islam, you have to look at the first three generations of Muslims." But when "authentic Muslim sources" are scrutinized to understand

Muhammad's life, it becomes apparent that "he was a violent man." While there were "some good things about him," "his evil outweighs any good that you can point to in his character." And if Muslims "want to follow him wholeheartedly, emulate him, they will adopt his same spirit and mentality. The same spirit that demonized Muhammad is demonizing them." Over the years Mansur's perception of Islam due to its evil shifted from, "you know, there may be some bad apples" to "those good Muslims are good Muslims in spite of their religion." And he admitted that his fear was that if they become convicted "to want to really become Muslim, then we have a potential terrorist. See, that's the scary thing about Islam." "Muslims that I meet who are trying to be devout Muslims end up becoming like their prophet, and that's not a good thing."

Mansur contrasted this with those Christians who want to become true Christians: "Then it is inevitable that the same Holy Spirit that empowered Christ would transform me to be like Christ. So then my character goes from being nasty to loving, impatient to patient." Christians want to "imitate Christ, who was gentle, who was humble, sacrificial, laid his life down even for his enemy, let alone for the ones he loved. See, it is inevitable that you adopt that kind of spirit, that kind of mentality if Jesus is your model."

Q9: Based on your experience of engaging Muslims through your ministry, if you had the opportunity to share with American evangelicals about Islam and Muslims, what would you say? What do you wish they knew about Muslims and/or Islam?

Mansur offered three points of advice. First, "know your faith" so that you are able to "witness to Muslims effectively" by answering the objections that they raise. Second, "live it for the glory of Jesus Christ." To know your faith but to not practice it will bring "greater judgment and shame to your testimony" because "Muslims will spot a hypocrite." Third, "know they are victims, they are not our enemies." At the same time there are fanatical Muslims who will not "hesitate to slit my throat because of the stuff I say about Islam."

Mansur felt that we can see a person as a "vile enemy," or he can be seen "for what he is, a victim who has been taken captive by Satan, being convinced of the devil that this is the way to earn Allah's favor, to kill these infidels who are spreading mischief in the land." In order to define "spreading mischief," Mansur paraphrased Qur'an 5:33: "Those who spread mischief in the land, Muslim lands, and wage war against Allah's messenger, their punishment will be either crucifixion, crucify them, chop off the hands and feet of opposite sides, or banish them." Classical Muslim scholars assert that spreading mischief means disseminating a message or ideology that "opposes and contradicts Islam," "anything that goes against Islam." To preach the gospel in a Muslim country is to spread mischief; to label Islam as false is to spread mischief. "It's not just waging physical war, attacking Muslims physically. It's also waging war intellectually: the jihad of the pen, using discourse or dialogue, or using written media to try to convince Muslims Islam is false. That's spreading mischief." Mansur asserted that what I [Amit] was doing was spreading mischief, what he himself was doing was spreading mischief, and because of that our blood could be shed "without any guilt because this is what Allah demands." Mansur concluded his discussion by asserting that he wants Christians to know that "Muslims are victims and only Jesus can set them free because he came to set the captives free."

Mansur believed that American evangelicals need to become "intentional about raising up people from their midst to witness to Muslims," which include equipping them, training them, and giving them resources. In addition, the church needs to be mobilized to pray faithfully and intentionally for Muslims as well as for the whole world. It seemed to Mansur that after 9/11 for a "few months" Christians were "anxious about Islam" but then "went back to sleep," that "among evangelical Christians and churches in general there isn't that zeal to see Muslims saved." Mansur added that Islam is here in America for two reasons: either to give the church the opportunity to be used by God to be a witness to the Muslims; or for God to "use Islam as a tool of punishment and discipline upon the church and upon the nation as a whole for turning their back against the living God." He would much rather "be used of God to see Muslims get saved than try to ignore this problem and ignore these people who are victims that need salvation and then see something worse than 9/11 take place in America." God can use "unbelievers to punish a nation that professes to know him." Mansur went on to say,

This enemy is very patient. Maybe 15 years from now, he's patient, he will attack when he feels it's necessary, but we have got to do something. That would be my passionate plea to the evangelical churches and churches in general. Do something about reaching Muslims. America has become a mission field, and we are saturated with unbelievers, not just Muslims. What are we doing as Christians to combat that? We don't kill people, but our weapons are spiritual, they are mighty in the heavenly realms. Prayer, fasting, equipping, evangelizing, we need to do more of that. We're not doing very well as a church. I know there are some churches doing good, but realistically speaking, how many churches do you know are intentional about evangelism, let alone evangelism to Muslims?

Summarizing COMM's Ministry

COMM is a church-supported facility and a helps-based ministry that offers community-oriented services such as providing Bibles and various literature in three different languages, faxing and photocopy services to the community, ESL classes for those who want to learn English, and tutoring services for children. COMM was established with the goal of providing a "platform" in the marketplace to reach the Hindu and Muslim immigrants of the South Asian community who had just arrived in the US, seek to meet their needs, and help them get adjusted. They are an incarnational ministry whose raison d'être is to be a witness for Christ and share His love.

Central to the ministry of COMM is the teaching that Muslims need to come to faith in Christ in order to receive salvation and that by bringing the gospel to Muslims, they are fulfilling the Great Commission. They also believe that, in accordance with Acts 17:26, God has brought Muslims to this country so that they may have the opportunity to find Christ. Their hope is that some of these Muslims will become saved and take the gospel back to their countries of origin, just as Acts 2 describes Jews from all nations who came to Jerusalem came to saving faith in Christ and then took the gospel back with them.

COMM's model of ministry includes five steps: survey, contact, evangelism, conversion, and discipleship. They serve in the community by informally finding out the needs of the people in the neighborhood through prayer, which they called a "strategy," and through living in the community. Contact is made with people through the various services offered at COMM; this kind of contact creates the opportunity for them to present the gospel "in a real and living way." In addition to sharing the gospel in the context of meeting their physical needs, they also engage in street evangelism. Their hope is that through this they would be able to make converts and establish churches. This cycle keeps going as contact is made with new people and they keep discovering new things through the informal survey. Many COMM leaders have also lived in India or Pakistan and speak Hindi or Urdu, which puts the

Muslim visitors at ease and allows them to develop trust, as a result of which the Muslim visitors open up more quickly.

The general consensus was that the COMM leaders enjoy the activities they are involved in because they are doing it as a ministry for Christ. Some of the challenges they face include opposition in public from some Muslims in the community who accuse these leaders of trying to proselytize, but the leaders asserted that God gives them the grace to come out of the challenges in a "triumphant" manner. The most intense challenges took place early in the ministry, but after 10 years opposition has greatly reduced. The reasons for this included their becoming established in the community, caring for and loving the children, intentionally speaking to their community on behalf of COMM, Muslims attending some of their programs, and Muslim women being served by COMM. While many Muslims in the community may never accept them, the leaders at COMM refuse to water down the gospel and are convinced that there is no new method of doing mission among Muslims in the 21st century that is devoid of "pain and persecution."

The leaders shared their views of Islam as a vile, wicked, violent, and satanic system that is not a religion of peace, though it is packaged and presented that way in the West. The leaders viewed Muslims as victims of Islam. Most Muslims are ordinary people and are interested in nothing more than working, taking care of their families, etc., though some Muslims hate Christians and even have a long-term agenda to make America an Islamic nation. They asserted that many evangelicals are afraid of Islam, but they should not allow this to be a hindrance to developing relationships with Muslims and sharing the gospel with them. Evangelicals need to see Muslims as lost people who are in bondage to Islam, overcome their fears, and engage with them for the sake of the gospel.

COMM leaders considered their ministry a success because in keeping with what God had called them to do they had been serving in that community faithfully, by God's grace, for approximately fifteen years. Their success was evident because they had been able to plant a lot of seeds of the gospel, some of which had borne fruit, and others were in the process of growing. In spite of the fact that they are a Christian organization, Muslims keep bringing their children back to their ministry and keep coming back for prayer because they have experienced the love of the leaders at COMM. They have also seen fruit come out of their Internet apologetics ministry, through which a Muslim woman living in Saudi Arabia, upon moving to Ohio, came to faith in Christ. They have also had the opportunity to train many Christian college students, fruits of their labor, who are doing ministry in numerous countries all over the world. And failure from their perspective would constitute people seeing them instead of seeing Christ, and glory not going to Christ.

Some of the leaders have experienced hatred and persecution from the "enemy," i.e., Muslims, and even the death of a brother at the hand of Muslims—experiences which have the tendency of making a person bitter, resentful, and angry toward Muslims; the staff apologist stated that his experience of engaging Muslims over the Internet and being at the receiving end of a lot of "vitriol and hatred" has caused him to view Islam as more evil than when he first began his ministry. The leaders find themselves intentionally having to stop and pray when they see Muslims on the streets so that they do not become bitter, and they see their need for praying daily for grace to love people who hate them, praying for Christ to give them His heart, praying for God to open the Muslims' blind eyes and set them free from bondage and oppression. Their experience has made them cognizant of the brevity of life and the urgency to evangelize Muslims for whom Christ died and become intentional in reaching out to Muslims.

The leaders of COMM asserted that there is no "sleek methodology" for evangelizing the Muslims in the 21st century except that evangelicals need to have a biblical foundation. This includes recognizing that Muslims are lost and need Christ and that they are victims of Islam and not our enemies. Evangelicals should not be intimidated by or be in fear of Islam, but love Muslims with the love of Christ and boldly present the message of the cross. Evangelicals should not be afraid of Muslims and as a result keep them at arm's length but recognize that Muslims are in bondage to sin and Islam and that they should boldly engage them in dialogue. Evangelicals should seek to develop long-term relationships and trust with Muslims and create an environment conducive for Muslims to engage in dialogue. Evangelicals should know a little bit about Islam but spend a lot of time knowing the Bible, knowing their faith, studying about Jesus and living for His glory, and learning how to deal with hang-ups of Muslims. God will empower evangelicals to evangelize Muslims, and evangelicals need to become "intentional about raising up people from their midst to witness to Muslims," as Mansur said, which includes equipping them, training them, and giving them resources. In addition, the church needs to be mobilized to pray faithfully and intentionally for Muslims as well as for the whole world.

As with the evangelical church respondents, the COMM leaders expressed dissonance in their perspectives and attitudes toward Islam and Muslims. Although they have dedicated their lives to ministering to Muslims and feel great compassion toward them, they also exhibited negative views of Islam and mistrust of some Muslims. One conclusion that may be safely drawn from this dichotomy is that it is possible for ministry leaders to espouse views characterized by negativity and mistrust as well as compassion, and yet still be effectively engaged in long-term ministry to Muslims. While the COMM leaders experienced the challenges of ministering in a sometimes hostile Islamic context, they did not allow their mixed perspectives and attitudes to keep them from actively engaging Muslims in dialogue, developing relationships with them, and meeting their physical needs. With God's help, as they would put it, they rose above their negative and mistrusting views to serve Muslims in the name of Christ. And, quite unlike the American evangelical respondents, the COMM leaders did not display any fear of Muslims.

Personal Reflections

We will analyze these responses, as well as the responses by the American evangelicals in the two preceding chapters, in detail in Chapter 9. However, one observation that is worth mentioning at this point is that the positive response that the helps-based ministry has received is in sharp contrast to the vitriol that the staff apologist has to endure from the Muslims he engages. Furthermore, while the helps-based ministry is conducive to developing friendships with Muslims, the apologist's ministry is not. Perhaps you, the reader, can identify with some of the experiences and sentiments expressed by these ministry leaders. Once again, it would be helpful at this juncture for you to reflect on what your own perspectives, attitudes, and practices are toward Muslims and Islam, as well as how they were formed and justified.

We turn now to a detailed discussion of theology of religions with the goal of developing some basic principles for an evangelical theology of religions toward other religions in general as well as an evangelical theology of religions regarding Islam and Muslims in particular.

PART III:

Future Directions for American Evangelical Relationships with Muslims

CHAPTER 8

EVANGELICAL THEOLOGY OF RELIGIONS

Over the years I have visited a Sikh gurdwara, Hindu temples, Islamic mosques, and Buddhist meditation centers, observing how devotees of these religions pray, worship their respective gods through singing and dancing, and teach from their scriptures. I have watched Hindus and Buddhists practice meditation and yoga. To the casual observer the practices of adherents of different religions look similar in many respects. They may all believe in a supernatural power of some kind, read their own religious texts, worship at a religious site, have a system of morality, pray, etc. For the careful observer who scrutinizes the various religions closely, along with many similarities, fundamental differences also emerge. Broadly, and very simply, speaking, differences include the following: Christianity teaches the existence of a personal God who is triune in nature; Islam teaches that God is one, rejecting the Trinitarian nature of God; and Hinduism teaches the existence of an Ultimate Reality that is impersonal and unknowable. How should evangelicals account for the similarities and differences among the world's religions? Theology of religions is the branch of religious study that concerns itself with this question. Veli-Matti Kärkkäinen (2003) explains:

> Theology of religions is that discipline of theological studies which attempts to account theologically for the meaning and value of other religions. Christian theology of religions attempts to think theologically about what it means for

Christians to live with people of other faiths and about the
relationship of Christianity to other religions. (p. 20)

Furthermore, when we think theologically about other
religions, we need to take into account both the similarities and
differences between the various religions. My goal in this chapter is to
develop some basic principles for an evangelical theology of religions,
regarding non-Christian religions in general and Islam and Muslims in
particular. Because as evangelical Christians we believe that God has
given a revelation of Himself through His Word, an evangelical
theology of religions must necessarily take into account what God has
revealed in the Bible (Netland, 2001, pp. 312-13), including what the
Bible says about God and human beings.

Defining "Evangelical"

Before we move into developing an evangelical theology of
religions, it would be helpful to define what I mean by the term
evangelical. McDermott and Netland (2014), drawing from Alister
McGrath, offer the following six basic beliefs of evangelicals:

1. The supreme authority of Scripture as a source of knowledge
of God and guide to Christian living.

2. The majesty of Jesus Christ, both as incarnate God and Lord
and as the Savior of sinful humanity.

3. The lordship of the Holy Spirit.

4. The need for personal conversion.

5. The priority of evangelism for both individual Christians and
the church as a whole.

6. The importance of the Christian community for spiritual
nourishment, fellowship and growth.

While most Christians would agree with these "six convictions," what sets evangelicals apart is their emphasis on evangelism and personal conversion (McDermott & Netland, 2014, pp. 5-6).

Teachings of the Bible

In his book Encountering Religious Pluralism Netland (2001) opines that a genuine evangelical theology of religions, one that affirms "the authoritative revelation of God in Scripture," must be characterized by the "teachings, values and assumptions of the Bible" (p. 313) and must adhere to the cardinal doctrines of the church throughout its history. Netland discusses six fundamental themes that encompass this criterion. First, "the one eternal God is holy and righteous in all his ways" (p. 315). The Bible unambiguously reveals that God is morally pure and completely free of "all evil and corruption," that he is completely separate from any kind of sin and moral impurity, that he is wholly "righteous and just" in all his ways, and that He deals fairly with all human beings (p. 315).

Second, "God has sovereignly created all things, including human beings, who are made in the image of God" (Netland, 2001, p. 315). While this image of God in human beings has become corrupted because of sin, sinful human beings—both Christian and non-Christian—still bear this image of God and continue in some sense to reflect what God is like (pp. 315-16).

Third, "God has graciously taken the initiative in revealing himself to humankind ... Although God's revelation comes in various forms, the definitive revelation for us is the written Scriptures" (Netland, 2001, p. 316). This revelation of God needs to be viewed from the perspective of general revelation and special revelation. General revelation is knowledge about God that human beings are able to gain through the created world. Through general revelation it is possible for people to know that God does indeed exist, that he has created this

universe, that he is a righteous God who must be worshiped, and that
human beings must act rightly and "refrain from doing what is wrong"
(p. 317). Special revelation is God's self-revelation to a specific group of
people at a specific point in history and typically refers to the written
revelation of God, i.e., the Bible. At the same time, Jesus Christ is "the
highest and fullest revelation from God" (p. 317). Given this
understanding of special revelation, it is also imperative to recognize
that according to the Bible, God has at different times in history given a
self-revelation directly to specific individuals who were outside of the
"covenant community of Israel" (p. 318). For example, God revealed
Himself to non-Israelites such as Abimelech of Gerar; the Pharaoh of
Egypt; Balaam, the pagan priest; Nebuchadnezzar, the king of Babylon;
and Cornelius, the Roman centurion, among others (p. 318).

Fourth, "God's creation, including humankind, has been
corrupted by sin" (Netland, 2001, p. 318). All of the major religions of
the world recognize that there is something essentially wrong with our
world, and the evil, pain, and suffering that people experience is due to
the sinfulness of the entire human race. Sin permeates the human heart
and impacts every aspect of our being, which includes our thoughts, our
attitudes and desires, our actions and relationships with other human
beings. Not only that, but the result of sin is that we are in rebellion
against God and separated from Him. Netland (2001) asserts that it is
imperative that we understand the gravity of the Bible's teaching about
sin because it is only then that the "Christian teaching on salvation
makes sense" (p. 318), a point that often gets left out of the discussion
of non-Christian religions. In other words, in order to adequately
understand the religiosity of individuals and cultures, we need to
understand fully the Bible's teaching about sin and its effects and also
"God's terrible wrath against sin" (pp. 318-19).

Fifth, "in his mercy God has provided a way, through the atoning work of Jesus Christ on the cross, for sinful persons to be reconciled to God" (Netland, 2001, p. 319). Here Netland (2001) describes in detail the gospel of Jesus Christ, which he calls "one of the great mysteries in Scripture;" God loves all people and cares for them; God's wrath against sin and his love for people intersect in the "life, death and resurrection of Jesus;" in the one-time unique event of the incarnation of Christ God took the initiative for human beings to be reconciled to Him; God's love for all people is revealed most clearly through the substitutionary death of his Son, Jesus; "salvation is rooted in the sinless person and atoning work of Jesus Christ;" and for this reason "Jesus is the only Savior" for all human beings, including adherents of other religions (p. 319). The only way for anyone to be reconciled to God is through the cross of Jesus Christ (p. 319). Netland (2001) explains that while the person and work of Jesus is the "objective basis for our salvation" (p. 319), salvation has a subjective element as well. In order to obtain salvation, which is through the grace of God and not through any human effort or good works, individuals must put their faith in God. For this reason the Bible encourages us to repent of our sin and turn to God to receive forgiveness and salvation, and anyone who does so will find that God is merciful and willing to forgive.

Sixth, "the community of the redeemed are to share the gospel of Jesus Christ and to make disciples of all peoples, including sincere adherents of other religious traditions, so that God is honored and worshipped throughout the earth" (Netland, 2001, p. 323). Netland asserts that any view of other religions that is biblically acceptable must espouse an urgency for preaching the gospel, as evident in the New Testament and in the life of Jesus' disciples. It is imperative that the church be engaged in global missions so that all peoples have the opportunity to "worship and give glory to the one God and acknowledge Jesus Christ as Lord and Savior" (Netland, 2001, pp. 324).

Describing Other Religions

Having discussed the first criterion for developing an evangelical theology of other religions, Netland (2001) discusses the second criterion: It is imperative that the descriptions of the "beliefs, institutions and practices of other religious traditions" are "phenomenologically accurate" (p. 313), i.e., other religions are depicted accurately, without caricature or our preconceived notions. Engaging in this exercise means that "we must avoid reductionistic and simplistic generalizations as we give due attention to the enormous variety among and within religions" (Netland, 2001, p. 325). There are several components that comprise this criterion.

First, it is imperative that we take into account that there is "diversity across religions," which includes describing not only the major religions such as Buddhism, Islam, and Hinduism but also information from the "less prominent" religions, such as "shamanism, animism and polytheism" (Netland, 2001, p. 325) among others. This would also include studying new religious movements, "syncretistic movements" that emerge from a combination of elements from the major religions and "ancient indigenous traditions, the various folk religions, etc." (p.325).

Second, we also need to take into account the fact that there is "diversity within particular religions" as well (Netland, 2001, pp. 325-26). For example, within Islam there are several sects, including the Sunni, Shia, Sufi, and other traditions.

Third, in order for us to be phenomenologically accurate, we also need to take into account that there are similarities as well as differences between Christianity and other religions. Netland (2001) asserts that when Christians respond to other religions, they do so by looking at only the differences in order to emphasize the "uniqueness of Christianity" (p. 326). But evangelicals also need to take into account that there are "striking similarities between aspects of Christianity and aspects of other religions" (p. 326), such as monotheism--a concept that is common both to Christianity and to Islam.

While we are acknowledging the similarities among the different religious traditions, we also need to be cognizant of the fact that each of the concepts that are similar among the different religions need to be understood in the context of their own traditions "so that we are not misled by surface similarities that obscure deeper differences" (Netland, 2001, p. 326). For example, while both Christianity and Islam affirm a monotheistic understanding of God, a particularly contentious issue today concerning this similarity between Christianity and Islam is whether Christians and Muslims worship the same God. Some scholars, such as Miroslav Volf (2011) in his important book Allah: A Christian Response, have argued that Christians and Muslims worship the same God (p. 14). Based on their agreement on the "following six claims about God" (p. 110), Volf concludes that the object of worship is the same for both Christians and Muslims:

1. There is only one God, the one and only divine being.
2. God created everything that is not God.
3. God is radically different from everything that is not God.
4. God is good.
5. God commands that we love God with our whole being.
6. God commands that we love our neighbors as ourselves.

This issue has been addressed by many other scholars for whom the question "Do Christians and Muslims worship the same God?" is ambiguous and may be answered in numerous ways (McDermott & Netland, 2014, pp. 61-72). For instance, in response to the issue whether Christians and Muslims worship the same God, Sanneh (2004) asserts:

> Muslims and Christians agree on the great subject that God exists and that God is one. They disagree, however, about the predicates they use of God. Much of the Christian language about God affirms Jesus as God in self-revelation, and much of the Muslim language about God seeks exception to that Christian claim. (p. 35)

McDermott and Netland (2014) have also responded to Volf. They assert that many will agree that there is "significant commonality with respect to the first three claims and similarity in the fourth" (p. 64) and that because by definition there is only one Creator who has created everything apart from himself, when Muslims and Christians refer to this one Creator, they "are referring to the same God" (p. 64). On the other hand, an examination of Volf's fourth claim shows that it is not clear that "Christians and Muslims agree in any unqualified way that God is 'good'" (McDermott & Netland, 2014, p. 64). While Christians understand the goodness of God in terms of God's love and that God is love (1 John 4:16), in Islam "God is never said to be love" (McDermott & Netland, 2014, p. 69). And in this particular case, spelling out all the different ways in which this question can be interpreted and understood will give evangelicals an understanding on how to view Islam and develop an adequate evangelical theology of religions regarding Islam. The point that Netland (2001) is making is two-fold: We should not allow surface-level similarities to eclipse differences that are much deeper; and even though the various concepts in the different religions "are not identical" to each other, still there are "significant similarities" (p. 327). That is, when we are seeking to understand and describe other religions, both similarities and differences need to be taken into account (p. 327).

A related question is the issue of "continuity or discontinuity between Christianity and other religions" (Netland, 2001, p. 327). Instead of thinking about a complete "exclusive disjunction," i.e., either a complete continuity or a complete discontinuity, we need to accept both continuities as well as discontinuities, "depending upon the specific question and particular tradition at issue" (p. 327). Here it is important that the right balance be struck between continuities and discontinuities. Too much emphasis on the commonalities between Christianity and other religions will misrepresent the teachings of the Bible as well as the teachings of the other religion. The more inclusivist theologies of religion emphasize the continuity between religions so much that what emerges is not only a naïve picture of other religions, but the radical discontinuity between the Jesus of the Bible and the religious figures of other traditions is also obscured. And radical pluralism's emphasis on continuity eschews the real differences among the various religions with regard to truth and salvation (Netland, 2001, p. 327).

Furthermore, we can make an error toward the other extreme as well, emphasizing discontinuity to the extent that "there is no real point of contact or commonality between Christianity and other religions" (Netland, 2001, p. 327). Some observers try to explain away similarities between Christianity and other religions, including "aspects of truth and goodness" in other traditions, as "elaborate deceptions by the Adversary" (p. 327). Netland argues that if we are going to be faithful to the witness of the Bible and the "empirical realities" (p. 327), then we need to recognize that there are continuities between Christianity and other religions. Our evangelical theology of religions should be informed by this fact. Accepting and affirming it does not in any way detract from the fact that God's revelation in Christ is a distinctive and unique truth or from "the finality of Jesus Christ as the one Lord and Savior for all humankind" (p. 327).

Winfried Corduan's book A Tapestry of Faiths (2002) offers a helpful discussion to account for the various similarities and differences in the plethora of religions. He notes that scholars have proposed several models to account for ways in which the various religions interrelate with each other (pp. 25-30). The first two models—"complete continuity" and "complete discontinuity" (p. 25-27)—are similar to Netland's discussion regarding continuities and discontinuities among the various religions.

In the third model, which Corduan (2002) calls "continuity on the basis of superiority and inferiority," all the religions are categorically similar to each other and continuous and discontinuous with each other, with the distinctions having to do with "more or less, better or worse, closer or farther," etc. (p. 27). In this case one religion would be regarded as having more truth than the others, or would be considered "better at mediating between God and humanity than another, or closer to realizing an ideal than another."

The fourth model, "discontinuity on the whole with some commonalities," envisions Christianity as distinct from all the other religions while also overlapping in some areas with them. This is Corduan's (2002) preferred model to explain how there can be similarities between Christianity and other religions. In addition to the two traditional ways in which human beings gain knowledge of God (general and special revelation), Corduan notes that one may acquire knowledge of God through information about Him that has persisted throughout history. This knowledge creates an historical thread of "original monotheism" (p. 54). All religion began with God's self-revelation to human beings. As this information gets passed on and the various religions develop over time and generations, some religions retain more knowledge of Him than others; in some religions information retained is accurate, while in others it gets distorted; some religions remained monotheistic, while others became polytheistic (or even atheistic). In other words, "all other religions are deviations from this original starting point" (p. 17) of the religion that began with God's self-revelation. In fact, it is because of this idea of original monotheism that information retained in the various religions, accurate or distorted, may rightly be attributed to special revelation, which in turn is reinforced by the knowledge of God obtained through nature, i.e., general revelation (p. 41-44). Hence, for example, we see the persistence of the concept of monotheism in a variety of religious cultures—El as God in Semitic culture, Shangdi as the God of heaven in Chinese culture, Allah in Islam, etc.; and monotheism as well as many gods in Indo-European culture—devas Vishnu or Indra in Hinduism (p. 43.)

Explaining Human Religiosity

Netland (2001) goes on to assert that when developing a theology of religions, it is also necessary to explain "the phenomenon of human religiosity" (pp. 330-331), answering questions such as: Why are human beings by nature religious?, Are non-Christian religions satanic or evil or "benign expressions" (p. 331) of human beings searching for God?, etc. The fact of human religiosity must be understood in terms of three interconnected biblical themes. First, creation and revelation (pp. 331-32). Religious expression and religious interest exist in all cultures and are universal. People of all cultures reflect upon issues such as the fact that we exist, that there is a universe, that there is a creator, that there is life after physical death, that there is something inherently wrong with the world that we live in; and all cultures exhibit the universal need to connect to God or gods and to live a better life, etc. All of these themes are readily apparent in

Islam. Reflecting upon issues of this nature, which are commonly identified with religion, is only possible because God has created human beings with the ability to think about such things.

A second biblical theme to consider is sin (Netland, 2001, pp. 334-35). Human beings in all their aspects have been corrupted by sin, which includes their capacity for expressions of religiosity and the religions they create as well. The Bible teaches that even though human beings have some knowledge of the reality of the existence of God and their responsibility toward him, people have universally lacked an appropriate response to this knowledge, and have chosen to suppress this knowledge of God, and have failed to do that which is right in the eyes of God (Rom 1:18-20). At the same time, it is quite often the case that the religiosity of human beings, evident among both Christians and Muslims, includes human beings' efforts to try to impress God and "earn his favor through following carefully prescribed religious rituals and rules" (p. 335). This tendency is what keeps us the furthest away from God.

A third biblical theme to consider is satanic influence (Netland, 2001, pp. 335-37). Netland wants us to see that it is imperative that a Christian perspective on other religions acknowledge that many religious rituals and beliefs are influenced by Satan. While it is erroneous to assert that "all non-Christian religious phenomena" are satanic in its origin, it is "equally naïve" to assert that none of the religious phenomena are satanic in its origin (p. 335). The apostle Paul says to his readers in 1 Corinthians 10:20 that the sacrifices offered by the pagans in the religious rituals in Corinth were actually being offered to demons, "a sobering warning that should caution us against undue optimism concerning non-Christian religious practices" (p. 335). According to Netland, satanic influence becomes apparent in the religious dimension when there is a blurring in the distinction between the divine and human beings. For example, in the West the New Age movement's teaching that human beings are essentially divine "is merely an echo of Satan's deception: 'You will be like God' (Gen 3:5)" (p. 336).

In summary, Netland (2001) explains that the Bible is quite clear on the "major issues" so that we can put together a basic paradigm within which "human religiosity" may be understood (p. 315). It is imperative that a sound evangelical theology of religions be formed by the "clear and dominant themes" in the Bible that inform us of the characteristics of "God, the created world, humanity, sin and redemption" (Netland, 2001, p. 315).

Sacred Scriptures

While we began the task of developing an evangelical theology of religions by looking at the teachings of the Bible, other religions also have writings that they consider sacred. How should evangelicals view scriptures of other religions? Corduan (2002) offers an insightful perspective of "special revelation" (p. 55) as it relates to the Scriptures of the Christian faith and other religions. He begins his discussion regarding special revelation by arguing that while the various religions may have their own scriptures, the way they view their religious books internally is fundamentally different from the way in which Protestants regard the Bible. For an evangelical the Bible is the inspired Word of God. The principle of sola scriptura asserts that there is no other source of revealed truth other than the Bible. Any assertions of truth must by necessity have been revealed also in the Bible and cohere with what the Bible says. Viewing the Bible in this way has various practical implications (Corduan, 2002, p. 58). We read it and study it to develop our faith, we base our encounters with God on the understanding acquired from the text, truths about salvation may be gleaned by studying the text, we derive our understanding of Christianity from the study of the Bible, etc. Corduan argues that we commit the "Protestant fallacy" (p. 58) when we apply the same understanding of the Bible to the books of other faiths; i.e., we think that adherents of other religions approach their scriptures the same way evangelicals approach the Bible. Corduan's point is that, because the "self-reported nature and function" (p. 70) of the sacred texts in the different religions is distinct from the other(s), in order to understand other religions it is necessary to begin by understanding how their scriptures function within their own religious context(s).

From this perspective, Corduan's (2002) discussion of the sacred scriptures of Islam (pp. 61-63) is particularly relevant to a theology of religions as applied to Islam. Corduan asserts that Islam also relies on "deuterocanonical literature in addition to the central revealed Scripture, the Qur'an" (p. 61). While in Islam the Qur'an is given a "truly exalted status," very shortly after this revelation was given to Muhammad it was supplemented by a body of "secondary literature" (p. 61). The reason for this was that even though the Qur'an contains many specific directives, it did not go far enough to clearly delineate for the Muslim community how they were to live. For the Islamic community, the best place to turn for this information was the life and sayings of Muhammad himself. These were compiled into a set of books called the Hadith, which, while not considered a revelation in the sense that the Qur'an is, are still considered "authoritative and binding" (p. 61) as the Qur'an itself. In other words, in order to do justice to the way in which the Islamic community understands scripture, it is crucial that we understand their view of this secondary literature. Corduan asserts that "Islam without the Hadith could be construed as a slight on the prophet because it would ignore Muhammad's life and example" (p. 62).

However, continues Corduan (2002), the true distinctiveness of the Islamic understanding of the Qur'an lies in recognizing that its significance has less to do with its content and more with its "occurrence" (p. 62). The Islamic understanding of the Qur'an is that it is the incarnation of the divine word of God, given to Muhammad in its perfect form and preserved in perfection since that time. Muslims believe God gave revelations to other prophets as well—Moses was given the Law, David was given the Psalms, and Jesus was given the Gospel. However, the Islamic understanding is that these revelations were distorted over time by the followers of Judaism and Christianity. The Qur'an, on the other hand, still remains in its perfect form. For Muslims it is more important to recognize the holy character of the Qur'an than to read it; it is more important to recite its words than to understand it; and it is more important to practice its teachings than to study it (Corduan, 2002, p. 62). Furthermore, as significant as these actions are, "they are eclipsed by the very phenomenon of the Qur'an itself, the divine word revealed to the world, and, by comparison those other practices are secondary" (Corduan, 2002, p. 62). The event of the Qur'an has been compared to the incarnation of God in Christ in order to show that in each of these instances the "Word of God has come into the world" (Corduan, 2002, p. 62). This understanding, asserts Corduan (2002), gets to the crux of the understanding that Muslims have of the Qur'an as the self- revelation of God (p. 62).

There is a clear difference here with the Christian understanding of the inspiration of the Bible. The Qur'an is not considered a human book but rather a divine book, and its main significance does not lie in what it teaches, as crucial as that is, but in the fact that it exists. Muslims do not consider the Qur'an as an object of worship because that constitutes idolatry, which according to Islamic understanding is the "most terrible sin of shirk" (Corduan, 2002, p. 63), but they do regard it as mediating God's presence into their lives. The significance of this understanding is highlighted through the practice of reciting the Qur'an in Arabic even in countries where people may not know Arabic. In fact, asserts Corduan "the most important function of the Qur'an in the Muslim community is just this: to recite it" (p. 63).

It is evident, then, that the scriptures of other religions in general, and of Islam in particular, are not like the Bible. Muslims do not regard the Qur'an in the same sense that Christians regard the Bible. While it is true that both these religions "in a looser sense" do have scriptures that they make use of in their own way, it is problematic to reduce the scriptures of Christianity and Islam "to a common denominator" (p. 70). In other words, it is erroneous both from a theological as well as a practical standpoint to regard the Bible and the Qur'an as being exactly the same in "content, function or perception" (Corduan, 2002, p. 70).

Having laid this foundation, Corduan (2002) asks five questions that elucidate whether other religious scriptures contain revelation from God. First, "Do other religions contain truth?" (p. 70). In answering this question, Corduan argues we need to view truth from two vantage points: the correspondence theory of truth and the coherence theory of truth. When the truths in other religions "correspond" to reality as it is, then they do contain truth (p.71). For example, the Qur'an affirms the existence of God, and the Upanishads encourage the reader to "look beyond the material realm of existence" (pp. 70-71)—in so doing they make affirmations that correspond to reality and hence, in those statements they are true. From the perspective of the coherence theory of truth, an assertion is true if it coheres with the system in which it was made. However, even if two statements are exactly alike, if they are made in different contexts, then the meaning and significance of the statements also differ. From this perspective different religions "cannot share any truths" (p. 71). For example, the Qur'an's teaching that there is one God can never cohere with the Bible's teaching that there is one God because the oneness of God means different things in the overall theology of each of these faiths. In sum, Corduan's (2002) point is that at least in the correspondence theory of truth we clearly find that the scriptures of other religions do "contain (some) truths" (p. 72).

Second, "Do other religious Scriptures contain wisdom?" (Corduan, 2002, p. 72). Corduan (2002) answers with a qualified "yes." If we view wisdom as more than just a mere assertion but as providing insight into life: "moral exhortations, advice on how to get along with others," then understanding the theological system within which the particular saying appears that gives it meaning becomes significant. There are plenty of these kinds of insights in the scriptures of other religions, and they can, with caution and within limits, be appropriated by Christians.

Third, "Do other religious Scriptures contain religious truths?" (Corduan, 2002, p. 72). Corduan (2002) believes that they do. For example, the Qur'an attests to the virgin birth of Christ. But he notes we must keep in mind that the scriptures of other religions also contain teachings that are incompatible with the Bible; for example, the Qur'an clearly denies the deity of Christ. Hence, to argue that if the other scriptures contain some religious truth then the writings are inspired in their entirety would be to commit the "fallacy of composition" (p. 73). Corduan suggests that although we may find wise insights in other religious writings, we need to remember according to the doctrine of inspiration, there can be "no new revealed truths" (p. 73), general or special, outside those already revealed in the Bible. For this reason, we must measure new information encountered in the scriptures of other religions by the standards of the teachings already revealed in the Bible.

For evangelicals, religious truths that emerge from other scriptures "can only be duplications of biblical truth" (p. 74). For example, the Qur'an exhorts God's people not to "despair over matters that pass you by, nor exult over favors bestowed upon you. For Allah does not love any vainglorious boaster" (Surah 57:23). The "contentment and humility" (p. 74) taught in this passage is compatible with similar biblical exhortations in passages such as Phil 4:10-13. Corduan thus argues that while teachings such as these may appear in the scriptures of other religions, the content must be evaluated based on the teachings of the Bible. Nonetheless, there can be value in encountering these truths in other religious scriptures. For example, it "may be different enough from the biblical phrasing" (p. 74) that it may be possible for people to gain new insight in the application of the truth in question. It also gives rise to the fascinating question of how it is possible for "true religious insights" to exist in religions that are in general "opposed to the truth" (Corduan, 2002, p. 74).

Fourth, "Do other religious Scriptures contain special revelation?" (Corduan, 2002, p. 74). Since Corduan has already dismissed the notion that it is possible to regard the non-Christian scriptures as a whole to be inspired because they have some religious truths that they affirm, he narrows the focus here and asks instead, "Can those statements of religious truths be considered to be inspired individually?" (p. 74). In order to answer this question, Corduan makes his point based on statements made in the Qur'an, which from a Christian perspective "presents a mix of truth and falsehood" (p. 75). The Qur'an is an interesting case study because it is quite reasonable to believe that Muhammad learned some truths from Jews and Christians and hence paraphrased some material from the Bible (p. 75). If this is the case, should not such statements in the Qur'an be accepted as being inspired in the Christian sense of the term? Corduan answers this question by saying that one cannot make such an inference because inspiration does not function in this manner. From a theological perspective, verbal inspiration works in conjunction with plenary inspiration: "The words are inspired, but they also have a setting in the larger text that gives them meaning and significance, and we say that the text as a whole is inspired as well" (p. 75). Corduan says that isolated statements of biblical truth appearing in other scriptures (e.g., the virgin birth of Christ in the Qur'an—Surah 19:19-21) cannot be considered as inspired individually. This is because a statement appearing out of its context and inserted into another paradigm where it is imbued with new meaning loses its original sense. So, in the context of the Qur'an, because it denies other teachings about Christ in the Bible, the assertion about the virgin birth of Christ, while accurate in and of itself, must not be considered as inspired. So then, while "true" religious statements may appear in other Scriptures, special revelation will not be found in these teachings.

Fifth, "Do other religious Scriptures contain general revelation?" (Corduan, 2002, p. 76). Keeping in mind that other scriptures cannot provide general revelation because, as Corduan (2002) says, by definition general revelation cannot be a book, he asks instead whether the scriptures of other religions could in part be based upon inferences drawn from general revelation. Corduan says that this is indeed the case, and in fact, this is the crux of the "overlap" (p. 76) between revelation in the Bible and in other scriptures.

There are several areas in which one can regard material in the scriptures of other religions genuinely to be inspired. First, in the awareness, inferred from the created order, that God exists. Other scriptures include information about the awareness of an "all-knowing, all-powerful" (Corduan, 2002, p. 76) God, consistent with the notion of original monotheism. For example, the Qur'an states: "And your God is one God. There is no deity [worthy of worship] except Him, the Entirely Merciful, the Especially Merciful" (Surah 2:163).

Secondly, we may find information about basic morality—prohibitions against lying and stealing, for instance—"to which all human beings are subject" (Corduan, 2002, p. 76). These moral injunctions function in several different ways in the scriptures of non-Christian religions. They lay out ways in which human beings as members of a given community may live harmoniously with each other so that "individuals can flourish and the community can thrive" (Corduan, 2002, p. 77). Further, because we may expect religious books in general to talk about a human being's relationship with the transcendent, we may expect them to delineate, in some sense, pathways to develop a connection with the spiritual realm. For example, we read in the Qur'an: "And those who are patient ... and prevent evil with good ... will have the good consequence of ... [Paradise]" (Surah 13:22).

Last, because human beings eventually fail to obey these moral injunctions, we may find in the scriptures of other religions "devices," "such as ceremonies, offerings or rituals" (Corduan, 2002, p. 78) to provide pathways in order to deal with this inadequacy. For instance, regarding prayer the Qur'an teaches: "And establish prayer and give zakah [charity], and whatever good you put forward for yourselves – you will find it with Allah. Indeed Allah, of what you do, is Seeing" (Surah 2:110). Corduan observes that scriptures of other religions outline "moral obligations" that work in the way that the law functioned in the Old Testament: as a "'schoolmaster' (KJV), 'tutor' (NASB) or 'guardian and teacher' (NLT). The law teaches us about our need for Christ by highlighting our failure to live up to the law's standards" (p. 78). In other words, general revelation, as it appears in the Scriptures of non-Christian religions, makes human beings aware of their own sense of spiritual and religious inadequacy.

So, how should evangelicals view scriptures of other religions? I believe we may expect that in reading and studying the sacred texts of other religions we are able not only to learn about the beliefs and practices of adherents of the different religions, but our increased knowledge and understanding will also serve as a way to build bridges with them. My experience has borne this out. As I have read from the Qur'an and dialogued with Muslims about it, I have found not only do they feel appreciated because I took the time to read portions of their scripture, but it has afforded me opportunities to share the gospel as well.

Learning from Other Religions

In his book Can Evangelicals Learn from World Religions? Gerald McDermott (2000) emphasizes that God wants the whole world to know that "He is the Lord" (p. 74). Throughout history there were "people outside the Jewish and Christian churches" (p. 77) who knew Him (pp. 74-80). Because this is the case, God's people learned things from "pagans" that gave them a better understanding of God's revelation through the Jewish and Christian communities (McDermott, 2000, p. 81). For example, the Hebrews adopted the name El used in Semitic culture to refer to God, and the authors of the New Testament used theos, a Hellenistic term for God. McDermott (2000) asserts that this should not surprise us, nor should it be "theologically problematic" because when the Holy Spirit "superintended the entire process of Scripture writing" (p. 81), He made use of the languages and the stories that the authors of the Bible were themselves familiar with and that were used in the culture to describe other gods. Similarly, Peter also learned something "new and profound" (McDermott, 2000, p. 88) about God from the way in which He was working in Cornelius' life even before Cornelius heard anything about Jesus: that God shows no partiality but accepts people from every nation who do what is right (Acts 10:34-35). In the end, Peter got a new and more complete understanding of "God's work of redemption" through God's encounter with Cornelius (McDermott, 2000, pp. 89).

Based on this line of reasoning, McDermott (2000) asserts that while there are significant differences between Christians and Muslims regarding revelation, there are numerous "striking lessons that Christians can learn from the Islamic tradition" (p. 194). He touches upon five themes, all of which are present in Christian thinking but are expressed in different ways in Islamic tradition. Hence, "these distinctives remind or inform us [Christians] of things we should see in our own tradition, perhaps in a new way" (McDermott, 2000, p. 194). First, "submission to God" (p. 194), by which McDermott (2000) is referring to God in the Qur'an (pp. 194-97). Muhammad taught that submission to the will of God is the supreme virtue, which forms the core of true religion. One's personal desires are of no relevance; the only duty a person has is to bow the knee in "humble obedience" (McDermott, 2000, p. 194). A Muslim should not "equivocate" about God's commands or regard them as anything other than being absolute because they come from God's infinite wisdom; the only proper response for a Muslim is to bow down in "meek deference" (McDermott, 2000, p. 195). McDermott (2000) admits that many Muslims submit to God only in order to gain Paradise, but also points out that Islamic tradition includes a "rich strand" encouraging Muslims to submit for the simple reason that "God is God" (p. 195). Islam teaches that God alone is great and he reigns with complete control over even the smallest part of the universe. For this reason the only sensible thing to do is to bring our entire life under submission to God's will, as made known to Muhammad, the greatest and last of all the prophets. For a Muslim to show loyalty to anything other than God, such as "money, family, race, success or earthly life itself, is idolatry (shirk), the unrelieved indulgence of which will merit the boiling water and searing wind of hell" (McDermott, 2000, p. 195).

Drawing from Harold Bloom's 1992 book The American Religion, McDermott (2000) describes American evangelical Christianity as being preoccupied with "self-affirmation and human freedom" (p. 196). All too often, American evangelicals show faith more in themselves than in Christ, concern themselves more with individual expressions of faith rather than caring for the community, and seek "more freedom for the self than freedom from sin" (McDermott, 2000, p. 196). McDermott (2000) says that getting a grasp of how Muslims understand the responsibilities that human beings have to God—"their theocentric dismissal of self-indulgence" (p. 197)—may assist us in breaking free from this narcissistic behavior that has potential to overwhelm us. If Christians pay more attention to the sense of reverence that Muslims show in the presence of the "majesty of God," it will help us to gain a greater appreciation of the "reverent fear of God with which Isaiah, Daniel and Cornelius served God" (McDermott, 2000, p. 197). To this statement McDermott (2000) adds a footnote, in which he admits that at one level this comparison between the worst of the Christians and the best of the Muslims is "unfair" (p. 197). There are many Muslims who live worldly lives, and there are many evangelicals who are dedicated to their faith. On the other hand, "it is instructive to see living examples of the best of what another tradition offers in order to clarify our own vision when it has become muddled" (McDermott, 2000, pp. 196-97).

Another theme that we can observe from interaction with the Qur'an is "creation as a theater of God's glory" (McDermott, 2000, p. 197). A common idea present in the Qur'an is that creation is full of indicators of God's reality—in the natural world, in human societies, and in individual human beings. Thus, Muhammad affirms that creation testifies and gives human beings evidence of the existence and the sovereignty of God. For human beings to "recognize the signs for what they are is close to what faith is all about" (McDermott, 2000, p. 197). Our chief responsibility as human beings is to "believe in Our [God's] signs" (Qur'an 30.53). McDermott (2000) quotes from numerous passages in the Qur'an to show that "God's signs are everywhere, especially in nature" (p. 197). For example, the Qur'an talks about the existence of heaven and earth, which has been called the cosmological argument for the existence of God by philosophers; alternation from light to darkness on a daily basis; rainfall that produces life from the "parched earth;" the abundance of animals on the earth; lightning that gives rise to fear as well as hope; and the stars in the night sky that give direction to "the darkness of land and the sea" (Qur'an 2.163-64; 6.97; 30.22-25). McDermott (2000) surmises that perhaps because Muhammad was living in a desert environment, he was particularly impressed "by the miracle of vegetation arising from lifeless sand" (p. 198). God's signs are evident in human culture as well: The diverse and complex human languages give evidence of the "existence, wisdom and power" of God (Qur'an 30.22). The beauty and the complexity of these languages for Muhammad seemed to provide evidence of the reality of God (McDermott, 2000, p. 199).

For Muhammad human beings in particular are signs of God. Similar to Paul's statement in Rom 2:14-15 that even nonbelievers have an "innate conscience," the Qur'an also makes a special note of the conscience of human beings as evidence of the moral nature of God (McDermott, 2000, p. 199). However, McDermott (2000) also lists some passages where we see the Qur'an lamenting the fact that most human beings "turn away" or "repudiate" (p. 199) this evidence because of their pride or unfathomable perverse nature (Qur'an 3.21; 7.36; 7.177; 30.10). This is the fundamental sin of human beings, which is simply another way of "naming, or perhaps the consequence of, the sin of shirk (idolatry)" (McDermott, 2000, p. 199). The Qur'an asserts: "they rejected the signs of God and took them for a joke" (Qur'an 30.10) and for this human beings are going to experience "excruciating pain" and become "inhabitants of fire;" human beings are "traitorous ingrates;" they "turn away" from the evidence of the reality of God and make themselves into a bad example (McDermott, 2000, p. 199). While McDermott (2000) does not explicitly explain what Christians may learn from what the Qur'an teaches regarding creation, his discussion indicates that the created order reveals the glory of God.

Third, we find in the Qur'an instructions on "regular and theocentric prayer" (McDermott, 2000, p. 199). A good Muslim is in the habit of praying five times a day, in the early morning, noon, midafternoon, sunset, and evening. McDermott (2000) explains: "A good Muslim washes his forearms, feet, mouth and nostrils three times before facing Mecca and reciting a memorized prayer of faith, praise and gratitude" (p. 199). Faithful Muslims begin their prayers by speaking a few prayers of worship, proclaiming the Islamic faith, and reciting the first surah of the Qur'an, which praises God as the creator, the sustainer, as being full of grace and mercy, the Lord of the day of judgment and petitions God to provide grace to keep one walking on the straight path. Only after these theocentric prayers have been uttered does the faithful Muslim present a brief petition for his personal needs. Thus, Islamic prayers focus attention on God's character and his attributes rather than the human being. This is evident in the fact that the main element of the prayer is worship and not supplication, as well as the notion that Muslims "need to take time at regular intervals throughout the day to acknowledge God's lordship over us and the world" (McDermott, 2000, p. 200). Having described the prayer of the faithful Muslim, McDermott (2000) asserts that Jesus instructed us to learn from the faith that pagan people display (Matt 15:21-28). He also draws from Bob McCahill's discussion in Dialogue of Life regarding the regular prayers that Muslims practice, asserting that evangelicals can learn from Muslims that at its core "prayer is worship and that a prayer life dominated by supplication is unbalanced and self-absorbed" (McDermott, 2000, p. 200). Evangelicals can also "relearn ... the importance of regularity in prayer and how set times can help check our inclination to forget about prayer entirely" (McDermott, 2000, p. 200).

A fourth theme is "charity to the poor" (McDermott, 2000, p. 200). The Qur'an places a special emphasis on the significance of helping the poor (McDermott, 2000, pp. 200-02), considering it one of the duties that defines righteousness for faithful Muslims. Numerous passages in the Qur'an touch on this theme: for example Qur'an 89.6-18, which criticizes the wicked for failing to honor orphans who were "among the truly needy in premodern society" (McDermott, 2000, p. 201) or for not exhorting each other within the Muslim community to feed the poor. Like Jesus, Muhammad also "condemned those who gave in order to be seen" (McDermott, 2000, p. 201), teaching that this nullified the act of charity, while doing charity in secret would "remove some of your stains of evil" (Qur'an 2.264, 2.271).

What does charity look like in the Islamic community? The Qur'an distinguishes between two types of giving. The first is called sadaqa, which is voluntary charity. The second is called zakat and includes giving 2.5% of the income by Sunni Muslims and 20% of the income by Shiite Muslims for alms. This giving is a "legal, obligatory act," a part of the Muslim's service to God and is considered "a technical part of worship" (McDermott, 2000, p. 202). It is comparable to paying a yearly tax on the various kinds of wealth that the Muslim has. McDermott (2000) adds: "One of the meanings of the word zakat is 'purity,' which suggests that money is 'unclean' until the proper percentage has been donated to the Islamic community" (pp. 201-02). While we do not know how many Muslims actually pay the zakat, we do know that most evangelicals do not tithe. Evangelicals might learn valuable lessons from Islam regarding giving: Until some of our money has been given to the community, it is not being used in the proper manner, and there is a vital connection between "faith and charity to the poor" (McDermott, 2000, p. 202).

Fifth, Islam addresses issues related to "faith and the public square" (McDermott, 2000, p. 202). To McDermott (2000), "Islam can help us understand why there is no such thing as a naked public square" (p. 202), a public square devoid of religious influence. Muslims believe that the heart of a human being was made to worship, and it will either worship the true God or regard something else as god and worship that (shirk). Even atheists are religious and worship some kind of a god, whether that is "nature, or happiness, or family or self" (McDermott, 2000. p. 202). Viewed from this perspective, when we remove religion from the public arena, including the government, we are actually embracing "a mythical vision of the human" (McDermott, 2000, p. 202). In doing this we are failing to recognize that when an explicit connection "to God or morality" is removed from the public life, a void is created that we try to fill with other gods, such as "race or nation or secular ideology" (McDermott, 2000, p. 202).

At this juncture McDermott (2000) draws from Lamin Sanneh, (pp. 202-05), who grew up as a Muslim in West Africa and became a Christian but continues to maintain a keen "appreciation for the integrity ... of Islam" (p. 202). According to Sanneh (1996), Muslims recognize that it is not possible to keep religion in the private and subjective arena. While we would never want to go back to Christendom and its oppressiveness that forces religion by coercing others and lacks tolerance for diversity in religious expression, the view of the modern Western world that religion is an expression of free speech without any objective basis in truth is a disaster "both in origin and in consequence" (p. 203). Sanneh continues,

> Standard Muslim sources are correct that a state that would deserve public loyalty and respect cannot be neutral with regard to moral principles; the state must in that case either cooperate with religion, or coopt and enjoin it, or worse still, proscribe it. (pp. 48-49)

Sanneh (1996) argues it is imperative to find a balance between the current Western mindset and the aspirations of Islam to establish a theocracy, while recognizing that the alternative that postmodernity presents in the long run could be even worse because it could strengthen "the status quo by driving religion from the public sphere into the private, with the weakening of religion going side by side with the growth of state power" (p. 49). Sanneh gives the example of Václav Havel, former president of the Czech Republic, who shared a similar view to many Muslims that a government that is not grounded religiously and morally will not have any instruments at its disposal to struggle effectively against "absolute and oppressive human pretensions" (McDermott, 2000, p. 203). Sanneh (1996) quotes from Havel's 1990 speech to the U.S. Senate: "the most dangerous enemy today is ... our own bad qualities ... we [human beings] have neither the right nor a reason to think we understand everything and that we can do everything" (Sanneh, 1996, p. 49). False absolutes that emerge from human idolatry are labeled "secular self-sufficiency" (Sanneh, 1996, p. 49) by Havel and shirk by Muslims. Havel's view is that "truth is not a matter of individual convenience" (Sanneh, 1996, p. 49) and that it is neither dependent upon consensus among the majority nor on the desire of the Congress or of the White House (McDermott, 2000, p. 204).

McDermott (2000) points out that radical postmodernity assumes it is not possible to have knowledge of anything outside of our own minds, and for this reason no one moral idea is any "truer" than any other—an assumption that "has chilling implications for public life" p. 204). Adhering to this worldview would keep us from being able to make any claims about what is morally right or wrong. We would not be able to go any further than making the claim that some people feel something is wrong because of their own personal moral context. Further, this assumption also creates space for people to think that if something is right for them, regardless of "centuries of moral consensus saying otherwise," then for them it is acceptable to do it (McDermott, 2000, p. 204).

Few people today would suggest that this is the situation currently in North America, at least in the public arena of "the media, courtroom and legislatures" (McDermott, 2000, p. 204). Most would still continue to assert that actions such as "rape, incest, murder and terrorism are morally wrong" (p. 204), and they would have no hesitation in declaring this publicly. Having said this, McDermott (2000) describes a "disturbing phenomenon" in his interactions with white American middle- and upper-middle-class students, a significant portion of whom are "convinced moral relativists" (p. 204). These students, says McDermott, are fairly certain that morality and religion are both matters of personal choice, having learned this from the social context in their homes and communities where they grew up. The students maintain that if they had grown up somewhere else, they probably would have had different beliefs. For this reason it is not reasonable for them to criticize someone else because they hold beliefs that are different from their own. In the final scheme of things what really matters is that a person is sincere about his or her own belief because it is not possible to ascertain "what is 'absolutely' or 'objectively' right and wrong" (McDermott, 2000, p. 205). For example, one student said to McDermott (2000) that even though she disagreed with what the Nazis had done and her personal opinion was that it was wrong, it was not legitimate for her to condemn the Nazis for what they had done if they "believed they were doing the right thing" (p. 205). McDermott says that a Muslim would respond to this woman by saying that objective morality does exist, regardless of whether a person is sincere or not. Hence, even if all of the Nazis thought that they were right, their actions were still wrong. This is so because Allah exists and "His moral law rules the world" (McDermott, 2000, p. 205). Furthermore, he has given signs in the created order so that Allah's existence and his moral character may be known. There is no excuse for the person who misses these signs and lives life "as if things were not clear" (McDermott, 2000, p. 205).

While evangelicals may not be willing to assert without qualification how clear these signs are, they do need to "recognize the power of the Muslim response to moral relativism" (McDermott, 2000, p. 205). In fact, some people are converting to Islam for this very reason: In a world that is replete with moral confusion, "Islam offers simple and clear answers" (McDermott, 2000, p. 205). Evangelicals also need to learn from Islam about the connection between religion and public life as well as the answers that strong faith has for the "moral and philosophical" threat that we are faced with (McDermott, 2000, p. 205).

Relating to Religious Others

A major component of developing an evangelical theology of religions is thinking about what it means for evangelicals to live with adherents of other religions. McDermott and Netland (2014) offer some helpful insight on the basis of three seminal teachings of Jesus: "All authority in heaven and on earth has been given to me. Go therefore and make disciples of all nations, baptizing them in the name of the Father and of the Son and of the Holy Spirit" (Matt 28:18-20); "You shall love your neighbor as yourself" (Matt 25:35-40); and the Golden Rule: "Whatever you wish that others would do to you, do also to them, for this is the law and the prophets" (Matt 7:12). Christians have three obligations based on these teachings: to "make disciples of religious others," to "love religious others," and to "treat religious others the way we would want to be treated by them" (McDermott & Netland, 2014, p. 270). As we do so, our witness for Christ should evidence the following, according to McDermott and Netland (2014): a manner that is "respectful and sensitive" (p. 271), without any coercion in trying to convert religious others; viewing them as our neighbors who are created in the image of God, and loved by God; living lives characterized by integrity, truth, honesty, compassion, grace and humility; in our witness eschewing violence or "abuse of power" (p. 274) of any kind and responding peacefully to acts of violence and persecution toward Christians; seeking to promote human rights and freedom of the practice of religion, denouncing religious persecution; and engaging them by listening and understanding their beliefs and acknowledging and appreciating what is true and good in them (pp. 270-275). Within this framework of relating to religious others in general, I turn now to Colin Chapman (2007), who offers some pertinent insights for the development of an evangelical Christian theology of religions regarding Islam. I will draw selectively from his work, touching upon issues that relate directly to the comments made by the American evangelical respondents interviewed.

Relating to Muslims

Chapman (2007) begins his discussions by offering several suggestions about how Christians should relate to their "Muslim neighbors" (p. 21). Christians should think about and approach Muslims first as human beings, as individuals, and as neighbors before we think about and relate to them as Muslims who are part of one of the great religions of the world and before we tell them that "we are Christians" (Chapman, 2007, p. 23). The key here is to develop meaningful relationships with them. This is significant because Jesus' command to love our neighbors comes before the command to make disciples. "It makes little sense to calculate how we are going to share the gospel with our Muslim neighbors if we have not begun to know them, love them and care for them as our neighbors," asserts Chapman (2007, p. 29).

Christians also need to develop an appreciation for Islamic culture. Chapman (2007) indicates four reasons Christians need to get an understanding of their culture before learning about their beliefs (pp. 31-34). First, Christians need to interact with Muslims as human beings, "rather than as representatives of the religion of Islam" (Chapman, 2007, p. 31), as putting too much focus on their beliefs could create barriers, and it could make relating to them as people more difficult. Second, because in Islam culture and religion are closely connected, learning about their culture can be helpful in learning about their beliefs. Third, understanding Islamic culture will help us better understand our own cultural biases. If we are having difficulty with some things in Islam, it may be related more with culture than with the religion. Fourth, Christians need to distinguish between "the gospel and culture" because what we think of as "the Christian way of life" may have more to do with our culture than with the gospel (Chapman, 2007, p. 31). Furthermore, we also do not want to give the impression to

Muslims that converting to Christ necessarily entails the rejection of Islamic culture and the adoption of a "foreign culture" (Chapman, 2007, p. 31). One way we can learn to appreciate Muslim culture is by asking our Muslim neighbors to explain in their own words aspects of their culture, such as their festivals, marriage and family life, dietary practices, clothing, social manners, etc. (Chapman, 2007, pp. 32-34).

Equally important is the necessity of examining attitudes that many Christians hold toward Islam and Muslims. Some of these attitudes may be theological, stemming from the fact that Islam poses a challenge to Christianity; others may be cultural and political, stemming from reactions by Christians to the Muslims in their midst who have a different lifestyle as well as a politically charged rhetoric. We as Christians need to reflect honestly on our attitudes and "examine them in the light of the gospel" (Chapman, 2007, p. 41).

Chapman (2007) offers some examples of attitudes Christians espouse that are reflected in the comments that they make about Islam and Muslims. Some Christians have negative attitudes because they have heard stories of persecution Christians face at the hands of Muslims in countries such as Pakistan and Iraq (pp. 41-44). While it is important to recognize that in some Muslim countries Christians are indeed being persecuted, it is equally important that evangelicals "do not allow the fact of persecution in these situations to create very negative attitudes in our minds toward all Muslims" (Chapman, 2007, p. 42). It is also important to recognize that not "all Christians living in Islamic countries are always suffering persecution" (Chapman, 2007, p. 44). When anecdotes of the persecution that Christians face are combined with political issues related to Islam and Muslims, Christians begin to fear Muslims, creating a hindrance to relationships. When Christians respond to Muslims "more out of fear than out of love," it is harder to "obey the command to 'love your neighbor as yourself' (Matt. 19:19)" (Chapman, 2007, p. 44).

Many Christians think because of terrorist activity carried out in the name of Islam that it is an "inherently violent" (Chapman, 2007, p. 44) religion. Indeed, there are passages in the Qur'an where God commands "Muhammad and his followers to fight and even to kill." For example, Qur'an 2.190-193 says,

And fight for the Cause of Allah those who fight you, but do not be aggressive. Surely Allah does not like aggressors ... Kill them wherever you find them and drive them out from wherever they drove you out. Sedition is worse than slaughter ... Fight them until there is no sedition and the religion becomes that of Allah.
Furthermore, Muhammad also fought numerous battles against the people of Mecca and treated violently three Jewish tribes in Medina. Muslims argue that Christians need to see these actions of Muhammad from the perspective of the local context of Muhammad, which espoused an "ethic of tribal revenge" (Chapman, 2007, p. 45), as well as to remember that there were times when Muhammad was generous toward his enemies. Muslims also frequently point out a verse in the Qur'an that teaches that "there is no compulsion in religion" (Qur'an 2.256).

Chapman (2007) offers a number of helpful suggestions to deal with this challenge (pp. 45-46). Christians need to recognize that Muslims have their own ways to deal with both sides of the issue. Some assert that the Islamic world "has been under attack from the West" for over two centuries and that they are in the same position as the first community of Muslims was in when they were being attacked by the pagans in Mecca. For this reason the verses in the Qur'an that talk about jihad apply to them today as well. Others assert that the word Islam means peace, hence Muhammad's commands to fight do not apply to the Muslim community today. While this defense may not be tenable, at the least Christians must be "willing to listen" (Chapman, 2007, p. 45) to moderate interpretations of these texts. Furthermore, Christians also need to recognize that similarly warlike passages are also found in the Old Testament. Historically Christians have in some instances engaged in violent acts toward Muslims, including the Crusades, meaning that accusations of violence in the name of religion cut both ways.

Christians often comment that "Islam wants to rule the world." Chapman (2007) points out that historically Islam has been a religion that has been interested in expanding not only through missionary activity but also through power, and with the rise of radical Islam some Muslims are seeking to "re-establish the Caliphate, make Muslim countries more genuinely Islamic and recover the political power of the Muslim world" (Chapman, 2007, 47). In response Chapman (2007) offers some helpful suggestions. One reason Islam is growing rapidly in the world is that Islamic communities often have a higher birthrate than many other people groups. Conversions of non-Muslims to Islam in the West are another factor in the religion's quick growth. However, while there are many Muslims in the West who have "a strong missionary vision," far more of them are simply interested "in the survival of the present Muslim communities" and in protecting their children from being influenced by the ungodly culture around them (Chapman, 2007, p. 48). For this reason, Christians need to be careful about making blanket assertions that Muslims want to rule the world because "expressions like these are highly inaccurate and only have the effect of stirring up fear and prejudice" (Chapman, 2007, p. 47).

Christians also need to recognize that in democratic countries Muslims have the same freedoms and rights to practice their faith as Christians do. These rights, Chapman (2007) says, which include freedom to build mosques; eat halal meat in public institutions, such as "schools, hospitals and prisons" (p. 48); have the services of Muslims chaplains in hospitals and prisons; make use of prayer rooms in airports; etc., need to be affirmed and supported. In all these instances, Christians need to keep in mind not only the necessity to defend civil rights of religious minorities on legal, constitutional grounds but to do so in order to observe our own faith's "principle of reciprocity" (p. 49): In keeping with the Golden Rule, Christians should treat Muslims as they themselves would want to be treated if they were living as minorities in a Muslim country.

Understanding Islam

Having asserted that one significant way in which Christians can relate to their Muslim neighbors is by learning about Islam from the perspective of Muslims themselves, Chapman (2007) discusses various aspects of Islam from their perspective (pp. 57-184). I highlight three here: political issues, the role and position of women in Islam, and Islam and terrorism.

Chapman (2007) discusses three political issues Muslims face that are especially pertinent to our discussion. First, is it possible for Muslims to accept pluralism, and "how should Muslims justify their existence as minorities in non-Islamic countries?" (Chapman, 2007, pp. 150). Chapman (2007) explains that although there are passages in the Qur'an that encourage Muslims to accept other religions, as long as some Muslims view the world as a two-part division of "dar al-Islam (the House of Islam) and dar al-harb (the House of War) and want to engage in jihad" (p. 150) to make the whole world Islamic, it will be a challenge for them to accept the presence of other religions along with Islam in a pluralistic context.

Second, can Muslims accept the existence of the state of Israel (Chapman, 2007, pp. 155-56)? Drawing from Nettler, Chapman (2007) says that many Muslims see the establishment of Israel as the "ultimate affront" to Arabs, with the result that the sentiments of "some Middle Eastern leaders" are strong enough to speak of this conflict in terms of jihad (Chapman, 2007, p. 155). They not only view this as another example of Western domination but also more significantly "as an attempt by Jews to do something that is not legitimate" (Nettler, 1978, p. 11)—seeking political independence right in the middle of Arab territory. For the Arabs this was even more shocking than the preceding displacement of Islam by Christianity in that region. Furthermore, Chapman (2007) says that while not all Muslims have the same feelings about Israel, there is "an Islamic dimension" (p. 156) to the Arab-Israeli conflict as well that has gained prominence over time with the emergence of groups such as Hamas and Hezbollah.

Third, are Islam and democracy compatible with each other? Chapman (2007) explains that while modern Western democracy emphasizes grassroots sovereignty and recognizes citizens' "inalienable right" (p. 158) to choose their own governments and establish their own laws, for Islam it is not possible to keep God out of the picture. Muslims insist, whatever society they live in, that society "should recognize the sovereignty of God"(Chapman, 2007, p. 158). At the same time, most modernist and traditionalist Muslims maintain that because Muhammad "clearly believed in and practiced the principle of consultation (shura), there can be no fundamentally Islamic objection to a nation electing its own leaders through democratic processes" (Chapman, 2007, p. 158).

The position of women in Islam is another significant challenge. The Qur'an and Islam teach that men and women are created from the same soul and are "morally equal before God" (Chapman, 2007, p. 161). Both men and women will be rewarded by God in Paradise, though it is described as a place that has "dark-eyed virgins"

(p. 162). God commands men to treat women well. While some verses do seem to suggest that men are superior to women, moderate scholars interpret them to mean that men are the leaders of their families and need to take care of their wives. Wives are to live chaste and obedient lives and can be beaten by their husbands if they are disobedient. Women should maintain modesty in their dress and, in some traditions, should veil themselves when they go outside, though most Muslims do not believe they must be completely veiled. Men may have up to four wives as long as they "treat them all fairly and equally" and may additionally according to the law have an unlimited number of "slave-concubines" (p. 161). Husbands may divorce their wives, but there is no provision in Islam for a wife to divorce her husband. Legally, one man's testimony is equal to the testimony of two women (Chapman, 2007, pp. 161-64).

Regarding the veiling of women, Chapman (2007) asserts that it comes as a surprise to people in the West that Muslim women who are veiled can be "highly educated, working women" (p. 169). He also talks about some of the reasons that women have given for wearing a veil: it liberates women and helps them escape from aggressive behavior of men in public and encourages men to respect women; it need not restrict the freedom of women; it shows that women are completely committed to Islam; it provides women with the "security and stability" (p. 169-170) of familiar social codes in a society that is always changing; it does not mean that women want to remain in seclusion in their homes, nor does it prevent them from working outside the home; it is an indication to men that women can interpret Islam in their own way and live consistently with it in a way that wins the approval of Muslim men (pp. 169-70). Chapman goes on to say that the status of women in Islam has changed significantly because of the influence of the West. At the same time many women in the West have also converted to Islam because of their distaste "of the promiscuity in Western societies" and their attraction to the "higher moral standards" in Islam (Chapman, 2007, p. 170). Christians may think that Christianity ascribes greater dignity to women, but in fact the church has not always had good attitudes toward women. While it is true that at some points in history Christians may not have had awareness of Christian teaching about women or Christians may have been influenced more by the culture than the gospel, Muslims often find it hard to separate "Christian teaching" from "Christian practice" (Chapman, 2007, pp. 170-71).

The third area that Chapman (2007) discusses has to do with the issue of Islamic terrorism. Islamists have numerous grievances with Western societies (pp. 176-78): The imperialism of the 19th and the 20th centuries has weakened and humiliated the Muslim world. Neocolonialism, which includes "political, military, economic and religious" influences, has replaced the old imperialism but it is even more "subtle and dangerous" (Chapman, 2007, p. 176). Because Western ideologies such as "capitalism, communism/socialism and nationalism" have failed, "the only solution is for Muslims to return to their own Islamic roots" (Chapman, 2007, p. 176-177). The western powers instigated the establishment of the nation of Israel in Arab territory. The presence of US troops in Saudi Arabia and the invasion of sacred territory by "infidels" (Chapman, 2007, p. 177) are inflammatory. Many Islamic governments are corrupt, autocratic, and have colluded with the West. Attempting to get Saddam Hussein to withdraw from Kuwait in compliance with UN resolutions but not attempting to get Israel to comply with UN resolutions to withdraw from occupied territory displays a double standard. In other words, asserts Chapman (2007), Islamism is the result of an "angry response"

(p. 178) by Muslims to the decline of Islamic societies and the ascendancy of the West.

Chapman (2007) also discusses three lines of thinking that Muslims espouse regarding terrorist activities carried out in the name of Islam (pp. 179-80) that would be helpful for American evangelicals to understand. Some Muslims think that these actions are carried out against those who oppose Islam and are "genuinely Islamic" (Chapman, 2007, p. 179) and in keeping with teachings of Islam. Other Muslims say that it is impossible to justify these actions in terms of teachings of Islam. Still others, while sympathizing with the motives of jihadists, will neither condemn nor support these actions.

Some Muslims as well as Christians also wonder how a religion that began with violent actions could today be called a religion of peace (Chapman, 2007, pp. 180-84). It would be helpful for Muslims to recognize and American evangelicals to understand that jihad has different meanings, including a spiritual struggle in a Muslim's pursuit of God, offensive war against those who refuse to submit to Islamic rule, defensive struggle that condemns "aggressive warfare" (Chapman, 2007, p. 181), and the concept that Muslim martyrs who die in jihad immediately go to paradise.

Dialoguing with Muslims

After presenting Islam from a Muslim's perspective, Chapman (2007) discusses ten "dos and don'ts" that Christians need to keep in mind when dialoguing with Muslims (pp. 197-99): Christians should be prepared to talk about anything, not just about religion; avoid starting arguments, and do not be concerned about winning the debate if you find yourself in it; avoid "the temptation to criticize Islam"; work at removing misunderstandings, e.g., the identity of Jesus; focus on what is more important rather than secondary issues, e.g., forgiveness rather than eating pork; be willing to acknowledge "the past and present mistakes and crimes of Christians"; exercise patience when talking about "political and social issues"; "do not underestimate the power of personal testimony"; be satisfied with explaining the gospel "one small aspect" at a time; and "be yourself, be honest and vulnerable, be open to learn" (p. 197-199).

When dialoguing with Muslims, Chapman (2007) asserts that we should "discover each other's humanity before we learn about each other's creed" (p. 227). In order to do that, our discussion should focus on two questions. First, "Who are we?" (Chapman, 2007, p. 229). Here we should emphasize that we, Christians and Muslims alike, are all human beings, belonging to a family and community of faith, and we are residents of a specific society. Second, "What are our basic human needs, and how are these met within our own faith?" (Chapman, 2007, p. 230). Here our discussion should focus on our common sense of "health and well-being" (Chapman, 2007, p. 230) our sense of values and morality, obtaining the forgiveness of God, loving other human beings and being loved by them, knowing the truth about our world and about ourselves, our common sense of humanity and the kind of people we should be in this world, and the nature of life after we die (Chapman, 2007, pp. 229-30).

In his discussion of some of the harder challenges that come to the foreground in the encounter between Christianity and Islam, Chapman (2007) asserts that Christians need an appropriate response to the political challenges that Islam poses (pp. 297-312). In his discussion he raises some important questions for Christians to think about:

- Why does Islam seem to be such a political religion—so much more political than Christianity as we know it today seems to be?

- What is the Muslim vision for the world? Do all Muslims want or expect Islam to triumph? If so, is it to triumph through persuasion, or force, or both?
- How are Christian minorities perceived and treated in Islamic countries? How should they respond, for example, to different kinds of discrimination? (Chapman, 2007, p. 297)

While Chapman's (2007) answers to these questions, and the sixfold Christian response to the political challenges posed by Islam, are tailored to countries where Christians are a minority in a Muslim-majority context, two responses are important for American evangelicals to consider. One, information that is presented must be accurate because, as Chapman asserts, people in the communities get influenced by what is passed on by the media, which is "often one-sided, misleading or hopelessly out of date" (p. 307), and making generalizations to describe two or more situations as though they were all the same is not helpful. Two, there is a need for outside governments and international organizations to protest unfair and harsh situations that Christian minorities in Muslim-majority contexts face (Chapman, 2007, p. 308). It is appropriate to add to Chapman's suggestion that American evangelicals should join such efforts when the need arises.

Basic Principles For A Theology Of Religions

From the discussion above three basic principles that shape my theology of religions emerge. First, it must be shaped by the teachings of the Bible. This includes recognizing that God is holy and His acts are righteous and that He deals fairly with adherents of other faiths. God has created human beings in his image, and while it is corrupted because of sin, God works to restore this image to its original state. Being created in the image of God also means recognizing the "common" humanity of all individuals, regardless of their religious beliefs. God has revealed himself to human beings through general and special revelation, and God wants people to know him through his final revelation of the incarnation of Christ. Human beings have been impacted by sin, which includes social relationships, cultures, and societies. Sin leads to human beings rebelling against God, which results in God's wrath and eternal condemnation of all human beings unless they receive salvation through Christ's forgiveness. God has made a way for human beings to be saved from God's wrath, which happens through Christ's atonement on the cross. While Jesus' death is the basis for salvation, this salvation is obtained through faith in Christ and not through any human effort. This salvation is available to all human beings regardless of their culture or religious background. Redeemed human beings have the responsibility of sharing the gospel with non-Christians.

Second, descriptions of other religions must be accurate as far as their beliefs and practices are concerned. This includes recognizing not only that within each religion there is internal diversity but also that each religion is different from the others. At the same time we need to be aware that each religion has aspects that are similar to aspects of other religions. While there are similarities among the various religions, concepts that are similar must be understood in the context of their own traditions, which also means that inherent differences between these concepts will emerge, and they need to be acknowledged. When aspects of other religions that are true and good are observed, they need to be acknowledged as such without characterizing them as satanic deceptions.

Third, while religious expression exists in all cultures, human beings and the religions they practice are impacted by sin and the work of Satan. This includes the variety of ways in which religiosity is expressed, for example inappropriate ways to respond to God; human efforts to please God; and Satan using other religions, as well as distortions of the "truth" within religions, to deceive people and move them away from the truth of Christ.

Additionally, as we think about the practice of religion at the grassroots level, it is significant to be aware that individual adherents are motivated by different cultural and family traditions, emphasize some doctrines of their faith over others, etc. In practice this means that their faith will not look exactly like the "textbook" version of their religion, and a person's lived-out faith will often appear different from that of their next-door neighbor(s). Thus, fully appreciating a person's daily faith practice means seeking textbook knowledge of their faith as well as gaining understanding about their faith from the individuals themselves.

The discussion above also yields some basic principles that inform my theology of religions with regard to Islam. First, there are elements in Islam that exist because of the concept of original monotheism, which should be affirmed by evangelicals as well as used as connecting points or a bridge for interacting with Muslims: the concept of monotheism in Islam; Islam's teaching about the imperative for human beings to submit to God; the strong sense of morality imprinted on the hearts of human beings and the resulting necessity to live an ethical life.

Second, evangelicals need to understand and appreciate the significance and reverence of the Qur'an in Islam, the role the Hadith plays in Islamic life, and the importance of Muhammad in Islam. This includes tempering our comments and not speaking disrespectfully about the Qur'an or Muhammad. It is crucial that we take the trouble to read and understand the Qur'an as well as the Hadith.

Third, evangelicals may safely affirm those teachings in the Qur'an that cohere with and correspond to the truths revealed in the Bible as well as through general revelation. For example, both the

Qur'an and the Bible teach that God exists. At the same time evangelicals need to understand that all that the Qur'an teaches, drawn from general revelation as well as what Muhammad may have picked up through his contact with Jews and Christians, must be understood in its larger context, the most significant aspect of which is that it explicitly denies the true nature of Christ; i.e., what the Qur'an teaches must be viewed with a great deal of caution. For example, the Qur'an's teaching that there is one God can never cohere with and correspond to the Bible's teaching that there is one God. But the teachings of the Qur'an can safely be used as connecting points or bridges, not new insights on biblical truth, to engage Muslims in dialogue and to proclaim the truth of the gospel.

Fourth, teachings we find in the Qur'an that come close to biblical truth may be used by the Holy Spirit to provide access to the complete revelation of Christ, with or without human intervention. For example, while the Qur'an denies Jesus' deity and that He is the Son of God, thus putting a great gulf between Christianity and Islam, it does say some true things about Him —His virgin birth, that He is a prophet sent by God, etc.—that can serve as bridges for dialogue. Evangelicals should use such teachings in the Qur'an as connecting points to engage Muslims.

Fifth, elements of Islamic tradition that are found in Christian tradition, while not serving as lessons for evangelicals, should be used as connecting points to engage Muslims. These include Islam's emphasis on submission to God; evidences of God's glory in and through creation; daily prayer; charity to the poor; and the intersection of faith with public life and contemporary culture. These elements of Islamic tradition are good and will have positive impact on the surrounding culture.

Sixth, evangelicals need to recognize that there are passages in the Qur'an that talk about Allah commanding Muslims to fight and kill infidels or idolaters, as well as the teaching that in matters of religion there is no compulsion. Evangelicals need to understand and take both of these into account and recognize that while the "violent" passages of the Qur'an do motivate some Muslims to engage in violent jihad, it does not motivate all Muslims to do so. Related to this issue is the understanding that Islam wants to rule the world. While some Muslims may want this and are willing to engage in violence to achieve this, the generalization that this is the mindset of all Muslims or that it characterizes all of Islam is inaccurate and has the propensity to stir up fear and prejudice.

Seventh, evangelicals need to be cognizant of and engage Muslims in the complexities of the various issues that characterize Islamic thought and the Muslim mindset: Muslims trying to live in pluralistic cultures; the existence of the state of Israel; the relationship of Islam and democratic governments; Islam's view of Muslim women; the different ways in which Muslims understand violence and terrorist activities in the name of Islam; etc. All of these can and should serve as points of dialogue and evangelism.

The discussion above also yields some basic principles that inform my theology of religions regarding Muslims. These principles are set within the framework that McDermott and Netland (2014) discuss above regarding religious others: that we are to make disciples of religious others, love them, and treat them as we would want them to treat us. While these principles also apply to Muslims as "religious others," we need to discuss some basic principles regarding Muslims because of the negative way in which Muslims via their association with Islamic terrorism are perceived. First, Christians need to have the proper perspectives toward Muslims, which includes thinking about and approaching Muslims first as human beings, as individuals, and as neighbors before thinking about and relating to them as Muslims who are part of one of the great religions of the world and before we tell them that we are Christians. That is, our perspective of Muslims, as well as the resulting attitudes and practices, should begin with the recognition of our common humanity rather than our different religious traditions.

Second, Christians need to inculcate the proper attitude toward Muslims, examining them in light of the teachings of the Bible. This includes recognizing our own negative attitudes that have the potential to be shaped by the violence toward society and persecution of Christians perpetrated by some Muslims and eschewing this attitude, as well as the fear that comes along with it, that are often unjustly generalized toward all Muslims.

Third, Christians need to engage in the proper practices toward Muslims, including moving beyond any negative attitudes and fear of Islam and Muslims we might harbor and developing relationships with them, treating them with compassion, and interacting and dialoguing with them as fellow human beings. In fact, dialoguing with them about the very issues that give rise to our animosity and fear would be a good way to not only deal with our attitudes but also engage Muslims about issues that are a source of consternation to many of them as well. Engaging in proper practices also includes developing an appreciation for Islamic culture as well as seeking to understand their beliefs from their perspective.

I will now use these principles for an evangelical theology of religions to analyze the perspectives, attitudes, and practices of the 21st century American evangelicals' toward Islam and Muslims that become evident through their responses to the questions they were asked during the interview and the focus group study.

CHAPTER 9

ANALYZING AMERICAN EVANGELICAL ENGAGEMENT OF ISLAM AND MUSLIMS

21st century American evangelicals' engagement of Islam and Muslims becomes evident through their responses to the questions they were asked during the interview. The analysis of this engagement is the subject of this chapter. I will use the basic principles for an evangelical theology of religions discussed in Chapter 8 to analyze the responses of the lay American evangelicals and pastors as well as the American evangelical leaders serving at COMM. I begin by offering some general observations about the responses of the lay evangelicals and pastors and the responses of the COMM staff. In Section II I offer an analysis of these responses, making explicit connections between the responses made by 21stcentury American evangelicals and the past experiences of Americans with religious others in the US that were discussed in PART II, Chapters 2, 3, and 4.

Section I: General Observations

A number of points emerged from this study that should be of concern to American evangelicals. First, the evangelical respondents tend to associate Islam with violence and even proactively look for teachings in the Qur'an that talk about violence in order to justify their preconceived notions. This association of Islam with violence has made them fearful of Islam and suspicious of Muslims, as a consequence of which the respondents "demonize" the religion and harbor a great deal of animosity toward its adherents. They tend to have a monolithic and static perception of Islam—supposing it has not changed since its inception in the 7th century and is implacably hostile toward Christians and Western culture. The unfortunate result of this has been that while the respondents claim they would be open to interacting with Muslims in social gatherings, some of their comments reveal a distinctly inhospitable attitude toward Muslims. Thus, their views are highly conflicted. This was especially evident as some of my respondents indicated that they know as Christians they are supposed to love Muslims but actually feel intense animosity toward them. Most respondents did not question whether their fear of Islam and hostility toward Muslims were justified. In light of this hostility, the counsel offered by the COMM leaders is especially apropos: "We never want to communicate a feeling of fear from Muslims or resentment or hatred of them. We want people to understand and have a compassion for Muslims. That's very important."

That some American evangelicals have negative perspectives and attitudes is not surprising, but it is problematic because it influences their practices toward Muslims. The interview of the COMM leaders revealed that it is possible to harbor extremely negative perspectives and attitudes toward Muslims and yet be able to act compassionately toward them when engaging them in the context of ministry. Clearly, negative perspectives and attitudes do not have to be debilitating, but in the case of some of my respondents they are.

A speaker at a Muslim-ministry conference, himself a convert to Islam, gave the following exhortation at a meeting of expatriate Christian ministry workers in the Middle East and North Africa You saw (and continue to see) Muslims go to their mosques for daily prayers. You knew (and know) that Muslims who do not come to faith in Jesus and find forgiveness through Him because of His death on the cross will spend eternity in Hell separated from God, but your fear of Muslims kept (and keeps) you from developing relationships with them and sharing the Gospel with them. Why were (and are) you moved more by a fear of Muslim retaliation and violence towards you as a Christian when you share the Gospel with them, than a fear of God to obey Him in evangelizing Muslims regardless of the consequences? (Identity withheld for security purposes).

We American evangelicals need to ask ourselves this question. Along these lines the COMM leaders also offered some helpful insight: The fear that some American evangelicals have is the "fear of being labeled as intolerant." But, in his view, what is intolerant "is to sit back and do nothing, keep your mouth shut while people are in bondage and going to hell right before our eyes."

Second, Christian theology is heavily influenced by the latest crisis unfolding in the world, and the respondents' understanding of Islam is primarily shaped by the information presented in the media. On the one hand, while it is not surprising that the respondents are influenced by the media and in fact this information needs to be taken into account as they engage their culture so that they are not naïve about what they are seeing and hearing, they do need to access better sources of information that provide a balanced view as well as a biblically grounded frame of reference.

Third, while it is good that the respondents hear from American Christian leaders about Islam and Muslims and are shaped by their teachings, several troubling issues emerge from this: American Christian leaders do not seem to exercise caution about what they say, and they inadvertently or unintentionally pass on perceptions that are inaccurate and that focus on the negative and violent aspects of Islam; the respondents do not exercise caution and discernment about who they listen to and whether to accept the information at face value and

how much of it to accept; and the respondents do not have access to the
voices of Muslim leaders and scholars or dialogue with Muslim friends
and acquaintances in order to help develop their perspectives and
attitudes toward Islam and Muslims. Furthermore, churches are not
doing enough to help educate congregants and help shape their
perspectives and attitudes toward Muslims within a biblical framework;
this lack of input from the churches is further exacerbated by the lack of
access to sources of information that describe and demonstrate proper
perspectives, attitudes, and practices. Churches are also not doing
enough to create the space and opportunity for their congregants to
engage directly with Muslims.

Fourth, given all the negative comments made by the 44
respondents, it is remarkable that only six respondents had strong
physical and emotional reactions to the information shared during the
course of the interviews: one expressed anger when talking about
Muslims being able to be good citizens of the US; one got defensive
when I pointed out that her perspective about Muslims was negative,
showing that she was not aware that her view of Islam was actually
negative; one wept over the conflicted feelings of hatred he harbored
toward Muslims, quite aware that based on the teachings of Jesus he
was supposed to love them; one gestured strongly while asserting that
she would not want to dialogue with Muslims because they may be
secretly radical and kill her; one wept when recalling the events of 9/11;
and one, gesturing strongly, asserted that Americans should "nuke" the
Muslim nations, and "when we do that once, they will not mess with us
again." The other respondents answered quite matter-of- factly, giving
the impression that their perspectives, attitudes, and practices are
neither unwarranted nor unusual, which is not the ideal frame of mind
for American evangelicals to be in.

There were also a number of points that emerged from this study that should be encouraging to American evangelicals. First, based on the information provided by the respondents as well as their pastors, the negative perspectives and attitudes espoused by the respondents are not being taught to them by the pastors of the churches they attend. Second, to a certain extent the perspectives, attitudes, and practices of the respondents are shaped by a biblical worldview regarding Islam and Muslims. This means that they view Muslims from a biblical perspective, are deeply concerned for the salvation of Muslims, and would share the gospel with them if they had the opportunity to do so. They also want to engage Muslims and would do so in deep and meaningful ways if they were given the opportunity. This desire to share the gospel and engage Muslims at a deeper level has resulted in their desire to learn about Muslims and Islam, and they are asking the right questions in order to do this.

Third, the respondents care about the US as a country and American cultural life, are deeply concerned about what influence Islam will have on American civic life, are concerned about the behavior of the "violent" Muslims, realize that the Muslim community does not always adequately denounce the violence that is perpetrated in the US as well as in other countries, and understandably complain about the absence of this voice.

Fourth, it is noteworthy and encouraging that COMM leaders are aware of their own negative perspectives and attitudes toward Muslims that have resulted from their experiences and acknowledge their need for asking God's help on a daily basis to repent so that they could engage Muslims in a Christ-like manner. It is also encouraging that in spite of the vitriol experienced by the COMM leaders by Muslims they engage, they are able to have a compassionate perspective and attitude, and the practices that they engage in are shaped by this compassion as well as a deep sense of hospitality. That is, in spite of the vitriol experienced, it is indeed possible for American evangelicals to live Christ-like lives in their relationships with Muslims. American evangelicals in general would do well to emulate the perspectives, attitudes, and practices of the COMM leaders.

Section II: Analysis Of Responses

When we situate the responses of the American evangelical respondents and the COMM staff within our discussion in Chapter 2 of the growth of religious diversity in the US, it becomes evident that their responses align well with what scholars have already observed in the past, in some cases agreeing with what has been observed and written, and in other cases showing that the perspectives of the American evangelical respondents and the COMM staff have changed. First, Wuthnow (2007) asserts that in the past American Christians could respond to adherents of other religions in several different ways: think that they are not present, or ignore them, or lump them into broad categories, or view them in ways that diminish the significance of their culture and tradition. The respondents and the COMM staff in some ways fit well with Wuthnow's assessment and in other ways diverge from it. Far from regarding Muslims as though they were not present or ignoring the presence of Muslims in their midst, they are actually very aware of them (contra Muck's 1990 observation). They are to a certain extent aware of what Muslims believe (contra Eck (2002)) and how they live and interact with others around them. At the same time, most respondents did tend to lump Muslims and Islam into broad categories—"Muslims are evil, Islam is an evil religion"; the COMM staff viewed Islam as evil but viewed individual Muslims as caught up in the system of Islam. Most respondents also diminished the value of Islamic culture and tradition—their negative perceptions of Islam, especially in regards to Islam's view of women and the lack of democratic freedom within Islam (which stands out to the American mind in light of the American constitutional right to freely practice religion), overshadowed or completely ignored the good social values that stem from Islam, which were not mentioned; the respondents also viewed Christianity, Christian culture, and American culture as superior to Islamic culture, thus lining up with Wuthnow's (2007) conclusions.

While Wuthnow (2007), Muck (1990), and Eck (2002) are correct in the conclusions they draw about the responses of American Christians that were made during earlier time periods, the change among the respondents, I would argue, has come about because Islam is much more in the forefront in US culture, and the respondents are "forced" to pay attention to Islam and how Muslims live and practice their faith. The respondents are not fully knowledgeable of the teachings of Islam and in most cases have an inaccurate understanding of it. However, judging from their expressed interest in learning about Islam and Muslims and the steps they are taking to acquire information, they do show a greater appreciation for religious diversity than what Muck said in 1990. They seem to be trying to get a deeper and more accurate understanding of Islamic beliefs and practices and the media reports about the relationship between Islam and the violence perpetrated in the name of Islam, which is contrary to Wuthnow's observations published in 2007. The COMM staff, on the other hand, by virtue of being directly involved in ministry to Muslims, is quite knowledgeable of Islam as a religion as well as the relationship of Islam and violence.

Second, again contrary to Wuthnow's observations in 2007 and Muck's in 1990, the respondents and the COMM staff are not satisfied by simply practicing their own faith within their own communities without thinking about ways in which Muslims practice their faith. That is to say, tolerance expressed by the respondents toward Muslims indicates that they have greater appreciation for the significance of interreligious understanding and interaction. Again, I would argue that the greater visibility of Islam in the media has been the catalyst for this change among the respondents, and the involvement in ministry to Muslims has been the catalyst for this change for the COMM staff. Perhaps one of the results of this will be, to answer the questions Wuthnow (2007) raises (whether American Christians will continue to ignore religious others or they would come to a deeper understanding of their own faith), that as the respondents think about Muslims, they will get a deeper understanding of what it means to live out the gospel, especially in relation to Islam and Muslims, as the COMM staff already is doing. And perhaps, as Eck (2002) suggests should happen but is not as yet happening, the result will be that the respondents, like the COMM staff, will take greater initiative to engage Muslims and to understand them and their beliefs more deeply, so that some of the stereotypes of Muslims and Islam may be eschewed and that the respondents may get a better grasp of the similarities and differences between Christianity and Islam and between Christians and Muslims.

Third, the responses very clearly show, as Eck (2002) also pointed out, that the respondents tend to be mistrusting, fearful, and suspicious of Muslims as well as recognize that their interaction with Muslims would be beneficial to themselves as well as to Muslims. The fear that the respondents have shown has resulted in hostility toward Muslims, which is in line with Marty's (2005) analysis; the COMM staff, on the other hand, did not show any fear or hostility toward Muslims. Given this, it would be helpful for the respondents to engage in healthy introspection, which includes trying to understand the reasons for their underlying fear, mistrust, and suspicion of Muslims so that they can better understand them, as Marty asserts. Furthermore, the responses also show that the respondents and the COMM staff are very willing to show hospitality toward Muslims, as Marty (2005) defines hospitality: expressing their faith in its fullness and expecting Muslims to do the same; being open about their own tradition as well as expecting Muslims to be open about theirs; regarding Muslims with civility and welcoming the diversity of Christian and Muslim beliefs, recognizing that dialogue is a continual process and that faith impacts social issues; engaging Muslims in open and honest dialogue on a personal level; and being willing to live with the conflict that comes with having starkly different religious beliefs.

That the respondents fit in well with Marty's (2005) definition of hospitality is indicated in a number of ways. One, those respondents who had interacted with Muslims did express their faith in its fullness and listened, even when they disagreed, when Muslims articulated their faith. Two, they regarded Muslims with civility, welcoming the diversity of the beliefs of each other's religions, and recognized that dialogue is an ongoing process and that each other's religious beliefs significantly impact social issues. Three, of those respondents who had discussions with Muslims, most engaged Muslims openly and honestly in dialogue. Four, most of the respondents engaged Muslims on a personal level in their interactions with them. Five, as long as the respondents felt that Muslims recognized that they should live out Islam within the broader umbrella of the American value of freedom of religion, the respondents were willing to live with conflict that comes from the practice and living out of faiths that are very different.

At the same time, while most of the respondents enthusiastically articulated that they would be willing to get together with Muslims if their church hosted events with their Muslim friends and neighbors, which indicates at least in their mind they are hospitable, all of the respondents also articulated negative perceptions of Muslims and Islam along with attitudes characterized by mistrust, fear, and suspicion from a variety of perspectives, and some of them even stated outright that they would not want to talk to Muslims and/or get together with them for social events; i.e., in actual fact the respondents do not display perspectives, attitudes, and practices that would be characterized as hospitable. This conflicting attitude is indicative of a great deal of inner discord that the respondents feel. Some of the respondents even articulated that they feel this way even though they know that as Christians who are seeking to live out the teachings of the Bible they should not espouse these kinds of negative perspectives and attitudes.

Fourth, Muck (1990) claims that the growth of non-Christian religions has gone unnoticed by Americans because non-Christian religions are still a minority and lack political and economic clout. While this assertion is accurate for the 1980s timeframe in which Muck made his observation, the responses of the interviewees show that the respondents and the COMM staff, because of the space that the media devotes to reporting on Islam and violence, are quite aware of the political involvement of Muslims and are actually concerned what impact the increasing numbers of Muslims will have on American life, especially in relation to sharia law. The respondents were also concerned that with the increase of Islamic influence on American life there will be limitations on religious freedoms and American evangelicals may not be able to live out their Christian faith fully, especially regarding the freedom to evangelize other religious groups. Furthermore, this research also demonstrates that the respondents partially fit in well with Eck's (2002) definition of pluralism, which includes: as opportunities arise, they actively engage Muslims; they are committed to their own faith as they engage Muslims; and they recognize that their engagement of Muslims is an ongoing process. At the same time Eck asserts in her definition of pluralism that American Christians should take initiatives to understand religious others. The responses of the interviewees show that the respondents, while wanting to do this with Islam and Muslims and in some cases indeed doing so, the sources that they access and the kinds of information they look for prohibit them from getting an accurate understanding of Muslims and Islam. The COMM staff, on the other hand, fits in well with all the components of Eck's definition of pluralism.

Fifth, based on his research Numrich (2009) put American Christians into two groups: those who respond to religious others keeping in mind Christian truth claims and doctrine and those for whom other issues, such as freedom of religion, take priority over religious truth claims in their interactions with religious others. This research demonstrates that the respondents actually fall into both these groups in that in considering Muslims they thought of them in terms of their need for sharing the gospel and Muslims coming to faith in Christ, i.e., Christian truth claims and doctrine were a priority, as well as recognized that Muslims have the right to practice their faith and build their mosques anywhere in the US, i.e., the basic civil right of the freedom of religion was a priority for the respondents. The COMM staff fit the first group quite well in that their entire raison d'être is their desire and goal to present the gospel to Muslims. The COMM staff also fits in well with the second group, which emerges from the focus of their helps-based incarnational ministry to meet the physical needs of Muslims in their community.

Sixth, Wuthnow (2007), through information gathered via qualitative interviews of over 50 pastors across the US who talked in detail about what their churches have done in order to respond to religious diversity, asserts that evangelical Protestant churches have been involved in, or sponsored, some kind of interfaith program in order to encourage more understanding among the various religions. Eck's 2002 work pointed out that engaging in interfaith dialogues and providing appropriate education would be an important response to the increase in religious diversity. This research project demonstrated that some of the congregations had created a forum for interfaith dialogue or specifically set up a conference to educate the congregants about ministry to Muslims. That is, the fact that not all congregations had created some kind of forum for discussing issues related to Islam and Muslims highlights the need for education, as Eck points out. The reason that not all congregations had created programs for interfaith dialogue and understanding, I would argue, is that evangelicals put a great deal of emphasis on individuals reaching out to individual Muslims, and put more emphasis on sharing the gospel than on establishing forums for interfaith dialogue and interaction across an array of areas of mutual interest. Another reason for this is that American evangelicalism is very inconsistent and conflicted about hosting these kinds of programs in their local congregations, as indicated through the comments of one pastor, who said that he was not sure how well his congregation would receive the hosting of such an event, as well as the comments of one respondent, who said that she would not be open to hosting such an event in her church because it would communicate the wrong message to other Christians and they may think that her church was liberal in its theological convictions.

Seventh, this research seems to indicate that the congregations fall into Wuthnow's (2007) category of "strategies of avoidance" (p. 244) in that only one of the congregations had organized a program where the congregants could hear from a Muslim speaker in the context of broader teaching about the Middle East, Islam, and war. The other three pastors would all be open to this within certain limitations: Two said that it should not be anything more than a social event for the purpose of building relationships, one of whom said that there should be no form of worship, and another that there should be no proselytism; the fourth pastor spoke about this in terms of encouraging his congregants to express their friendship towards their Muslim neighbors. But, these three pastors had not done anything concrete in their congregations as the first pastor had to facilitate deeper understanding of Muslims, Islam, and issues related to Muslims and Islam, highlighting the inconsistent and conflicted nature of organizing these kinds of programs in their congregations. This perspective also seemed to emerge through some of the comments made by the respondents: they did not want mosques in their neighborhoods, one respondent was completely unwilling to dialogue with Muslims, and some of the respondents expressed discomfort at the idea of sitting down for dinner with Muslims.

Eighth, this research also demonstrates that the respondents and the COMM staff in some respects engage in what Wuthnow (2007) calls "reflective pluralism" (p. 289): the respondents recognize that Muslims are different and why they are different and have good reasons for engaging Muslims—want to understand them better; are interested in the specifics of Islam; are, or are in the process of becoming, "studiers" of Islam (however, in this case it would be important for the respondents to draw information about Islam and Muslims from sources that are more balanced and that provide a biblical frame of reference to interpret Islam and Muslims and violent events related to Islam and not just from news media); recognize that their viewpoint, or that of Muslims, is not arrived at arbitrarily or disconnected from the truth of Christianity; and respect Muslims. Furthermore, the sixth characteristic of reflective pluralism, which Wuthnow (2007) calls "willingness to comprise" (p. 292), talks about individuals making the decision to interact with religious others at a level where the differences come to the fore and become important instead of thinking that religious beliefs and values are insignificant. This research demonstrates that those respondents who did engage Muslims displayed a clear willingness to compromise in that they were willing to interact with them at a level where Christian and Muslim differences would become prominent. This was true of the COMM staff as well.

Ninth, the responses by the COMM staff align very well with Muck's (1990) approach to the response of American evangelicals to religious pluralism. One, COMM staff love their Muslim neighbors unconditionally—sharing with the Muslims the common courtesies of life, loving those Muslims who regard the COMM staff as "enemies," not judging them, recognizing that Christians and Muslims are equally sinful, and removing cultural barriers that would impede the development of relationships. All of this stems from COMM staff's love for Christ. Two, glorifying God through their institution: a bookstore that offers a variety of services to the community, all of which is done in the name of Christ and to honor Christ. This is fulfilled to the extent that they glorify God through their ministry but does not include cooperation with institutions of other religions. Three, COMM staff, recognizing that the presence of Muslims in their community is an opportunity to preach the truth to them, is unashamedly involved in the activity of the verbal proclamation of the gospel, including Muck's (1990) nine principles that characterize the proclamation of the truth to Muslims: COMM staff is intimate with their faith so that they can articulate it well to Muslims; expect conflict in dialogue with Muslims; recognize that Muslims believe and proclaim absolute truth but do so with only a partial understanding of the truth; make sure that their motives are right—wrong motives could include gaining converts, manipulating others to believe, or arrogantly believing that they are better than Muslims; the goal of their discussion with the Muslims they encounter is to clearly communicate the gospel to Muslims and understand them; do not create their own ideas but rather stick with God's theology—knowing their faith, being firmly established in the love of their faith, and committed to transforming this world; rather than trying to disprove Islam (although by virtue of definition, Mansur, the COMM staff apologist, engages in disproving Islam), they focus on proving Christianity; and adopt an attitude of humility toward Muslims. At the same time, all of the COMM staff members strongly emphasized Islam as an evil religion. No one mentioned if there were any "good" or "true" aspects within Islam. Their perspective was developed through their interactions with Muslims in the US, many of whom opposed COMM staff members strongly, as well as their interactions with Muslims in various ministry contexts outside of the US and a biblical understanding of religions that "deny" Christ. Their perspective was reinforced by what they see in the media.

At the same time they also recognized that not all Muslims are radical and/or violent but many of them are like "us," simply seeking to live out their lives as ordinary citizens, and that they are in bondage to the system of Islam. While there probably are certain aspects of Islam that are "good" or "true," and it would be significant for them recognize that, I maintain that for the most part their perspective, shaped both by what they have seen and experienced in their culture regarding Islam and Muslims as well as Christian theology, is balanced. At the same time, the clear evidence of both positive and negative perspectives and attitudes espoused by COMM staff is indicative of the conflicted perspectives and attitudes espoused by them, just as it was with the American evangelical respondents.

In Chapter 4 I presented a brief summary of some influential literature on Christian-Muslim relationships in the US, including perspectives, attitudes, and practices of Christians toward Muslims.

These non-evangelical American and evangelical scholars discussed a plethora of topics, both negative and positive in tone, many of which were also brought up by the respondents during the course of the interviews. Firstly, I mention topics discussed by non-evangelical American writers. Themes pertaining to Islam that Said (1997) mentioned, all of which were negative in essence, included: Westerners, Americans included, think that Islam is a demonic religion, filled with hostility and fear and characterized by violence; Islam is one monolithic entity; Islam is a threat to Western culture and wants to destroy Christianity; Christians have a fear of Islam; and terrorism has been linked directly with Islam. Other themes in Said's book mentioned by respondents refer to Muhammad: that he was a false prophet who sowed discord, was given to sensuality, was a hypocrite, and represented the devil; these understandings about Muhammad are not derived from the Qur'an but are shaped by real events of terrorism in the name of Islam happening in the real world, all of which make Islam a significant force in the political world. Said also discussed the numerous avenues through which Americans' perspectives were influenced, all of which emerge from the comments made by the American evangelical respondents: American Christians continue to rely on the press and on Christian leaders who, during this period where much terrorist activity is carried on in the name of Islam, focus on sensational crises and jihad; and Christian leaders continue to disseminate information that portrays Islam and Muslims in a negative light, giving the impression that Islam is characterized by violence.

Themes that Kidd (2009) mentioned that were brought up by the respondents included: the growth of Islam in the US and the corresponding increase in the respondents' fear of Islam; evangelization of Muslims; Islam does not offer assurance of salvation as Christ does; Jews and Israel on one side and Islam and Arabs on the opposing side as enemies; the Palestinian crisis and US foreign policy serve as hindrances to evangelism among Muslims; the desire to better understand evangelism among Muslims; an interest in insider's literature on Islam that not only reveals the true nature of Islam but also helps Christians evangelize Muslims; the linking of Satan and Islam; Arabs are regarded as descendants of Ishmael, whereas interviewees considered Muslims as descendants of Ishmael; Ishmael was Satan's plan; Islam's role in the end-times has been "re-energized"; and Muslims are the enemies of God who oppose God's plan.

Secondly, themes, both positive and negative, that appeared in American evangelical writings on Islam and Muslims in the US included: Islam is the stronghold of the devil, a masterpiece of delusion, an intolerant religion; Islam is a religion of violence; Islam engages in jihad in order to expand; Islam plans to take over the world; Islam is violent toward and persecutes Christians; Muhammad was a pedophile, was possessed by devil, and was violent; Islam talks about responsibility toward family and community, and Christians and Muslims share similarities in culture and morality; negative comments about Islam, and America's unquestioned support of Israel and the Jews are a hindrance for evangelism of and dialogue with Muslims; Christians should not demean Islam or Muhammad; Christians should empathize with Muslims; Muslims are just like "us" Christians; our enemy is not Muslims but Satan; it is imperative that Christians maintain a moral and ethical lifestyle; etc.

The clear links of the themes that appear in these writings with the topics brought up by the respondents suggest that there has not been a notable change in what American evangelicals think and say about Islam, the reason for which is that overwhelmingly American evangelicals are shaped by the negative aspects of Islam portrayed in media and popular literature as well as by their biblical understanding of religions that deny Christ. While it is necessary to be shaped by the teachings of the Bible and to take serious stock of the violent actions of some adherents of Islam, it appears that American evangelicals are too quick to view and portray Islam as a monolithic entity that is for the most part characterized by violence.

From the principles that emerge from the discussion in Chapter 8 of the literature on theology of religions, the responses evidence that American evangelicals are influenced by some of these principles: teachings of the Bible, including the nature of God, human beings, and the created world; human beings, as well as the religions they practice, are impacted by sin and the work of Satan; God has revealed Himself to human beings; God seeks the salvation of all human beings, and He has provided a way through the death of Christ; it is the imperative of the Christian community to take the gospel to all non-Christians; and the starkly different ways in which the monotheism of God is understood in Christianity and Islam.

Other principles from the discussion of the literature on theology of religions that are not as prominent in influencing the American evangelical respondents include: descriptions of other religions must be accurate as far as their beliefs and practices are concerned; all religions have some things in common and are different in many ways, and all non-Christian religions have some true claims as well as aberrations of the truth; there are commonalities between Islam and Christianity, including submission to God, God's purpose in and through this created world, the importance of prayer, helping the poor, and the significance of faith in public life as well as aberrations of biblical truth found in Islam, all of which can serve as connecting points to engage Muslims in dialogue; the significance of having the proper appreciation for the importance of the Qur'an for Muslims and speaking about it and about Muhammad less disrespectfully; and Islam is not one monolithic entity but has a great deal of internal diversity. The reason that these are less prominent in the understanding of the American evangelical respondents is that Islam is viewed as a monolithic entity, lumped as a whole into the category of "negative," "deficient," or "evil" religion. That is, respondents' view of Islam is not as nuanced as it needs to be.

Other topics brought up by the respondents that were not as nuanced as they need to be, thus highlighting their deficient understanding of Islam, include: Islam and the Muslim community in general advocate violence, and Islam is an inherently violent religion; whether the Muslim community wrestles with the violent actions of some radical Muslims apparent in our world; that all Muslims want to rule the world; and that Muslims' view of women within Islam is characterized by the perspective that men are superior to women. This deficient understanding of Islam also brings to the fore the need for the respondents to become more knowledgeable about issues regarding Islam and Muslims, which includes: viewing Muslims first and foremost as fellow human beings and the basic needs they have as human needs and only secondly as followers of Islam; developing an appreciation for Islamic culture and the connection between the culture and the religion; the numerous ways in which Muslims view jihad and terrorism; the role of violence in the Old Testament and the Crusades in the history of the church; how the Muslim community as a minority attempts to live in democratic nations; the Islamic perspective of the nation of Israel; Muslim perspective of Western culture; and recognizing that quite often the information that the media presents is one-sided and that when we present information, it must be accurate because people get influenced by the information disseminated by us and the media.

Some of the sources of information that the American evangelical respondents have access to also show the mixed nature of information they are exposed to. On the one hand the information had to do with relating to Muslims in different ways, including doing evangelism among Muslims, understanding Islamic culture, etc.; and on the other hand the information consistently touched on the negative aspects of Islam, including violence, terrorism, poor treatment of women, etc. That is, the information that the American evangelical respondents access and receive is not only mixed but also extremely negative and strikingly harsh in tenor. For this reason it should not be surprising that the perspectives and attitudes of the American evangelical respondents are quite conflicted, but for the most part extremely negative, and their practices are characterized by inhospitality.

CHAPTER 10

CONCLUSION AND IMPLICATIONS

Since the terrorist attacks of 9/11, many world events have drawn attention to the intersection of Islam and Christianity. I began my qualitative interviews just after the Boston Marathon bombings in April 2013, and I was writing the conclusions and implications of the two-year study when news broke in Paris of the terrorist attacks on Charlie Hebdo to the cries of "Allahu Akbar" in February 2015. Most recently, on July 14, 2016, during the annual Bastille Day celebration, a truck driver plowed a 19-ton truck through the crowd that had gathered to watch the fireworks display. ISIS claimed responsibility for this terrorist attack that killed 86 people. Given the results of this study, it is not hard to ascertain what impact these events will have on the perspective of American evangelicals, whose understanding of Islam and Muslims is shaped by the violence reported by the media more than by a careful study of Islam or personal engagement with Muslims.

Without having access to balanced sources that would provide sound knowledge about Islam, it would be difficult to understand Islamic culture accurately, since to a large extent the media presents a negative picture. Balanced sources that provide sound information are overshadowed by the cacophony of a ratings-seeking media. Evangelicals tend not to consider the violence explicitly commanded by God in the Old Testament or the Crusades performed at the instigation of the Christian church. In their minds, contemporary occurrences of religiously motivated violence by Muslims stand out in a more immediate way. As long as popular evangelical writers focus on the negative aspects of Islam without presenting a sound framework within which to interpret these aspects, they will greatly hamper accurate knowledge of religious others and will influence the perspectives, attitudes, and practices of American evangelicals in such a way that they are hindered from fully living out Jesus' exhortation to "love your neighbor as yourself" (Matt 19:19).

How does one withstand the effect of the virulent comments made by American evangelical leaders who are in the position to influence the evangelical church in America? Islam is but one of the many religions and cultures to which Americans are increasingly exposed. How does one understand them all, and what should individuals and churches do to understand religious others? The analysis of the responses by lay evangelicals and pastors and the helps-based incarnational ministry of the COMM staff yields several helpful insights, both of which in combination with the discussion of the literature on theology of religions facilitate the development of pertinent missiological recommendations for evangelicals as they seek to engage Muslims and Islam in the US.

Missiological Recommendations

It is helpful to organize the missiological recommendations for American evangelicals in terms of their perspectives, attitudes, and practices regarding Islam and Muslims, the heart of which is the Golden Rule: American evangelicals should treat Muslims the way in which they themselves would want to be treated (Matt 7:12).

Perspectives

Evangelicals must view Muslims from a biblical perspective, recognizing that God is holy and His acts are righteous and that He deals fairly with the adherents of Islam. God has created Muslims in His image. This image is corrupted because of sin, but God is working to restore His image to its original state. Being created in the image of God also means recognizing that Christians and Muslims share a common humanity, that they have similar needs as human beings living together in a shared community, and that Christians must look at Muslims as human beings first and Muslims second. God has revealed Himself to human beings through general and special revelation, and God wants Muslims to know Him through his final revelation of the incarnation of Christ. Muslims have been impacted by sin, which includes negatively influencing social relationships, cultures, and societies within Islam. The impact of sin also means that Muslims, rather than being in submission to God as they believe, are in fact in rebellion against Him, resulting in God's wrath and eternal condemnation unless they receive forgiveness and salvation through Christ's atonement on the cross. This salvation is obtained through faith in Christ and not through any effort by Muslims.

Evangelicals must also be informed by their observations of Muslim actions in the wider culture, which includes recognizing that most Muslims are not radicalized and are not driven to engage in violence but are "peaceful" Muslims. Pertinent here is the understanding that while there are some passages in the Qur'an that speak of violence, Islamic teaching influences many Muslims to live lives characterized by peace and good morals; it is equally important for evangelicals to recognize that the Qur'an also asserts that in matters of religion there is to be no compulsion (Qur'an 2.256). At the same time, evangelicals must not have a naïve view that all Muslims are peaceful but recognize that there is a minority of Muslims that is hostile to Christians and Christianity and the wider American culture. That is, evangelicals need to espouse a more nuanced view of Muslims rather than categorize all Muslims into one camp, whether that is "peaceful Muslims" or "violent Muslims." Here it is well worth noting the comment made by one of the pastors who asserted that Islam is a "broad tent" and saying that "Muslims are bad, Muslims are evil" or that "Islam is a religion of peace, everything is good" are both inaccurate. "It is not helpful for you to have a narrow snapshot of what Islam is like." Islam has more than one billion people and "everything you think about it is true somewhere in the world. There are wonderful, open-minded, highly educated, moderate Muslims. There are mean, trying-to-kill-you, fundamentalist, hate-women Muslims."

Evangelicals must have a more robust understanding of the Qur'an and what it teaches. Evangelicals need to affirm that both the Qur'an and the Hadith are authoritative for the Islamic community as well as be cognizant of the understanding that Muslims have of the Qur'an as the revelation of God, which is similar to the Christian understanding of the incarnation of God in Christ. Regarding whether the Qur'an contains revelation from God, evangelicals can safely affirm that the Qur'an talks about the existence of God, but it is not exactly the same as the Bible's teaching of the One God; that the Qur'an contains religious truth, e.g., attests to the virgin birth of Christ, but also recognize that religious truths that emerge from the Qur'an are only duplications of truth taught in the Bible, e.g., the Qur'an's teaching about contentment and humility are also taught in the New Testament; and that while the Qur'an may contain "true" religious statements, it is not inspired and does not contain any special revelation. Furthermore, evangelicals can safely affirm that there is some truth in the Qur'an, such as God's justice and transcendence, and that it came into the Qur'an through the avenues of general revelation and the knowledge of the teachings of the Bible that people in the time of Muhammad, including Muhammad himself, were cognizant of through their contact with the Jewish and Christian communities in that region of the world.

Evangelicals must recognize that within Islam there are several sects, including the Sunni, Shia, Sufi, etc., traditions. There are several points of similarity between Islam and Christianity, such as both Islam and Christianity are monotheistic and teach good moral values to their adherents; both Christianity and Islam teach that human beings must submit to God; and both have a strong sense of morality imprinted on the hearts of human beings with the resulting imperative to live an ethical life. At the same time there are also significant differences, such as while both religions espouse a monotheistic understanding of God, Christianity has a concept of the triune God while Islam does not. Also significant is recognizing that there are elements in Islam that exist because of the concept of original monotheism, which should be affirmed by evangelicals as well as used as connecting points for interacting with Muslims, such as submission to God, the concept of monotheism, etc. Here it would be important to point out that while these are similarities, Islam and Christianity are fundamentally different from each other, and giving assent to both similarities and differences is necessary for genuine and meaningful dialogue to take place.

Furthermore, regarding satanic influence in Islam, while it is erroneous to assert that the entire religious phenomena of Islam, as well as the Qur'an, is satanic in its origin, it is equally naïve to assert that none of the religious phenomena of Islam, or the Qur'an, are satanic in its origin. For example, Muhammad himself thought that he was possessed by an evil spirit during the course of receiving revelations, and this needs to be taken into account. The way to navigate through this issue when dialoguing with Muslims is by focusing on the facts that human beings have a natural propensity to seek after God and reflect on spiritual matters; that the Qur'an as a book and Islam as a religion emerged out of this quest that Muhammad was on; and, not unlike other non-Christian religions, Islam and the Qur'an developed out of both a human and a spiritual influence. Evangelicals must also recognize the impact of sin and Satan on Muslims as individuals in that they respond to God inappropriately, sincere as their response may be. Here the Muslim's desire to seek God must be affirmed while also pointing out that God has sought out sinful human beings through His Son Jesus. Evangelicals also need to recognize the impact of sin and Satan on Islam as a religion in that Satan uses the incorrect teaching about Jesus in the Qur'an to lead Muslims away from the truth of the gospel. Having an accurate understanding of Islam, as well as Islamic culture, is crucial for cultivating a proper view of Muslims and developing healthy relationships with them.

It also imperative that evangelicals espouse the perspective that, in the words of one of the COMM leaders, "there is no new methodology for doing mission among Muslims ... [except to] confront them with the love of Christ" and "to be bold." That is, they need to be proactive in sharing the gospel with Muslims they know, regardless of the negative reactions and opposition they may/will experience as a result. Furthermore, Christians need to recognize that Muslims tend to have greater respect for Christians who are sincere about their faith; a perspective which should lead Christians to be direct in their proclamation of the gospel.

Attitudes

Evangelicals must eschew their fear of Islam, and animosity and mistrust of Muslims, as well as any inhospitable attitudes so that these do not become a hindrance to developing relationships with Muslims who are in their sphere of influence. This is significant in light of the fact that the community of the redeemed are to share the gospel of Jesus Christ and to make disciples of all peoples, including sincere adherents of other religious traditions, so that God is honored and worshipped throughout the earth. If evangelicals live with fear of Islam and animosity toward Muslims as well as an inhospitable attitude toward them, they will not be able to develop relationships and create space for Muslims to enter into the evangelicals' sphere of influence to hear the gospel of Christ. An attitude of fear and mistrust toward Muslims will also preclude genuine dialogue with Muslims, which is essential for the mutual education of Christians and Muslims. One of the insights that the COMM leaders gained through their ministry experience is that while initially the American church is very interested in learning about Islam and Muslims, their fear paralyzes them. COMM's response to this is that "disengagement from or with Muslims and Islam is not an option."

Another helpful observation offered by the COMM leaders is that because Muslims are part of the larger system of Islam which by its very nature tries to change "other cultures so that they all become Islamic and everyone accepts Islam and is forced into Islam," the average American is confused because they think that all Muslims are attempting to "turn America" into part of the Islamic world. This kind of thinking leads American evangelicals to espouse a negative attitude. It would be helpful for evangelicals' attitude to be characterized by the notion that while there certainly are Muslims who are driven with the long-range goal to make America an Islamic nation, "the average Muslim you meet in America is just a good guy trying to make a living"; they are just normal people trying to get a job, go to school, drive a taxi, visit the hospital, etc. and are not "affecting America in a bad way." This kind of an understanding will go a long way in helping evangelicals eschew their negativity. Espousing the proper attitude begins by recognizing their own negative attitude toward Muslims and inculcating an attitude that is shaped by Jesus' command to love others as ourselves.

Espousing the proper attitude also entails recognizing that Muslims are not enemies but lost individuals who are in bondage to Islam. Here the strategy that the COMM staff has inculcated in their own lives and ministry to deal with their own negative attitudes is very helpful: praying and asking that God would give them grace so that they don't become bitter, that God would fill their hearts with compassion for Muslims, and that God would help them see Muslims the way Jesus sees them.

Preparing people to minister to Muslims, which needs to be viewed under the broader umbrella of having a good understanding and knowledge of the Bible and a vibrant relationship with Christ, must be done with the recognition that effective ministry to Muslims can only happen in the context of a strong relationship with Christ and empowerment by the Holy Spirit. That is, it is imperative that American evangelicals espouse an attitude of dependence on the Triune God for effectiveness in ministry. In the words of one COMM leader, it is evangelicals who are "passionate, who are burdened [for Muslims], who depend on the Lord" that will reach Muslims.

Practices

Evangelicals must present Islam accurately in terms of its beliefs and practices, the starting point of which is having an accurate understanding of Islam. One effective way of learning about Islamic culture, as well as the ways individual Muslims practice their faith on a daily basis, is by asking Muslims themselves about their religion. It will serve evangelicals well to take the posture of a "learner" of Islam and develop the art of asking questions as they walk on the journey of genuine inquiry. Asking Muslims questions about their faith is something that Muslims appreciate, rather than something that offends them, as we are all sometimes prone to filling in gaps in our knowledge with imagination. Incidentally, this also gives Muslims permission to ask us questions, thus allowing us to tell them about our faith and share our lives with them.

Evangelicals need to take an interest in Muslims and actively engage those Muslims who have been sovereignly put by God in their sphere of influence, whether that is in their places of work or in their neighborhoods. This engagement includes praying for the salvation of Muslims and for Christ to empower and equip evangelicals to minister to Muslims; developing healthy relationships; dialoguing about issues that are important to both Muslims and Christians; and seeking to understand their Muslim neighbors, including getting a first-hand understanding of their neighbors' religious life. Points of dialogue can include themes that are common to both religions, such as: submission to Allah; creation as a theater of Allah's glory; regular and theocentric prayer; charity to the poor; and faith and the public square. Evangelicals also need to engage Muslims regarding the complexities of the various issues that characterize Islamic thought and the Muslim mindset, such as: Muslims trying to live in pluralistic cultures; the existence of the state of Israel; the relationship of Islam and democratic governments; Islam's view of Muslim women; the ways in which Muslims understand violence and terrorist activities in the name of Islam; ministering to the "peaceful" Muslims they know and reassuring them when radical Muslims act violently; etc. Engagement at a deeper level will also create space for evangelicals to help Muslims get a better understanding of American cultural, political, and religious life, thus helping them better assimilate into the American pluralistic context. And evangelicals need to recognize that as they seek to get a better understanding of Islamic teaching through these kinds of interpersonal, face-to-face encounters and relationships, this engagement will in turn create space to share the gospel with their Muslim friends. Furthermore, this kind of engagement will help alleviate prejudices and negative perceptions that evangelicals have about Muslims and will help them develop and inculcate more positive perspectives, as evidenced through this research study. In the context of their dialogue with Muslims, it is critical that evangelicals refrain from making incendiary comments about Islam and Muslims, such as talking disrespectfully of Muhammad or the Qur'an, but rather communicate a welcoming attitude toward Islam as one of the religions that may be practiced with the same freedom that is accorded to other religions such as Christianity, Hinduism, and Buddhism, to name just a few, within the American religious pluralistic context. Especially apropos here is the encouragement offered by the COMM leaders: "Instead of belittling Islam, talk about Jesus, [share] your testimony."

Furthermore, some kind of context is needed where evangelicals can dialogue with "peaceful" Muslims about the issue of violence and Islam. Perhaps one kind of setting to do this would be bringing together evangelicals and "peaceful" Muslims, those who are concerned and vexed about the violence in the name of Islam, in a church-based discussion forum in order to dialogue together. This would help alleviate the chagrin expressed by evangelicals because of what they see as a lack of a loud-enough voice from the "peaceful" Muslim community in America condemning violent actions by radical Muslims in the name of Islam. In fact, Arsalan Iftikhar, Senior Editor at the Islamic Monthly Magazine and a leader from the American Muslim community, did condemn on CNN the events surrounding the Boston Marathon in 2013, expressing the view that what was being seen on the media does not represent "true" Islam (CNN, 2013). CNN's report titled "I'm Muslim, and I hate terrorism" (Obeidallah, 2013) is another example of American Muslims denouncing terrorism. And the website

The American Muslim (http://www.theamericanmuslim.org) presents letters condemning the Boston Marathon bombings as well as words of condolence offered by a plethora of Islamic organizations, such as Muslim Public Affairs Council, The Islamic Society of Boston Cultural Center, Muslim Peace Coalition USA, Council on American-Islamic Relations, to name just a few.

Because one way in which evangelicals can meet and befriend Muslims is through helps-based ministries like COMM, those evangelicals who feel called to minister to Muslims should be proactive in finding and becoming a part of such a ministry, and pastors should consider leading their congregations into partnering with a ministry of this kind so that congregants have an avenue to engage in this kind of ministry to Muslims. Serving in ministries of this nature will open up avenues for evangelicals to engage Muslims in multi-faceted ways, including: come alongside Muslims and support them as they adjust to life in the US; join them in their daily activities, such as shopping, etc.; find out their needs and pray for them specifically, and when God answers your prayers, Muslim begin to view Christians as godly and spiritual people and as "acceptable" and "attractive" in their eyes, as one COMM leader asserted. Helping them meet their daily needs in this way is the kind of interaction that has brought Muslims to trust Christians and deepen relationships, which facilitate the sharing of the gospel and living it out. As evangelicals are building relationships, it would be helpful to keep in mind COMM staff's experience that many Muslims who move to the US are out of their comfort zone, are lonely, are struggling, and sometimes they have a hard time connecting with other Muslims when they first come here. Offering them love and care by inviting them into our homes helps develop relationships. At the same time we can also receive hospitality from them, not unlike what Jesus did when He was a guest in people's homes while doing ministry.

Receiving hospitality from Muslims means communicating to them that we too have needs that arise out of living in a fallen world and becoming willing to receive the care that Muslims have the ability to offer us; this will go a long way in the development of meaningful relationships. And it is in the context of building trust and deep relationships that our Muslim friends will ask questions. Muslims are searching for the truth, and we should not be afraid of presenting the truth to them but be willing to open God's word, which is "alive and it goes deep," as one of the COMM leaders asserted. Muslims have questions that they want to ask about Christianity but may have no one they can trust and talk to. If we establish trust and answer their questions, "we clear those misconceptions ... And then the veil is removed." This is especially significant in light of what of one of the COMM leaders said: Muslims who have been educated in mosques think that they know Christianity and that they know "about the Bible." These Muslims have been taught a lot of things, and they have "been told a lot of things." But, what they have been told are lies, and Christians need to show them that the things that they have been taught "are not true."

As evangelicals are developing relationships, it is also important to "have a vision of hope for Muslims": to believe that while Islam is "a barrier, it's a block, it's a stronghold of Satan," as a COMM leader said, God can break down and "release the captives" and to pray that Jesus would move Muslims towards Himself. In the context of befriending Muslims, evangelicals need to keep in mind that developing relationships and establishing trust takes time and a person may never see for themselves the harvest that may result from the breaking down of barriers that have been set up by Islam. Here it is important to keep in mind, as the COMM leaders counseled, that evangelicals may be involved in ministering to their Muslim friends over a long period of time, and they should not let a lack of fruit in the short-term in the lives of Muslims become a source of discouragement to them. At the same time, while Christians need to "look for the long-term relationships," they should not "forget the chance encounter, the individual short brief encounter" with Muslims. For example, when filling your car with gasoline at a gas station, instead of paying at the pump, go inside, meet that person behind the counter, and engage them in conversation, encouraged one COMM leader. This is a practice he engages in regularly with great success.

Evangelical pastors should avail themselves of resources regarding ministering to Muslims and train and equip congregants to be hospitable toward Muslims and evangelize Muslims. Training their congregants must include: educating them about the proper perspective toward Islam and Muslims and Islamic teaching; teaching them that Islam is not what it was in the 7th century when it was first established but has changed and continues to change as it engages other religions and cultures; and teaching them to espouse a healthy understanding of the events that they see in the news regarding Islam and Muslims, especially as their understanding relates to the violence associated with Islam and the undeniable way in which evangelicals are shaped by this. That is, evangelical pastors must provide a biblical lens through which their congregants can view and understand Islam and Muslims. Evangelicals must also be made aware that some Christian leaders disseminate perspectives and attitudes about Islam and Muslims that are erroneous in nature as well as taught to develop discernment so that they are able to differentiate between information about events and evaluations of these events without using these events and evaluations to caricature all of Islam and all Muslims. All of this could easily be done in the context of discipling congregants to evangelize non-Christian others, which includes Muslims, via Sunday school classes or evangelism seminars. Sunday school series on Islam that one respondent was part of, or seminars such as the Muslim Summit Conference or the Equip seminar, or the class titled "Middle East, Islam and War" are excellent examples of the kinds of educating that can be done in churches.

In training and equipping congregants, it is imperative that congregants are made aware that their perspectives and attitudes are conflicted in terms of their views of Islam and Muslims, which include the deep fear, and mistrust of, and animosity toward Muslims as well as negative views of Islam which sometimes go hand in hand with their positive views of Muslims they know. It is also imperative that congregants are encouraged and taught to eschew this inner conflict that they feel toward Islam and Muslims. Congregants also need to be helped in dealing with the dissonance that they feel toward Muslims in that they know that as Christians they are supposed to love them, yet they harbor a lot of animosity towards them. One way in which to do this is through regular dialogue about this, which would include helping congregants repent of this fear, mistrust, and animosity, praying for God's help to change their attitude of animosity toward Muslims and developing a sense of trust in God to sustain evangelicals in these kinds of hostile situations. A second component that is crucial to dealing with their fear, mistrust, and animosity is to pray regularly for Muslims in general as well as individual Muslims that they are in relationships with, a practice that COMM leaders engage in with great intentionality, which consequently keeps them from becoming bitter toward Muslims that they interact with in their ministry. Prayer for grace on a daily basis is crucial because bitterness can easily develop into hostility and anger toward Muslims and hinder the development of relationships with and ministry to Muslims. It is well worth noting what COMM leaders have to do regularly: They "draw on the Lord" and say to Him, "Give me your heart."

Final Reflection

I serve at a ministry that reaches out to Muslims. On most occasions, Muslims I interact with are kind, polite, and friendly, willing to dialogue peacefully when I have the opportunity to engage them with the gospel. In one of my roles at this ministry during an annual event I sit at a literature table and dialogue with Muslims as they stop by to peruse our Islam-oriented evangelistic resources, such as books and pamphlets, Jesus DVDs, the Bible in a variety of languages, testimonies of Muslims who have come to faith in Jesus, etc. Every year I have done this, most encounters are characterized with equanimity. But each time I have also encountered one or two Muslims who have seemingly come with the intent of raising objections against, and heaping abuse on, Jesus, the Bible, and Christianity, sometimes uttering statements that are very crude. In these kinds of encounters I find myself in need of turning to Jesus in prayer to ask for His grace and discernment so that I respond wisely.

Over the past year since completing this research project I have reflected much about my own perspectives, attitudes, and practices toward Muslims and Islam in the US. My mindset is shaped by my background, being born in India, hearing about my family's experiences with Muslims, growing up among Muslims, and engaging them in India and the US, first as a Hindu and then as a Christian. As I take to heart the lessons garnered through my experience and research, the most significant for me is the importance of prayer. I cannot overstate the significance of prayer. Without prayer we will not be able to display Jesus' perspectives, attitudes, and practices toward Muslims as we engage them in our daily life and in ministry. My prayer for myself is that Jesus would give me His eyes so that I would see Muslims as He sees them; that Jesus would give me His heart so that I would be moved with compassion for Muslims as He is; that Jesus would give me His hands to serve and bless Muslims even if they do not reciprocate, as Jesus served and blessed even those who later took his life. And most of all, I pray that as I interact with Muslims in ministry and daily life, I would never fail to pray for Muslims to come to know Him. I pray all this for you, the reader, as well, and invite you to join me in this prayer and this ministry.

APPENDIX I

RESEARCH METHODOLOGY

The research project was comprised of four steps, the first three of which helped me gather qualitative data for step four. First, I reviewed literature in three areas: one, growth of religious diversity in the US (Chapter 2); two, growth of Islam in the US (Chapter 3) and Christian-Muslim relations in the US (Chapter 4); and three, theology of religions that evangelicals have developed as to how evangelicals should view and respond to other religions—as well as their adherents—in general and Islam in particular (Chapter 8). The literature not only provided the framework for the focus of this research study: perspectives, attitudes, and practices of American evangelicals towards Muslims in the US but also served as the basis for the development of the set of principles that were used to analyze the information obtained through the two research questions and the focus group study.

Second, I did a study based on qualitative interviews of 40 lay American evangelicals (23 men and 17 women) and four American evangelical pastors (all male) to gather information on their experience with Muslims focusing on areas stated in the two research questions. The qualitative study was conducted via one-on-one interviews (Bernard & Ryan, 2010, pp. 27-37), which allowed me to gather information about the respondents' "thoughts, behaviors, emotions" (Bernard & Ryan, 2010, p. 5). In the interviews, in order to draw out the emic perspectives (Madden, 2010, p. 19), I asked open-ended questions (Bernard & Ryan, 2010, pp. 34-35) so that the participants could respond freely from their own thoughts and experiences, i.e., using their own discretion, while also asking other probing questions when I felt I needed more "in-depth" information (Bernard & Ryan, 2010, pp. 31-33). The study helped me to understand the perspectives, attitudes, and practices that American evangelicals have toward Muslims in the US and how these perspectives and attitudes are formed and justified. Gathering this information was a two-step process through the "nonprobability sampling method" (Bernard & Ryan, 2010, p. 358), which works well because my research sought "to study a small subset" of American evangelicals, who are part of the "larger population" of American evangelicals, and the members of the subset of American evangelicals were easy to identify, whereas studying all American evangelicals "would be nearly impossible" (Babbie 2007, p. 184). First, four American evangelical congregations located in four different suburbs of Chicago were selected, and congregants and their pastors were asked to participate in the research study. The four congregations, comprised primarily of white-collar workers, are from three different theologically conservative traditional evangelical denominations located in four different suburbs in the Chicago area. The sole criterion for selecting these congregations was that they are "evangelical" in their theological commitment. While three of the congregations have some ethnic diversity, they are predominantly white American congregations. The fourth congregation is self-described as a "multi-cultural and multi-generational" congregation with "a wide range of age groups," with half the adults below the age of thirty-five, and "a wide range of racial and ethnic diversity," with no ethnic majority and more than half of the congregants described as "people of color."

Second, the 40 respondents that were selected through "purposive sampling" (Bernard & Ryan, 2010, p. 358) were the first 40 who responded and expressed interest in participating in the study, two of whom I was put in touch with by one of the interviewees. Even though I did not get "an unbiased sample" (source) of American evangelical respondents because the respondents were for the most part self-selecting, the data that I collected allowed me to answer my two research questions (Bernard & Ryan, 2010, p. 366; Babbie, 2007, p. 184) because the information came from respondents who had read and dialogued about as well as reflected on the issues related to the research topic. Since three of the four congregations are predominantly white and the information that was communicated to the congregants explicitly stated that I was looking for "American evangelicals," the respondents from these three congregations were white Americans, with two respondents from two different European countries, but they had lived in America for over ten years, hence meeting my criteria of focusing on "American evangelicals." Even though the fourth congregation has no ethnic majority and over half of the congregants are people of color, all the respondents from this congregation were white Americans. The ages of the respondents ranged from mid-20s to late-70s, and three fourths of them had contacts of some kind with Muslims, with some contacts even overseas. In order to protect the identity of the respondents, the names of the respondents have been changed.

The third step in the research involved a focus-group-based study with ministry leaders of COMM in a major metropolitan city in the US, an organization that began in the fall of 1997 and whose leaders have actively engaged Muslims with the "friendship" model of doing ministry (Wilch, Clark, & Naaman, 2001, p. 125), which is one of several kinds of models of outreach to Muslims in the US (Wilch at al., 2001; Philip, Stewart, Jr., & Blincoe, 2001; Morton & Katz, 2001). It is a helps-based, incarnational ministry that seeks to meet the needs of the Hindu and Muslim immigrants in the community.

This ministry was selected for three reasons. One, they have made concerted efforts, both as an organization and as individuals, to engage Muslims from an evangelical perspective, which was the case for some of the 40 individuals I interviewed in step three but not most; none of the individuals I interviewed in step three were part of this group. Two, this is an American evangelical ministry, and the individuals comprising the leadership are also American evangelicals, which is the group I sought to study in my research project. Three, the group comprised of six men and four women: three of the leaders are from an Asian background, two women from India and one man from Pakistan; three of the white American evangelicals (two men and one woman) have done mission work among Muslims in Pakistan; two leaders are white Americans (one man and one woman) and have been involved in ministry to Muslims in the US; one male leader is from a Syrian background and has been engaging in Christian apologetics to Muslims for a number of years; and one male white American leader serves as a security guard for this ministry and has engaged Muslims in the US. Hence, the information that I obtained from this group, which is similar in content to the information I gathered from my interviewees, came from a group of evangelicals who are different from the interviewees in that they are from a variety of ethnic backgrounds. In order to protect the identity of the COMM leaders, their names have been changed.

This focus group study (Bernard & Ryan, 2010, pp. 40-41; Yin, 2014, pp. 111-12) was designed to provide additional information for the fourth step; that is, this ministry serves as an example of the perspectives, attitudes, and practices that evangelical ministries, and individual evangelicals, should espouse regarding Islam and Muslims; furthermore, this ministry's practices were also evaluated in light of the information obtained through the study of the literature on evangelical theology of religions. On a secondary level the focus group study also provided information about why evangelicals have the perspectives, attitudes, and practices that they do toward Muslims.

My study of COMM was a three-step process that facilitated the gathering of data from numerous sources. One, I interviewed the leaders of this ministry in a focus group, with an opportunity given for people to respond to my questions in a group setting. Gathering data in this setting was helpful because respondents fed off each other, providing information from different perspectives. Two, in order to familiarize myself with COMM, over a period of several months I attended as a participant-observer certain activities at COMM that are geared to reaching out to Muslims, including their annual block party where I manned the literature table and engaged Muslims in dialogue, the annual fund-raising banquet, and daily ministry of services provided at the ministry location where I spent time in the bookstore observing leaders engage visitors and also engaged the visitors myself. Participant observation, which puts the researcher in the same space as the participants and facilitates the observation of "behavior in a natural context" (Bernard & Ryan, 2010, p. 41), allowed me to observe and collect data in the context where COMM is located, including how to engage Muslims, what to say and what not to say, proper attitude to display, etc. Two of the leaders also gave me instructions on the proper ways to engage Muslims, such as always putting the Qur'an on top of other books as opposed to underneath other literature to show proper respect for the Qur'an and to not offend Muslims and to have some conversations with other leaders in private rather than in earshot of Muslims because of the sensitive nature of the topics. Three, I also studied the flyer provided to me by COMM, with information listing the various services offered by COMM. This is a flyer that is given out to Christians who may be interested in doing ministry as volunteers at

COMM and also to non-Christians who are interested in finding out about the kinds of services COMM provides.

Finally, in step four I developed a model for how evangelicals should respond theologically and missiologically to the perspectives, attitudes, and practices of American evangelicals toward Muslim immigrants in the US. This model is discussed in Chapter 10.

APPENDIX II

INTERNET RESOURCES

The following Internet resources are recommended as a starting place for the reader who would like to become better prepared to share the Christian faith with Muslim friends:

- 30 Days of Prayer (http://pray30days.org/)
- Answering Islam (http://answering-islam.org/)
- A Coalition of Ministries to Muslims in North America (http://commanetwork.com/)
- Crescent Project (https://www.crescentproject.org/)
- PrayerCast (http://prayercast.com/)
- Billy Graham Center for Evangelism (http://wheaton.edu/BGCE)

REFERENCES

Abusharaf, R. M. (1988). Structural adaptations in an immigrant
    Muslim congregation in New York. In R. S. Warner & J. G.
    Wittner (Eds.), Gatherings in diaspora: Religious communities
    and the new immigration (pp. 235-62). Philadelphia, PA:
    Temple University Press.

Allison, R. J. (2000). The crescent obscured: The United States and the
    Muslim world, 1776-1815. Chicago, IL: University of Chicago
    Press.

Aubin, P. (1797). The noble slaves [Google Books version]. Retrieved
    from
    http://books.google.com/books?id=I2VsjZhqKrIC&printsec=fr
    ontcover#v=onepage& q&f=false

Austin, A. D. (1984). African Muslims in antebellum America: A
    sourcebook. New York, NY: Garland.

Babbie, E. (2007). The practice of social research. Belmont, CA:
    Thomson Wadsworth.

Bagby, I. (2012). The American mosque 2011: Basic characteristics of
    the American mosque. Attitudes of mosque leaders, report
    number 1. Retrieved from
    https://www.cair.com/images/pdf/The-American- Mosque-
    2011-part-1.pdf

Bagby, I. (2012). The American mosque 2011: Activities, administration
    and vitality of the American mosque, report number 2.
    Retrieved from http://cair.com/images/pdf/The-American-
    Mosque-2011-part- 2.pdf

Bagby, I., Perl, P. M., & Froehle, B. T. (2001). The mosque in America: A national portrait. Retrieved from http://cair.com/images/pdf/The-American-mosque-2001.pdf

Bailey, S. P. (2015, December 5). Jerry Falwell Jr.: 'If more good people had concealed-carry permits, then we could end those' Islamist terrorists. The Washington Post. Retrieved from https://www.washingtonpost.com/news/acts-of-faith/wp/2015/12/05/liberty-university-president-if-more-good-people-had-concealed-guns-we-could-end-those-muslims/?utm_term=.27ead110764f

Baptist Standard. (2003). Full Text of Missionaries' Letter on Islam. Retrieved from http://assets.baptiststandard.com/archived/2003/1_20/pages/letter_fulltext.html

Bernard, H. R., & Ryan, G. W. (2010). Analyzing qualitative data: Systematic approaches. Thousand Oaks, CA: SAGE.

Bill, J. A. (1978-79, Winter). Iran and the Crisis of '78. Foreign Affairs 57(2), 323- 42.

Brimelow, P. (1995.) Alien nation: Common sense about America's immigration disaster. New York, NY: Random House.

California State Department of Education. (1991). Moral and Civic Education and Teaching about Religion. Handbook on the Legal Rights and Responsibilities of School Personnel and Students in the Areas of Moral and Civic Education and Teaching about Religion. Retrieved from http://files.eric.ed.gov/fulltext/ED341613.pdf

Caner, E. M. & Caner, E. F. (2009). Unveiling Islam: An insider's look at Muslim life and beliefs. Grand Rapids, MI: Kregel.

Chapman, C. (2007). Cross and crescent: Responding to the challenges of Islam. Downers Grove, IL: InterVarsity.

Cimino, R. P. (2005, December). 'No God in common:' American evangelical discourse on Islam after 9/11. Review of Religious Research, 47(2), 162-74.

CNN. (2013, April 24). Please God, don't let it be a Muslim [Video file]. Retrieved from https://www.youtube.com/watch?v=lA-EH6ckPE4

Colson, C. (2002, November). Terrorists Behind Bars. First Things, 127, 19-21.

Columbus, C. (1989.) The diario of Christopher Columbus's first voyage to America, 1492-1493. Abstracted by Fray Bartolomé de las Casas. Trans. Oliver Dunn and James E. Kelley Jr. Norman, OK: University of Oklahoma Press.

Connor, P. (2016, October 5). US admits record number of Muslim refugees in 2016. Retrieved from http://www.pewresearch.org/fact-tank/2016/10/05/u-s-admits-record-number-of-muslim-refugees-in-2016/

Cooper, B. M. (2006). Evangelical Christians in the Muslim sahel. Bloomington, IN: Indiana University Press.

Corduan, W. (2002). A tapestry of faiths: The common threads between Christianity and world religions. Downers Grove, IL: InterVarsity.

Cox, H. (2001, December 24). Religion and the war against evil. The Nation, 273(21), 29-31.

Cragg, K. (2000). The call of the minaret. Boston, MA: Oneworld.

Culbertson, William. (1968, June 7). Perspective on Arab-Israeli Tensions. Christianity Today XII (12), 6, 8.

Curtin, P. D. (1969.) The Atlantic slave trade: A census [Google Books version]. Retrieved from http://books.google.com/books?id=4uEWuoGwwhkC&printsec= frontcover#v=onepage&q=islam&f=false

Darwish, N. (2011 Feb. 1). The joys of Muslim women. Retrieved from http://israelpalestine-speedy.blogspot.com/2011/02/joys-of-muslim-women.html

DeHaan, Martin R. (1950). The Jew and Palestine in prophecy. Grand Rapids: Zondervan.

Doumato, E. (1985). Celebrating tradition in Rhode Island. In E. Hoogland (Ed.), Taking root: Vol. 2. (pp. 101-24). Washington, D.C.: Arab American Anti-Discrimination Committee.

Ebaugh, H. R., & Saltzman Chafetz, J. (2000). Introduction. In H. R. Ebaugh & J. Saltzman Chafetz (Eds.), Religion and the new immigrants: Continuities and adaptations in immigrant congregations (pp. 13-28). Walnut Creek, CA: AltaMira.

Eck, D. L. (1993). Foreword. In R. Hughes Seager (Ed.), The dawn of religious pluralism: Voices from the World's Parliament of Religions (pp. xiii-xvii). Lasalle, IL: Open Court Press.

Eck, D. L. (2002). A new religious America: How a "Christian country" has now become the world's most religiously diverse nation. San Francisco, CA: HarperSanFrancisco.

Estes, J. R. (1967). A Baptist look at Islam. Atlanta, GA: Southern Baptist Convention.

Evangelical Lutheran Church in America. (2016). Talking points. Retrieved from http://download.elca.org/ELCA%20Resource%20Repository/TP_CM_Users_Guide.pdf?_ga=1.244322177.500654476.1485185087

Evangelical Lutheran Church in America (Producer). (2016). Discover Islam [DVD]. Available from http://download.elca.org/ELCA%20Resource%20Repository/DI_Study_Guide_Introduction.pdf?_ga=1.42984225.500654476.1485185087

Falwell, J. (2002, June 15). Muhammad, a 'demon-possessed pedophile'? WND. Retrieved from http://www.wnd.com

Ferris, M. (1994). To 'Achieve the Pleasure of Allah': Immigrant Muslims in New York City, 1893-1991. In Y. Yazbeck Haddad & J. I. Smith (Eds.), Muslim Communities in North America (pp. 209-30). Albany, NY: State University of New York Press.

Finnie, D. H. (1967). Pioneers East: The early American experience in the Middle East. Cambridge, MA: Harvard University Press.

Fisk, E. G. (1951). The prickly pear: Mission stories from Moslem lands. Chicago, IL: Moody Press.

Fortner, M. (2006). The scarlet beast: Islam and the beast of Revelation. Lawton, OK: White Stone.

Foss, J. (1798). The Journal of the captivity and sufferings of John Foss; several years a prisoner at Algiers: together with some account of the treatment of Christian slaves when sick:-and observations of the manners and customs of the Algiers [Google Books version]. Retrieved from http://books.google.com/books?id=zCRXAAAAcAAJ&pg=PA161&lpg=PA161&dq=the+Journal+of+the+captivity+and+sufferings+of+John+Foss&source=bl&ots=tDHLeS6jbP&sig=2ywrtqa9ABNAColIj3_ChUNPgCs&hl=en&sa=X&ei=8kXsUvHFAufPsASSiYD4Dg&ved=0CF8Q6AEwCTge#v=onepage&q=the%20Journal%20of%20the%20captivity%20and%20sufferings%20of%20John%20Foss&f=false

Gabriel, B. (2006). Because they hate: A survival of Islamic terror warns America. New York, NY: St. Martin's Press.

Glidden, H. W. (1972). The Arab World. American Journal of Psychiatry, 128(8), 984-988.

Graham, F. M. (1969). Sons of Ishmael: How shall they hear? Nashville, TN: Convention.

Hammonds, P., Dr. (2005). Slavery, terrorism & Islam: The historical roots and contemporary threat. Cape Town, South Africa: Christian Liberty Books.

Hermansen, M. K. (1994). The Muslims of San Diego. In Y. Yazbeck Haddad & J. I. Smith (Eds.), Muslim Communities in North America, (pp.169-94). Albany, NY: State University of New York Press.

Hertz, T. (2002, October 1). Riots, Condemnation, Fatwa, and Apology Follow Falwell's CBS Comments. Christianity Today. Retrieved from http://www.christianitytoday.com/ct/2002/octoberweb-only/10-14-41.0.html

Hirsi Ali, Ayaan. (2013, May 27). The Problem of Muslim Leadership. The Wall Street Journal. Retrieved from http://www.wsj.com/articles/SB10001424127887323475304578503613890263762

Hunt, D. (2005). Judgment day! Islam, Israel and the nations. Bend, OR: The Berean Call.

Hutchison, W. R. (2004). Religious pluralism in America: The contentious history of a founding ideal. Ann Arbor, MI: Sheridan.

Inner-City Muslim Action Network. (2014). About us. Retrieved from http://www.imancentral.org/

Kärkkäinen, V.-M. (2003). An introduction to the theology of religions: Biblical, historical and contemporary perspectives. Downers Grove, IL: InterVarsity.

Kershaw, R. M. (1978). How to share the good news with your Muslim friend. Colorado Springs, CO: International Students Inc.

Kelso, James L. (1968, June 7). Perspective on Arab-Israeli Tensions. Christianity Today XII (18), 7, 9.

Kidd, T. S. (2009). American Christians and Islam: Evangelical culture and Muslims from the colonial period to the age of terrorism. Princeton, NJ: Princeton University Press.

Kimball, C. (1991). Striving together: A way forward in Christian-Muslim relations. Maryknoll, NY: Orbis.

Koenig, M. (2009). How Nation-States Respond to Religious Diversity. In P. Bramadat & M. Koenig (Eds.), International migration and the governance of religious diversity (pp. 293-322). Kingston, ON: School of Policy Studies, Queen's University.

Kumar, P. P. (2006). Religious pluralism in the diaspora. Leiden: Brill.

Library of Congress. (n.d.). Colonial settlement, 1600s-1763. American Memory Timeline. Retrieved from http://www.loc.gov/teachers/classroommaterials/presentation sandactivities/ presentatons/timeline/colonial/

Lutzer, E. W. (2013). The cross in the shadow of the crescent: An informed response to Islam's war with Christianity. Eugene, OR: Harvest House Publishers.

MacArthur, J. (2001). Terrorism, jihad, and the Bible: A response to the terrorist attacks. Nashville, TN: W Publishing Group.

Madden, R. (2010). Being ethnographic: A guide to the theory and practice of ethnography. Thousand Oaks, CA: Sage.

Mahfouz, N. (2001). The Cairo trilogy: Palace walk, Palace of desire, Sugar Street. (W. M. Hutchins, O. E. Kenny, L. M. Kenny, & A. B. Samaan , Trans.) New York, NY: Alfred A. Knopf. (Original work published 1956 and 1957).

The Majlis Ash-Shura. (2016). About us. Retrieved from http://shuranewyork.us/

Mandryk, J. (2010). Operation world: The definitive prayer guide to every nation. Colorado Springs, CO: Biblica Publishing.

Marger, M. M. (2012). Race and ethnic relations: American and global perspectives. Belmont, CA: Wadsworth Cengage Learning.

Marty, M. E. (2005). When faiths collide. Malden, MA: Blackwell.

McCord, K. (2012). In the land of blue burqas. Chicago, IL: Moody Publishers.

McDermott, G. R. (2000). Can evangelicals learn from world religions?: Jesus, Revelation and religious traditions. Downers Grove, IL: InterVarsity.

McDermott, G. R., & Netland, H. A. (2014). A Trinitarian theology of religions: An evangelical proposal. New York, NY: Oxford University Press.

McDowell, B. A., & Zaka, A. (1999). Muslims and Christians at the table: Promoting biblical understanding among North American Muslims. Phillipsburg, NJ: P&R.

McKay, M.-J. (2002, October 3). Zion's Christian soldiers: Conservative Christian says founder of Islam set a bad example. 60 Minutes. Retrieved from http://www.cbsnews.com/news/zions-christian-soldiers/

Means, E. L. (1955). World within a world. Nashville, TN: Convention Press.

Medearis, C. (2008). Muslims, Christians, and Jesus: Gaining understanding and building relationships. Bloomington, MN: Bethany House Publishers.

Merryweather, F. (1925). The Easy Way. The Sudan Witness IV(6), 13-14.

Mohamed, B. (2016, January 6). A new estimate of the U.S. Muslim population. Retrieved from http://www.pewresearch.org/fact-tank/2016/01/06/a-new-estimate-of-the-u-s-muslim-population/

Morey, R. (1992). The Islamic invasion: Confronting the world's fastest growing religion. Las Vegas, NV: Christian Scholars.

Morton, J., & Katz, J. (2001). Interfaith Dialogue Models. In R. Oksnevad & D. Welliver (Eds.), The gospel for Islam: Reaching Muslims in North America (pp. 155-64). Wheaton, IL: EMIS.

Muck, T. (1990). Alien gods on American turf: How world religions are evangelizing your neighborhood. Wheaton, IL: Victor.

Muslim Community Network. Retrieved from http://mcnny.org/

Naff, A. (1985). Becoming American: The early Arab immigrant experience. Carbondale, IL: Southern Illinois University Press.

Netland, H. A. (1991). Dissonant voices: Religious pluralism and the questions of truth. Grand Rapids, MI: Eerdmans.

Netland, H. A. (2001). Encountering religious pluralism: The challenge to Christian faith and mission. Downers Grove, IL: InterVarsity.

Nettler, R. L. (1978). Islam and the Minorities: Background to the Arab-Israeli Conflict. Jerusalem, Israel: Israel Academic Committee on the Middle East.

Neusner, J. (1991). Jews and Christians: The myth of a common tradition. Philadelphia, PA: Trinity Press International.

New-York Tribune. (1893, October). Christianity and Other Religions, 1, 6.

Numrich, P. D. (2009). The faith next door: American Christians and their new religious neighbors. New York, NY: Oxford University Press.

Obeidallah, D. (2013, April 24). I'm Muslim, and I hate terrorism. CNN. Retrieved from http://www.cnn.com/2013/04/24/opinion/obeidallah-muslims-hate-terrorism/

Oksnevad, R. (2001). Preface. In R. Oksnevad & D. Welliver (Eds.), The gospel for Islam: Reaching Muslims in North America (pp. v-vi). Wheaton, IL: Evangelism and Missions Information Service.

Parshall, P. (2002). The cross and the crescent: Understanding the Muslim heart and mind. Waynesboro, GA: Authentic Media.

PCID. (2016). The Pontifical Council for Interreligious Dialogue. Vatican City: The Holy See. Retrieved from http://www.vatican.va/roman_curia/pontifical_councils/inter elg/documents/rc_pc_int erelg_pro_20051996_en.html

Pew Research Center. (2011). Muslim Americans: No signs of growth in alienation or support for extremism. Retrieved from http://www.pewforum.org/2011/08/30/muslim-americans-no-signs-of-growth-in-alienation-or-support-for-extremism/

Pew Research Center. (2015, May 12). America's changing religious landscape. Retrieved from http://www.pewforum.org/2015/05/12/americas-changing-religious- landscape/

Philip, D., Stewart, A. T., Jr., & Blincoe, R. (2001). Models for Ethnic Ministries. In R. Oksnevad & D. Welliver (Eds.), The gospel for Islam: Reaching Muslims in North America (pp. 131-54). Wheaton, IL: EMIS.

Poston, L. (2001). The Current State of Islam in America. In R. Oksnevad & D. Welliver (Eds.), The gospel for Islam: Reaching Muslims in North America (pp. 3-20). Wheaton, IL: Evangelism and Missions Information Service.

Poston, L. A., & Ellis, C. F., Jr. (2000). The changing face of Islam in America: Understanding and reaching your Muslim neighbor. Camp Hill, PA: Horizon.

Presbyterian Church (USA). (2010). A study on Islam. Retrieved from
https://www.presbyterianmission.org/resource/study-islam/

Price, R. (2001). Unholy war: America, Israel and radical Islam.
Eugene, OR: Harvest House.

Prideaux, H. (1698). The true nature of imposture, fully displayed in the
life of Mahomet. Retrieved from
https://archive.org/details/thetruenature00priduoft

Register, Jr., R. G. (1979). Dialogue and interfaith witness with
Muslims. Fort Washington, PA: WEC.

Richardson, E. Allen. 1988. Strangers in this land: Pluralism and the
response to diversity in the United States. New York: Pilgrim.

Robertson, P. (2002, November 11). Islam [Web log post]. Retrieved
from
http://www.patrobertson.com/pressreleases/bushresponse2.a
sp

Rushdie, S. (1989). The satanic verses: A novel. New York, NY: Viking
Penguin.

Said, E. W. (1979). Orientalism. New York, NY: Vintage.

Said, E. W. (1997). Covering Islam: How the media and the experts
determine how we see the rest of the world. New York, NY:
Vintage.

Said, E. W. (2003). Orientalism (Rev. ed.). New York, NY: Vintage.

Sanneh, L. (1996). Piety and power: Muslims and Christians in West
Africa. Maryknoll, NY: Orbis.

Sanneh, L. (2004, May 4). Do Christians and Muslims Worship the
Same God? Christian Century, 121(9), 35-36.

Schlesinger, A. M., Jr. (1998). The disuniting of America: Reflections on
a multicultural society. New York, NY: W. W. Norton &
Company.

Shoebat, W. (with Barrack, B.). (2013). The case FOR Islamophobia: Jihad by the Word; America's final warning. [n.l.]: Top Executive Media.

Smith, J. I. (2007). Muslims, Christians, and the challenge of interfaith dialogue. New York, NY: Oxford University Press.

Smith, J. I. (2010). Islam in America. New York, NY: Columbia University Press.

Solomon, S., & Al Maqdisi, E (2009). Modern day Trojan horse: Al-Hijra, the Islamic doctrine of immigration, accepting freedom or imposing Islam? Charlottesville, VA: Advancing Native Missions.

Taber, S. (2004). Muslims next door: Uncovering myths and creating friendships.. Grand Rapids, MI: Zondervan.

The American Muslim. 2013. American Muslims Respond to Boston Marathon Bombings. http://theamericanmuslim.org/tam.php/features/articles/americans-respond-to-boston- marathon-bombings/0019758 (accessed October 1, 2016).

The Mother Mosque of America. The dream of the Mother Mosque of America. The Mother Mosque of America. http://mothermosque.org/page.php?2 (accessed January 19, 2014).

Tibawi, A. L. (1966). American interests in Syria, 1800-1901: A study of educational, literary and religious work. Oxford, UK: Clarendon.

Volf, M. (2011). Allah: A Christian response. New York, NY: HarperCollins.

Wagner, W. (2004). How Islam plans to change the world. Grand Rapids, MI: Kregel.

Warner, R. S. (2004, February 10). Coming to America. Christian Century, 121(3), 20-23.

Warner, R. S. (2005). A church of our own: Disestablishment and diversity in American religion. New Brunswick, NJ: Rutgers University Press.

Warren, R. (1995). The purpose driven church: Every church is big in God's eyes. Grand Rapids, MI: Zondervan.

Warren, R. (2002). The purpose driven life: What on earth am I here for? Grand Rapids, MI: Zondervan.

Wortley Montagu, M. (1893). The letters and works of Lady Mary Montagu. Retrieved from http://www.questia.com/read/82408790/the-letters-and-works-of-lady-mary-wortley- montagu

Wilch, G., Clark, M., & Naaman, S. (2001). Organizational Models. In R. Oksnevad & D. Welliver (Eds.), The gospel for Islam: Reaching Muslims in North America (pp. 111-30). Wheaton, IL: EMIS.

Wilder, R. G. (1861). Mission schools in India of the American Board of Commissioners for Foreign Missions, with sketches of the missions among the North American Indians, the Sandwich Islands, the Armenians of Turkey, and the Nestorians of Persia. New York, NY: A. D. F. Randolph.

Williams, R. B. (2004). Williams on South Asian religions and immigration. Burlington, VT: Ashgate.

Wilson, J. C. (1950). Introducing Islam. New York, NY: Friendship Press.

Wilson, J. C. (1950). The Christian message to Islam. New York, NY: Fleming H. Revell Company.

Woodsmall, R. F. (1936). Muslim women enter a new world. New York, NY: Round Table.

Wuthnow, R. (2007). America and the challenges of religious diversity. Princeton, NJ: Princeton University Press.

Yin, R. K. (2014). Case study research: Design and methods. Thousand Oaks, CA: Sage.

Youssef, M. (1991). America, oil, and the Islamic mind: The real crisis is the gulf between our ways of thinking. Grand Rapids, MI: Zondervan.

Author Bio

Amit Bhatia has a passion for the development of college students. In his current role as adjunct faculty at Trinity he is regularly involved in motivating students as they pursue an education keeping in mind Trinity's vision of fostering a "vibrant community" that facilitates the development of students, both academically and spiritually.

Since Fall 2011 he has served as Adjunct Faculty in the Biblical Studies and Christian Ministries Departments, with course topics including intercultural ministry, contextualization, world religions, race and ethnic relations, global missions and the missional church, intercultural communication, etc. Prior to this he spent 9 years serving as a pastor in multi-ethnic congregations, which included engaging people from Hindu, Muslim, and Jewish backgrounds.

In addition to teaching at Trinity, he serves as the Director of Outreach at Village Church of Lincolnshire in Lincolnshire, IL, and he also volunteers at South Asian Friendship Center in Chicago, IL, where he serves and engages Hindus and Muslims from India and Pakistan.

INDEX

Made in the USA
Las Vegas, NV
08 March 2024